GOLD
experience
2ND EDITION

TEACHER'S BOOK

Pearson Education Limited
KAO TWO,
KAO Park
Hockham Way,
Harlow, Essex,
CM17 9SR
England
and Associated Companies throughout the world.
pearsonELT.com/goldexperience

Written by Clementine Annabell.

First published 2018

Second impression 2019

ISBN: 978-1-292-23974-3

Set in Camphor Pro

Printed by Neografia, in Slovakia

Acknowledgements
The publishers would like to thank Lindsay Warwick and Jacky Newbrook for the classroom teaching ideas and Louise Manicolo for creating the Grammar Presentations.

Picture Credits
The publisher would like to thank the following for their kind permission to reproduce their photographs:

123RF.com: Katarzyna Bialasiewicz 30, Orlando Rosu 133, Pavlo Vakrushev 80; **Alamy Stock Photo:** Ian Shaw 90; **Getty Images:** Artur Debat / Moment Open 122, Blend Images - KidStock 22, Ghetea Florin / EyeEm 54, Hero Images 42, 101, PhotoAlto / Laurence Mouton 112, Qi Yang / Moment 68.

Cover Image: Getty Images: EyeEm / Stefanie Wenk

Every effort has been made to trace the copyright holders and we apologise in advance for any unintentional omissions. We would be pleased to insert the appropriate acknowledgement in any subsequent edition of this publication.

CONTENTS

Introduction to Gold Experience 2nd Edition　　**4-7**

  Course components　　**5-6**

  Teaching pathways　　**7**

Unit walkthrough　　**8-12**

  Student's Book unit　　**8-11**

  Workbook unit　　**12**

Classroom teaching ideas　　**13-21**

  How to teach for exams　　**13-15**

  How to flip the classroom　　**16-17**

  How to present grammar　　**18**

  How to teach class projects　　**19**

  How to teach with readers　　**20**

Starter　　Welcome to my world　　**22-29**

Unit 1　　Come in　　**30-41**

Unit 2　　What a week!　　**42-53**

Unit 3　　Animal magic　　**54-67**

Unit 4　　Let's explore　　**68-79**

Unit 5　　Fun with food　　**80-89**

Unit 6　　Back in time　　**90-100**

Unit 7　　Bright sparks　　**101-111**

Unit 8　　Top to toe　　**112-121**

Unit 9　　School's out　　**122-132**

Unit 10　　Films and friends　　**133-138**

Switch on videoscripts　　**139-141**

Workbook answer key　　**142-165**

A1 Movers: Wordlist　　**166-168**

A2 Key for Schools: Topic Lists　　**169-173**

A1 Movers Exam Overview　　**174**

A2 Key for Schools Exam Overview　　**175**

GOLD EXPERIENCE 2ND EDITION

Gold Experience second edition is an 8-level course that prepares students for the Cambridge English exams while building their language and real-world skills. The course gives students thorough exam preparation in terms of both strategy and language, while simultaneously developing the life skills that students will need to use English successfully beyond the classroom. Real-world, engaging materials ensure students are switched on and curious to learn more. This second edition is fully updated with new content and a new design.

The A1 level

Gold Experience A1 is aimed at students aged 9–12 years old, who are at the beginning of their journey learning English, and may be working towards one of the *Cambridge for Schools* qualifications. The A1 introduces students to the task types and strategies that they'll need when they do sit an exam, whether it is *Pre A1 Starters*, *A1 Movers*, *A2 Flyers* or *A2 Key for Schools*. However, the engaging activities and themes also make *Gold Experience A1* suitable for students who are not preparing for an exam.

Gold Experience A1 provides students with a solid grounding in the basics of English grammar, and will begin to develop students' confidence in speaking in English. It includes themes accessible to pre-teens, and gives them achievable yet challenging tasks.

The principles and methodology

Reliable

First and foremost, you need your course to help you help students build language skills and pass exams. With *Gold Experience* second edition, the syllabus is based on a combination of exam requirements and the Global Scale of English, ensuring comprehensive language coverage. Meanwhile, we have brought together highly experienced authors and exam consultants to ensure accuracy and rigor in exam preparation, as well as managing the balance of general English, exam English and life skills. This means you can rest assured that your students will be learning the right language with suitable practice to help them excel in their exams and communicate with confidence.

'Under-the-hood' exam preparation

We believe that students need training and practice to excel in exams, but that this doesn't need to be the overarching feel of a class. In Gold Experience second edition, exam tasks are woven seamlessly into the flow of the lesson, but can be easily identified by the **e** icon. Each unit includes activities based on exam task types to develop familiarity with these while building on the target language of the unit. Over the course of the book, students build their exam strategies and their confidence through the step-by-step core activities and task-based exam tips. For those classes or individuals wanting more targeted exam preparation we have a full practice test in the Workbook, and an additional Exam Practice book for practice of full papers.

Engagement

Gold Experience second edition aims to bring new experiences to students, and encourage students to bring their own experience to the classroom. We believe that any text or discussion topic should be interesting regardless of the language, and at A1, we have used a range of light, quirky topics that students will have fun with.

Where possible, we have used authentic texts and real people in reading texts allowing students to investigate anything that takes their interest. Authentic broadcast video from a variety of sources, and grammar 'vox pop' interviews with the general public, introduce students to authentic accents and real experiences and stories.

As every teacher knows, when students are engaged with the topic and the material, they are engaged with English and everything else is just that little bit easier.

'Whole student' development

As well as language and exams, we know you care about developing your students as citizens of the world. This means helping them develop their ability to think critically, assimilate new information and points of view, and formulate, express and defend their opinions. This means helping them develop research techniques, work both alone and with others, and reflect on their own learning. In Gold Experience second edition, these skills are developed throughout each unit in the Speak Up sections, where students are encouraged to express their own views, and in a more focused way, at the end of each unit in the Project section. The Projects are designed to be flexible and you can decide to do them quickly in class, or expand them into longer-term projects over several classes or weeks.

Flexible resources

We know that the real classroom can often be far more complex than the ideal classroom we imagine. For that reason, we've provided a wealth of materials to provide extra support or further challenge for students who need it, plenty of additional and alternative ideas and resources for you, and a full suite of components to allow you to tailor your teaching package to your classroom.

COURSE COMPONENTS

For students

Student's Book with App

- **Nine topic-based units** divided into 8 main teaching lessons, plus video, project, wordlist and unit check.

- Initial **Starter** unit to review and consolidate the very basics of English which may or may not have been covered by students before starting this course.

- Final **tenth unit review** provides revision of language and skills from the course.

- Training and practice for the *Cambridge For Schools* exams is seamlessly integrated into every unit.

- Students and teachers can easily **identify exam-like tasks** with the **e** icon.

- Students are encouraged to begin to communicate their ideas, opinions and knowledge of the world from the first lesson, through frequent **discussion opportunities**, for example through Speak up activities.

- **Video clips** expose students to a variety of authentic broadcasting formats, accents and ideas, and encourage students to think critically about what they watch.

- Where appropriate, **grammar vox pop** interviews give authentic examples of target grammar in use.

- End of unit **projects** can be adapted depending on the time available, and encourage students to explore a topic, collaborate and work creatively with classmates, and present back to the class.

- The back of book **Grammar file** gives a full page of detailed grammar and language explanation, plus a full page of practice activities for every unit.

- **Writing file** and **Speaking file** give additional exam-related practice for students.

- **Student's App** gives access to videos and the extensive class and workbook audio, as well as additional fun practice of course vocabulary. Accessed via a code in every Student's Book.

eBook for students

- Full Student's Book in digital format with embedded audio, video and interactive activities.

- Suitable for computer or tablet.

Workbook

- **Mirrors the Student's Book** lesson-by-lesson and consolidates learning with targeted practice.

- Additional **topic-related practice** of reading, writing, speaking, listening and use of English skills.

- Extensive practice of course grammar and vocabulary.

- General language revision and practice in **Unit 10**, including extensive **Cambridge A1 Movers and A2 Key for Schools Exam** practice tasks.

- Designed for either independent study at home or in-class extra practice.

- Audio for listening lessons available on the **Student's App**.

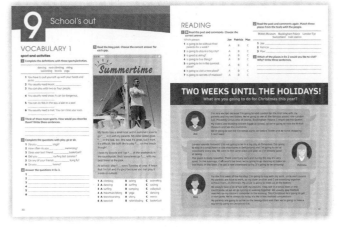

Online Practice for students

- **Fully interactive digital version** of the Workbook, which complements and consolidates the Student's Book material.

- **Remediation** videos and activities powered by MyGrammarLab.

- **Instantly graded** activities with supportive feedback.

- Personal **gradebook** for students to review their performance.

- Access to Student's Book video and audio for students.

Exam practice books

- Additional intensive practice for the *Cambridge Exams for Schools* exams.

- Two complete practice tests, one with tips and guidance for every task.

- Extensive support for productive tasks at the back of the book.

- Online answer keys, audio and speaking test videos with teacher's resources.

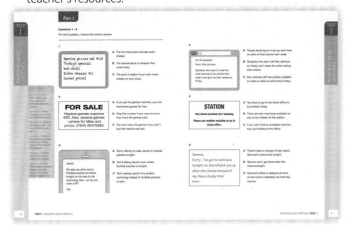

For teachers

Teacher's Book

- Teaching notes with a wealth of additional and alternative classroom ideas, including an idea for how to start and finish each lesson, and ideas for mixed-ability classes, fast finishers, and additional questions to encourage critical thinking.
- Exam information, including how Student's Book activities may differ from exam tasks (for example, shorter text length, fewer items, a focus on unit language meaning less variety of tested language than in the exam, etc.).
- '*How to*' sections in the introduction, giving advice on teaching for exams, flipping the classroom, teaching with projects and teaching with readers.
- Photocopiable videoscripts at the back of the book.
- Workbook answer key.
- Access code for all *Gold Experience* digital teacher tools.

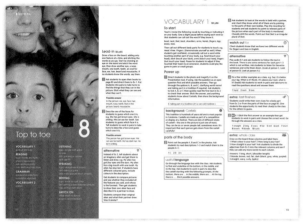

Teacher's Online Resources

All the support a busy teacher needs in one place, accessed via the access code in the back of the Teacher's Book or via your Pearson consultant.

Presentation tool

- Front-of-class teacher's tool with fully interactive version of every Student's Book and Workbook activity with integrated audio and video.
- Planning mode, including teacher's notes, and teaching mode.
- Easy navigation via either book page or lesson flow.
- Additional whole-class game activities – plus score and timer tools for teacher-led games.

Resources

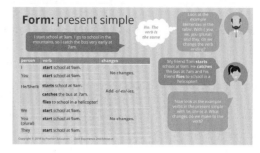

- Teaching notes (digital teacher's book).
- Detailed grammar PowerPoint presentations for each unit's grammar points (see above).
- Three photocopiable worksheets (Grammar, Vocabulary + skill or exam focus) per Student's Book unit, with full teaching notes and answer key.
- Class audio and video.
- Assessment package (see details below).
- Expanded Wordlists for each unit of the Student's Book, including example sentences and phonetics. These wordlists are editable, allowing teachers to add their own examples or translations.

Assessment package

- Extensive range of tests for use throughout the course.
- A/B versions of core tests to prevent copying.
- Versions for students dyslexia.
- Available as ready-to-print pdfs or editable word documents.
- Answer keys and audio files.
- Test pack includes:
  - Diagnostic test to help confirm place students and identify strengths or weaknesses.
  - Unit tests with two papers: Vocabulary and Grammar; Listening and Reading
  - Review tests every three units with three papers: Vocabulary and Grammar; Writing; Speaking.
  - End of Year test with three papers: Listening, Language and Reading; Writing; Speaking

Online Practice for teachers

- Teacher view of Online Practice provides a full learning management system.
- Assign tasks to the whole class, groups or individual students depending on their needs.
- Automatic marking to save time.
- Performance area lets you see how individual students and the whole class are progressing overall and by skill.

TEACHING PATHWAYS

We know that not every class is the same, and there are many influences, from your course hours, teaching context and personal style to your class size, and the needs of every one of your students. Gold Experience 2nd Edition has been designed to be as flexible as possible, allowing you to add relevant sections and support to the core content, and tailor the course to your classes and students.

Component		To focus on ...				
Print	Blended / Digital	Core material	Grammar and vocabulary	Exam preparation	21st Century skills	Fun activities
Student's Book + App	Student's eBook	Units 1–9: • core lessons	• Unit checks • Grammar file (reference & practice) • App: Vocab activities • Authentic 'on-the-street' interviews	• Unit 10 (review unit) • Writing file • Speaking file	• *Switch on* video project • *Speak up* & extended discussions • *Improve it* writing sections	• *Game on* activities in main units • *Switch on* video & project • Footers in main units
Workbook	Online Practice	Units 1–9: • core lessons	• Unit checks • Online Practice: MyGrammarLab videos & activities	• Unit 10	• Writing tasks	• Puzzles (e.g. crosswords)
Teacher's Book		Units 1–9: • core lessons	• Extra activities in teaching notes	• How to teach for exams • Extra activities in teaching notes	• How to teach with a flipped classroom • How to teach with projects • How to teach with readers • Critical thinking activities in teaching notes • Project extensions	• How to teach with projects • Extra activities in teaching notes
Teacher's Online Resources (including Teacher's Presentation Tool)		Units 1–9: • audio & video	• Grammar PowerPoint Presentations • Photocopiable activities	• Photocopiable activities		• Photocopiable activities • Presentation Tool games
Assessment package (Word or pdf - part of Online Resources)		Unit tests: Grammar & Vocabulary	• Diagnostic test • Review tests (main)	• Unit tests: Skills • Review tests: Writing • Review tests: Speaking • End of Year tests	Tests used as assessment *for* learning	
Exam practice booklet				Exam booklet (A2 Key for Schools) • 2 full practice tests • Guidance, tips & reference		

UNIT WALKTHROUGH

STUDENT'S BOOK UNIT

Each unit has a *lead-in* photo, quote and discussion questions to get students thinking about the unit theme, and using their existing topic vocabulary.

The *Unit overview* gives a brief outline of topics, key language, skills focus and exam tasks.

Exam skills and strategies are built up through both core activities and **exam tips.**

The main reading text **previews grammar** that students will meet in the next lesson.

Audio recording of all main **reading texts** for a more inclusive learning environment.

Power up sections get students thinking about the lesson topic.

Exam tasks are easily identified by the **e** symbol.

The *explore language* boxes provide explanation and examples of key language areas.

Fun footers, loosely connected to the topic, can be explicitly exploited or left for students to notice.

Sum up sections require students to think about the **text as a whole.**

Speak up sections develop critical **thinking,** asking students to think more deeply about the topic and consider different viewpoints, and provides extra **speaking practice.**

Editable **PowerPoint presentations** for each core grammar area save valuable preparation time for teachers and bring the grammar to life.

Active *explore grammar* boxes require students to engage with the taught grammar.

Language is **contextualised** in authentic **Grammar vox pop** interviews, scripted **conversations** or short texts. Grammar vox pops are provided as both audio and video.

Frequent opportunities for **personalisation** and **discussion** using new language.

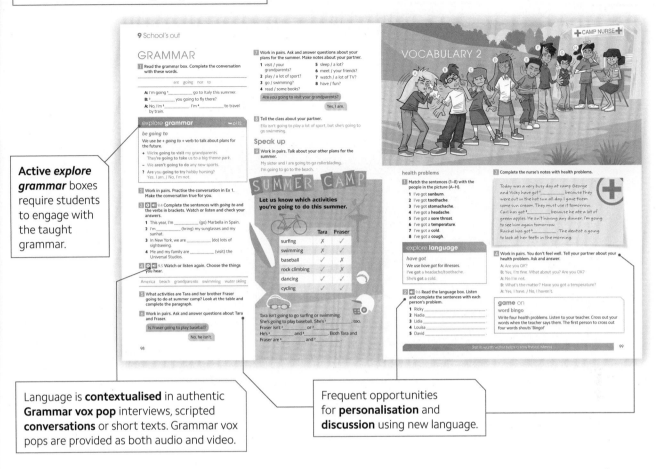

Speaking extra provides more **general** speaking practice on the topic.

Task **layout** reflects the exam.

All **audioscripts** are printed in the back of the book.

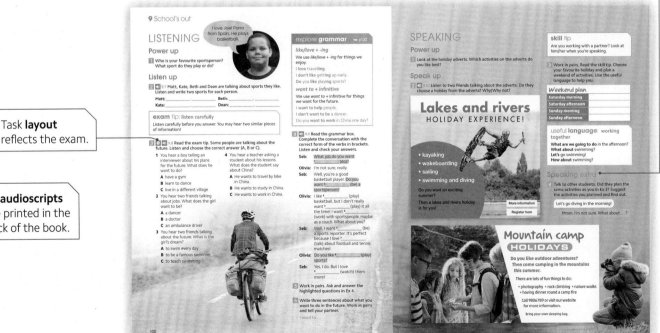

Step-by-step approach to exam tasks.

Plan on asks students to:
• **analyse** the exam task, with tasks and tips to help them;
• work on **appropriate language**;
• break down tasks such as **how to make an argument** in writing.

The *Switch on* video lessons provide authentic clips on a variety of engaging and thought-provoking topics.

Skill tips provide **important information** for students on particular writing genres.

Activities move from **gist** to **close watching** to general **discussion** questions.

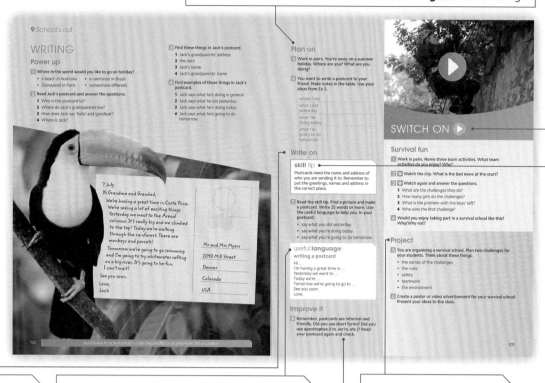

Write on walks students through **planning** and **writing** their own answer.

Useful language boxes provide a wide range of **language options** for a specific function.

Improve it encourages students to **reflect on** their work and make improvements.

Projects involve **research**, **collaboration**, **critical thinking** and **creativity**, and are flexible, allowing teachers to take a quicker or more in-depth approach.

Unit checks provide two pages of practice to review the unit language.

Wordlists include all the explicitly taught **vocabulary** from the unit.

Activities include **personalisation** and **sentence-level** writing.

Practice dedicated to the **unit vocabulary**, including **audio activities**.

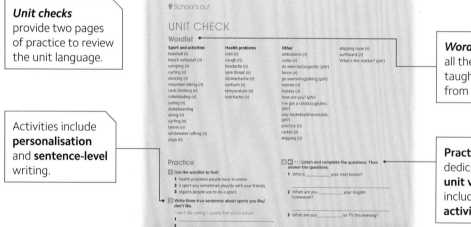

Real-life texts to engage students and contextualise language.

Some fun, game-like activities to give a variety of tasks throughout the review sections

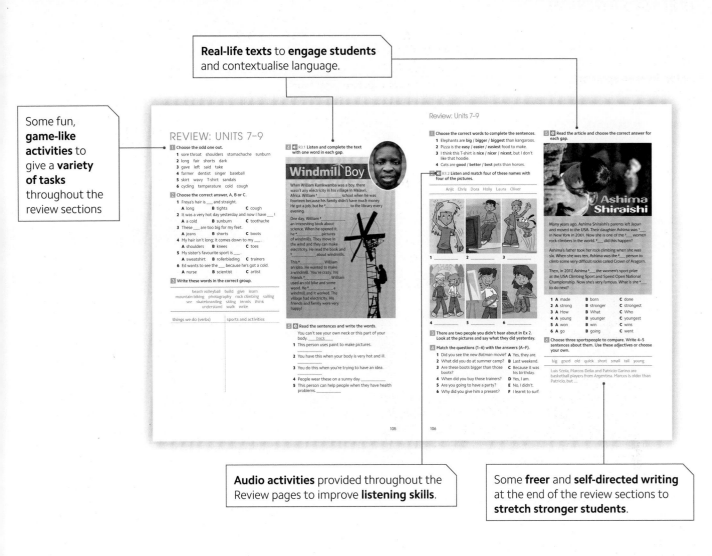

Audio activities provided throughout the Review pages to improve listening skills.

Some freer and self-directed writing at the end of the review sections to stretch stronger students.

Clear focus and practice on particular grammatical topics.

Each unit has one page of reference and one page of practice, which can be used for remediation, extra practice or in a flipped classroom scenario.

Grammar file at the back of the Student's Book gives detailed explanations for all grammar topics

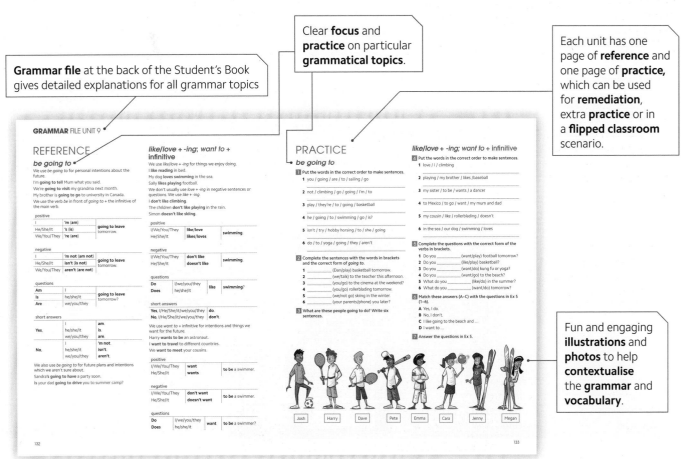

Fun and engaging illustrations and photos to help contextualise the grammar and vocabulary.

WORKBOOK UNIT

Workbook units mirror the Student's Book with additional practice of all language, skills and exams tasks.

Writing and **Speaking** pages focus on subskills, analysis and useful language, and include an optional productive task in every unit.

Unit check pages at end of each unit help students check they understand the core language from the unit.

Exam tasks are flagged with the **e** icon.

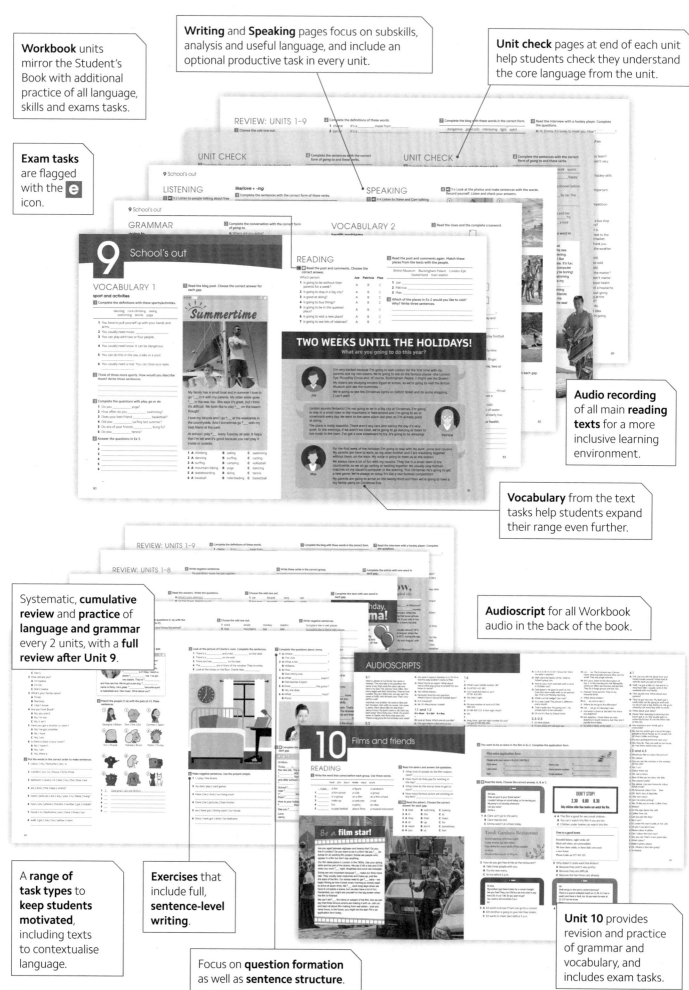

Audio recording of all main **reading texts** for a more inclusive learning environment.

Vocabulary from the text tasks help students expand their range even further.

Systematic, **cumulative review** and **practice** of **language and grammar** every 2 units, with a **full review after Unit 9**.

Audioscript for all Workbook audio in the back of the book.

A **range of task types** to **keep students motivated**, including texts to contextualise language.

Exercises that include full, **sentence-level writing**.

Focus on **question formation** as well as **sentence structure**.

Unit 10 provides revision and practice of grammar and vocabulary, and includes exam tasks.

CLASSROOM TEACHING IDEAS

HOW TO TEACH FOR EXAMS

What do teachers need to consider?

1 **What do you do when not all students in a class are taking the exam, or are taking different exams?**

Students using the A1 level of the course may be working towards either of the A1 Movers or A2 Flyers exams, or the A2 Key for Schools qualification. Teachers should make sure that students who are not taking the exam that a particular exam task relates to are still engaged with the work done in class and feel they can benefit from the specific practice it provides. This means explaining clearly exactly what is being tested in exam tasks and how these skills also benefit students outside the classroom. Cambridge exams test skills that are transferable to the real world, and this should be explained to students. Once an exam task has been completed, it could be followed by general discussion on the topic or extended vocabulary practice to maximise its usefulness for non-exam students as well.

2 **How is teaching for exams different from teaching general English classes?**

- Exam classes often place more emphasis on reading, writing and grammar. General courses often include more speaking activities and general listening tasks that aim to develop communicative skills and fluency.

- An exam course is fixed, with an exam syllabus that must be completed. This means the teacher may feel there's little time to do many extension activities from the Student's Book that are either optional or not in exam format, even though these are clearly useful. When doing these activities, it's important that teachers explain their value clearly to the students so that they understand how they relate to the exam.

- Exam students may not be interested in learning English for its own sake – they may simply want to pass the exam. This means they may be keen to do exam practice but may not see the value of spending time on communicative or fluency activities. Non-exam students, on the other hand, will want to do fluency work that improves their communicative ability.

- Students may feel under pressure to succeed. This could come from parents, teachers or from the students themselves, and leads to a feeling of frustration if they're not doing well.

- There can be problems if students are not at the level of the exam they're studying for. Students can become demotivated, and teachers can feel frustrated.

- There is a very clear end goal which creates a shared bond among exam students. It also means that non-exam students can see a progression through the course, and gain a sense of progress and achievement in their overall ability.

3 **What do exam teachers need to know at the start of a course?**

It's vital that teachers know about the exam before they start the course, so they can make crucial decisions about how much time to spend on the different aspects of the exam, when to start dedicated exam practice and so on.

Teachers should find out about student's priorities and how many students intend to take the exam. They should then find out about individual student's respective strengths and weaknesses in order to focus as much time as possible on those areas students have trouble with. Information they need includes:

a) The format and content of the exam.

- How many papers are there, and what skills does each one test?

- How many different parts are there in each paper? Are they all compulsory or is there a choice?

- What is the grammar syllabus for the exam?

- How are the skills tested – multiple choice questions, gap-fill …? What techniques are required for dealing with each one?

b) The practicalities of taking the exam.

- How much time is allowed for each part of the exam? How should students balance their time?

- Where do students write their answers? Is there transfer time?

c) Marking the exam.

- What is the weighting of different papers within the overall qualification?

- How many marks are there for each question?

- What are the assessment criteria for each part where there is no 'right' answer, especially when testing the productive skills of writing and speaking?

d) What happens after the exam?

- How are the results presented? Do students receive feedback? Are the grades linked to the CEFR? What level are they linked to?

- What can your students do with the qualification? Is it recognised internationally?

- What is the next exam that your students should progress to?

4 **What makes a successful exam teacher?**

Teaching for an exam is very rewarding, but it is also challenging. A good exam teacher

- knows and understands the exam well, including the testing focus of each part and what techniques students need to deal with each one

- understands how to achieve a balance between developing skills and doing exam practice in lessons so as to engage all students in the work

- enjoys teaching towards a goal

- manages their own and their students' time effectively and efficiently

- listens to students' concerns and worries

- gives honest and direct feedback on students' performance

- motivates students and fosters confidence and independent learning

5 How important is balancing teaching and testing?

Students enrolled on an exam course will expect to go through a lot of practice tests and exam practice. However, if this is all you do you will produce excellent test takers but poor language users! You may also risk losing the interest of non-exam students. When time is restricted you need to make the most of the time you choose to teach, and the time you need to be testing. This balance is different with every class.

- **A class below the level**

    The priority is teaching. Students may lack both test taking skills and language knowledge, so you need to identify their needs and try to fill in the gaps. Testing too often might de-motivate them, although you may want to set progress tests for your own assessment of what they need to study more. Make sure that they have realistic aims and that they maintain a sense of progress. You may decide not to mark their work using exam criteria, but to mark constructively which will also benefit non-exam students.

- **A class at the level**

    Students have the basic test-taking and language skills, but they need to consolidate and review these as well as extend the range of structures and language they can use productively. Regular testing can give these students a sense of progress. However, you need to consider how you mark their work in order to provide positive feedback and foster improvement, possibly by not marking to the level of the exam too early.

- **A class above the level**

    The emphasis is on enabling students to achieve the highest mark they can. Their language and test-taking skills should be good, and the problem may be to keep them motivated. Challenge them by setting them tasks above the level of the exam, and involve them in understanding what they have to do to get a higher than average mark in the exam. They should be aiming high, extending their range of language and not settling for 'good enough'.

6 Helping exam students help themselves

Encouraging a collaborative approach to developing exam skills will improve students' confidence, enable them to help each other and make each task seem more familiar and achievable. By involving students in understanding what exam tasks involve, teachers can foster confidence and facilitate success. It is really crucial that students feel comfortable with the tasks, and that there are no surprises when they enter the exam room.

How does the Gold Experience series help with exam teaching?

Gold Experience works in a graded and supportive way, and provides a number of resources that help to develop the technical skills students need to deal with exam tasks, while also improving and extending their general language skills. The course is beneficial for both exam and non-exam students, and provides supportive and extended practice in real-life skills. The topics are engaging and age-relevant and give students the opportunity to read about and discuss interesting subjects.

Development of language

Exam tasks require students to demonstrate a range of language at the appropriate level. Gold Experience has grammar and vocabulary sections that develop this range in topic related units, which makes it easy for students to apply them to exam tasks and to the real world. For example, in Unit 3, the topic is *the world around us*, and students are asked to group new vocabulary into two thematic groups, in this case *land and water*. This grouping of associated vocabulary, helps facilitate learning, which in turn, enables students to use the language more effectively in real world situations, and also to apply it to exam tasks, such as Part 1 of the A1 Movers Reading and Writing paper.

Focus on the process as well as the goal

Learners are helped to understand not just the point of what they are doing but also how to be successful. Understanding the point of each task type, and the process they need to follow in order to complete it, enables student to reach the overall goal. For example, in unit 6, students learn strategies to help them complete the A1 Movers Reading and Writing Part 3 exam task. These strategies include reading the whole sentence around the gap, and thinking about what kind of word is needed in each gap. By following this process, students become more successful in achieving their goal.

Graded exam tasks

Exam tasks are introduced to students early in the course, but in a graded way. This may mean that a task type initially has fewer questions or a simpler text, or that it tests a more limited range of structures. This helps them to understand the exam task, and therefore deal with it more effectively. For example, as well as using texts of increasing difficulty, there is also progression in the type of reading exam tasks that are used. Most reading lessons focus on A1 Movers exam tasks, but by the end of the course, students are introduced to an A2 Flyers reading task (in Unit 7) and a A2 Key for Schools reading tasks (in Unit 9).

Developing confidence with exam tasks

The clear learning goals for each skill established at the start of each unit, plus the frequent models throughout the book for the productive skills, show students what they need to do in each task and how to do it. Students are often nervous about certain parts of the exam, such as the speaking and listening papers. There are often specific reasons for this:

- Speaking – students may be embarrassed about speaking in front of an examiner, or may be nervous so that their mind goes blank and they say too little.

- Listening – students often feel that they are not in control as they can't stop the tape to play it again, and this can cause them to panic if they are unsure of an answer.

Gold Experience provides plenty of practice in these two skills, and clear advice on how to deal with the problems students find with them. In this way students develop confidence. For example, in the listening lesson in Unit 4, which focuses on the A1 Movers Listening Part 5 task, students are encouraged to describe the picture first and think about how prepositions of place could be used to describe the location of objects. This builds students' confidence and prepares them for the kind of language they will need to respond to in the exam listening task.

Regular exam tips

There are exam tips in every unit which deal with specific exam tasks. The tips focus on aspects of the task that will help students deal with it effectively. These often precede practice in that particular task, so that students can see the tip in action. Some of these tips give factual information about the exam. For example, in Unit 2, p.26, the exam tip informs students that in A1 Movers Listening Part 2, they can write numbers in letter form (twenty) or using numbers (20) . Other tips offer helpful reminders. For example, in Unit 5, p.59, students are reminded to use the present continuous in A1 Movers Speaking Part 1 when describing weather conditions or people's actions. These tips build throughout the Student's Book and help students to understand exactly what is being tested, what to look out for, and develop a bank of appropriate exam techniques that they can refer to. As they work through the Student's Book and become familiar with the tips the tasks will become easier.

Focus on the process of writing

To help students identify good practice in writing tasks, lessons in the Student's Book provide model answers. There are also tasks that encourage students to analyse the model answers, which gives them greater understanding of how to complete the tasks themselves. These analytical tasks focus on the approach, content and language required by the different writing genres. In Unit 8, for example, students are introduced to story writing, which is Part 7 of the A2 Flyers reading and writing paper. Students are guided through the process of responding to picture prompts, selecting appropriate content and using appropriate punctuation such as speech marks, all before they are asked to attempt a Part 7 exam task on their own. There is a task at the end of each writing section which mirrors the model so that students can practise writing an answer themselves. There is also an *Improve it* section which guides students and helps them review and improve their work. In these sections, students are encouraged to work together to review and analyse each other's writing tasks, and to cooperate in understanding where improvement is required. There is a Writing file with further tips on how to approach the tasks, with further models.

Focus on speaking

Throughout the Student's Book there are discussion questions that encourage students to talk about ideas related to topics they have been reading or writing about. This is particularly beneficial for non-exam students. In sections specifically devoted to exam tasks, there are model answers for students to analyse. These answers give clear models for long turns and give examples of the best ways to interact with a partner. An example of this can be found in the speaking lesson in Unit 2. Students are given a model conversation about school and studies which they can then adapt to talk about their personal experience.

Explanatory answer keys

There are clear keys and model answers provided for the exam tasks. In the reading and listening tasks the lines where the answers can be found are quoted.

Practice test

As well as working through regular exams tasks in the Student's Book and Workbook units, students complete the course by doing further exam task practice in unit 10.

Resources for self-study

There are a number of resources which provide opportunities for further study and self-study, and also give supplementary information and further practice. These can be used in class or at home. They include:

- A wordlist at the end of each unit in the Student's Book
- A Speaking File section in the back of the Student's Book
- A Writing File section in the back of the Student's Book
- A Grammar File and Practice section in the back of the Student's Book
- Audioscripts for the listening tasks
- The Workbook
- Online practice activities and the vocabulary practice app

Extra suggestions

Here are five suggestions that might help your students with their studies for exams.

1 Watch videos of the speaking test

Videos are available of the Speaking part of the exam online. Watching another student sit the relevant exam can help students familiarise themselves with what to expect. Make sure students understand that the format will be the same but the content will be different.

2 Practice Speaking test

If students feel comfortable with the practicalities of taking the Speaking test they only have to think about the language they need, and an activity like this will help them relax. If you can, near the end of the course, give students opportunities to do a practise Speaking exam, either with yourself or another teacher acting as the examiner.

3 Encouragement from previous candidates

If you can, invite older students or alumni from your school who have taken the same exam the previous year to visit your class. Get them to talk briefly about what it was like, give tips, and give students the opportunity to ask questions. (Be aware that exam specifications do change, so make sure any specific task advice is relevant to the most up to date exam specifications.)

4 Exam tips

Make a point of discussing each exam tip and ensuring students understand how to apply it to the task.

5 Focus on building student confidence

Look for opportunities to build student confidence through actively looking for opportunities to give each student positive encouragement that is sincere and specific.

Emphasise that the Cambridge for Schools exams are an opportunity for students to demonstrate their progress in English.

HOW TO FLIP THE CLASSROOM

What is it and why try it?

The flipped classroom is an approach where classroom instruction is given to students at home via a video, and application usually given for homework is completed in class with the teacher's support.

Teachers began flipping their classrooms in subjects such as science when they became frustrated that many of their lessons were taken up with giving students information. Students who struggled to complete their homework without the teacher there to support them were unable to master the topic.

The teachers exploited new technologies by creating short videos that provided classroom instruction. Students watched these in their own time before a lesson and then class time was spent on applying that information with the teacher there to support them. The teacher could differentiate tasks for different learners to ensure that everyone was challenged and supported at an appropriate level.

In language learning terms, flipping the classroom means students listening to or reading information about language at home before a lesson, leaving more time for practice of that language in the classroom. Alternatively, it could be information about an exam technique or how to write an informal letter. Lessons then provide more opportunities for practice of language and skills development with the teacher there to support, correct and challenge the students as they complete tasks. Students can work on the same tasks, or work in groups on different tasks to ensure they work at a level suitable for them.

The flipped classroom is still a fairly new approach and so research on its efficacy is ongoing. Anecdotally, teachers who flip their classrooms believe that the approach allows students to become more independent in their learning. They learn how to learn. Rather than receive information in the classroom, they have to take more control and ensure they learn it outside the classroom, watching the video or re-reading written material several times if necessary. In class, they have time to ask the teacher questions if they still don't understand and choose when they need support. This autonomy motivates students and results in a higher level of engagement according to teachers. In terms of language learning, students can gain more practice time and receive more feedback from the teacher on performance.

Be aware that some pre-teen students may be only beginning to develop the self-study skills required to prepare effectively for a flipped classroom lesson. If you are using this approach, begin gradually and make sure you have a backup plan for students that haven't prepared, e.g. they must watch the video while the rest of the class enjoys a game to start the lesson.

You also need to be aware of possible barriers to watching videos at home, such as internet access.

Current best practices and methods

The following are the typical stages of a lesson when flipping the classroom.

1 Preparing the homework

Teachers can provide instruction through video or written material. These can be created by the teacher or sourced from an alternative source e.g. their coursebook or online. If teachers make videos, they are usually five to ten minutes long and comprise the teacher recording themselves with their device, standing at the board and explaining the language. Alternatively, a video can be made using screencasting software which allows voice recording over slides.

2 Students watch the video for homework

In the previous lesson, the teacher sets the classroom instruction task as homework, usually with an accompanying activity to check understanding. Students do the tasks at home. The task that checks understanding might be completed online as this allows the teacher to check understanding before the lesson and make adjustments to their lesson plan if students have found the language particularly easy or difficult. Alternatively students may bring the completed task on paper to discuss at the beginning of the lesson.

3 In class review

In the lesson, the teacher begins by checking students' understanding of the content of the video. It could be through checking answers to the homework task, oral questioning or a quick paired quiz. Students are given the opportunity to ask questions.

4 Practice, practice, practice

Students are then given several practice tasks to complete for the rest of the lesson while the teacher monitors and offers support. This practice might be individual at first as they complete written exercises. It can then be communicative as students work in pairs or groups to complete oral tasks. Fast finishers can move onto new tasks so that they are challenged. Weaker students can receive extra support such as prompts.

5 Reflection on performance

Finally, at the end of the lesson, students reflect on what they have learnt to help them identify progress and areas where they still need to improve. These reflections allow students to gain a greater understanding of their strength and weaknesses, and encourage them to set achievable learning goals for future lessons.

Efficacy

Keeping track of learner progress is one way of finding out whether flipping the classroom is effective or not. This could be through monitoring student's performance in language tasks or self-reflection. For example, you could ask students to feed back using questions such as the following, offering a ranking of 1–5 (1 = not, 5 = very). This can be via an anonymous questionnaire or orally in class (in L1 if necessary.)

- Do you like watching the videos at home?
- How easy is it for you to watch the videos at home?
- Do you think watching the videos at home helps you learn?

How does the Gold Experience series help me with that?

Gold Experience provides the following resources that will help you to flip your classroom.

Grammar presentations

The Presentation tool software contains presentation slides with step-by-step walkthroughs of the grammar points taught in each lesson. These can be used by the teacher in class, when explaining language, but they can also be printed out for students to read at home when flipping the classroom. The slides contain detailed information about the meaning, function and form of the target language with examples. There is a final task that checks students' understanding.

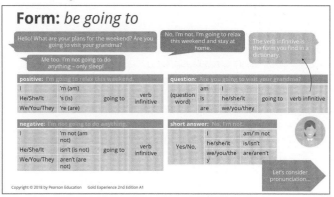

Workbook support

The workbook contains exercises on the grammar points taught in each unit. These can be used either as homework prior to the grammar lesson in order to check what learners already know. With students at this level, the grammar may be completely new to them and so a test, teach, test approach may be challenging, but you can make a decision about this when you get to know your class. can be used.

Alternatively, the workbook exercises can be completed in class to provide as much practice as possible while the teacher is available to offer support and clarify any confusing aspects of the language.

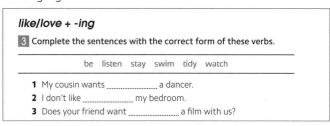

Teacher's Book support

In the Teacher's Book, prior to a grammar lesson, there are notes for the teacher on what materials are available when flipping the classroom.

> Find a short video clip of young people from Finland riding hobby horses to show the class. (Alternatively, show the picture of the hobby horses on Student's Book page 95.)

To take it further …

Here are some tips to help you to flip your classroom effectively:

Tip 1: If you create your own videos, personalise them

Just as we would try to personalise language in class when we clarify it for students, try to personalise it in videos too. For example, give a short anecdote about yourself using the target language. You can then use sentences from that anecdote to explain how the language is used, formed and pronounced.

Tip 2: Motivate student to want to complete the homework tasks

It's important that students complete the homework because if they don't, they'll find it difficult to complete the practice tasks in class. Pose a question and elicit answers but don't give the correct answer. Tell students that they have to do the homework task to find out. For example, before a lesson on past simple irregular forms write the following sentence on the board:

Yesterday I buyed a new book.

Tell students that this sentence is factually correct but ask if it's grammatically correct. Tell students to watch the video and come back to the next lesson, and say whether anything needs to be changed and why.

If you make your own videos, engage students by teasing the context so that they want to know more and have to watch the video to find it out. Let's imagine that you tell a short anecdote in the video using the target language before explaining it. You could show a photo that represents the anecdote or tell the beginning of an anecdote but not the end. Elicit what the anecdote is but don't tell the students the correct answer. They do their homework to find out.

Tip 3: What to do when students don't do the homework

If possible, arrange for students who haven't done their homework to go to the back of the class and do it while the other students start to practise using it. Make technology available there if the homework is a video. Once students get into the habit of a flipped classroom, they tend to do the homework but even the best students sometimes forget or are unable to.

Tip 4: What to do when students don't have the technology

Try to arrange for all students to have access to any online material they need do the homework after school or before school if not everyone in the class has a device or internet access at home. Alternatively, create study pairs or groups where at least one student has a device and can watch the video with someone who does not.

Tip 5: Help learners to become more independent in their learning

Students often need to practise to work independently. To help them do this, make learning goals clear so they know why they are doing the homework before the language lesson and how it will help them. At the end of the lesson, encourage students to reflect on their performance in the lesson so they can identify progress and recognise strengths and weaknesses. This can help them to set personalised learning goals and progress more quickly.

HOW TO PRESENT GRAMMAR

Gold Experience grammar presentations

Helping learners to understand language is one of the key roles of a language teacher. To make it easier for you to clarify language with your students, each grammar lesson in Gold Experience 2nd Edition is accompanied by a set of PowerPoint grammar presentation slides. Each grammar presentation covers the meaning/use of the language and how it is formed. It ends with a short practice task to check students have understood the key points.

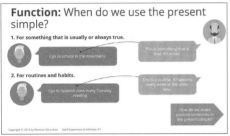

As you can see, the presentations do not just include information to be explained by the teacher. They very much involve the learner through questions designed to encourage students to work out meaning and form themselves. This aims to help learners internalise the language more readily.

You can download each grammar presentation from the Gold Experience teacher resources site or display it in class at the click of a button using the Front of Class tool. The presentations can be edited by you quickly and easily, meaning you can adapt them to suit the needs and interests of your class.

Exploiting the presentations

Using a grammar presentation in class

The grammar presentations are primarily designed to be used by teachers when presenting grammar in a lesson. Here are some tips on how to best exploit them in your lessons.

1 Ensure the level is right for your class

Each grammar presentation can be edited which means that you can add, edit or delete content to suit the needs of your class. It could be that you want to reduce the level of challenge with a weaker class, focus on the more challenging aspects of a language point or focus on just one aspect when addressing an issue in remedial work.

2 Personalise the presentation

You can personalise the content by changing the example sentences to make them relevant to your class. This can make the presentation more engaging and entertaining for learners and maintain their interest more readily. Just changing the names of people and places can make a difference.

3 Move through the slides at a pace suited to the class

The slides are designed to be controlled by you which means you can move at a pace relevant to the students in your class. You can spend more time on a slide that students are having difficulty with and less time on one which students have understood quickly.

4 Involve students and check understand effectively

The slides include questions to encourage learners to work out meaning and form themselves or to check their understanding of the content. Exploit these successfully by giving all students time to reflect on the questions and think of an answer, either alone or in pairs. Plan how much wait time you will allow for students to come up with an answer (e.g. 20 seconds) to ensure it is not just the fastest students who have this opportunity. Plan how you will gather answers to questions so that you can assess the understanding of the whole class rather than just a few students who put their hands up or call out an answer. One way of doing this is to use a voting system (coloured cards, hands up or a digital version e.g. Socrative) or mini whiteboards where learners write an answer and hold it up for you to see.

5 Use the practice slide to further check understanding

At the end of every grammar presentation is a slide which includes some practice questions. These help you and your students to further check understanding of the grammar presented. Give students time to do the task alone or in pairs and check answers thoroughly to identify problem areas and misunderstandings. You can then return to the relevant slide to clarify anything that is still unclear to students.

Using a grammar presentation out of class

The grammar presentations can be downloaded and then shared with your students, either by email, a document sharing site such as Google Drive, or any virtual learning platform you use with your students. You may wish to do this for the following reasons:

- To provide the material for the students who were absent from a lesson due to illness, etc.

- To provide revision and reference material for students after the presentation is used in class. Students can review it to consolidate their understanding of the language and refer to it when completing homework tasks.

- To flip your lesson. This means that learners work through the slides at home on their own before a lesson. In the next lesson, you spend time checking the learners' understanding of the language but soon move onto speaking activities that give learners a lot of practice in using the language. You could even create a video using a screencasting tool online (e.g. screencast-o-matic) so that your class see the slides and hear your explanation at the same time. To find out more about how to flip a lesson, go to the How to Flip the Classroom section on page 16.

HOW TO TEACH WITH PROJECTS

The benefits

Projects involve students working together to produce something in English. They can require students to research and present information, create something or design something. Students might do two or all of these things. For example, students might research museums around the world, design their own museum idea, and present it to the class.

Projects in the English language classroom provide several benefits:

1 Authentic use of language

Students work on an authentic task which requires them to use English authentically. Projects also often develop all four skills: reading, writing, listening and speaking. At A1 level, code-switching (i.e. using a combination of English and L1) is acceptable as students work on projects, but do encourage students to use English as much as possible.

2 Development of personal skills

Projects require learners to collaborate, enabling them to develop skills such as the ability to co-operate, solve problems and communicate.

3 Development of autonomy

As project work involves students making decisions about how to achieve their learning objective, they are able to develop learner autonomy with support and guidance from their teacher.

4 Development of thinking skills

Students can develop information literacy and media literacy when doing research online, determining what information is useful, biased, misinformed etc. They can also develop critical thinking skills when analysing that information, evaluating it and deciding how to use it.

5 Development of creativity

Many projects require learners to be creative in some way. Creativity, along with collaboration, communication and critical thinking skills are considered to be key skills for 21st century learning.

6 Increased motivation

Project work can provide a break from lessons which have a very specific language or skills focus. In addition to that, all of the other benefits mentioned here can make project work motivating for students.

It is important to note that while project work provides many development opportunities, students are likely to need support in exploiting those opportunities, such as advice from their teacher on how to work independently or feedback on their communication skills.

How to extend Gold Experience projects

At the end of each unit in Gold Experience, there is a Switch On lesson which provides video input and listening tasks followed by a project. These can be completed in one lesson, or students can work on them over a longer period of time e.g. one lesson a week over a month plus homework. By extending the project, students can more fully benefit from it.

Below is the project task from Unit 1.

> ## Project
>
> 6 Work in pairs. Design a tiny house. There are only four rooms. What things do you need? Draw your tiny house and present it to the class. Explain your ideas.
>
> This is our tiny house.
> There is a …
> There are …

To expand the project over a longer period of time, you could do the following:

Lesson 1

In class

Students watch the video and complete the listening tasks.

Homework

Each student goes away and researches examples of tiny houses.

Lesson 2

In class

Students work in their pairs and share their research. They discuss what rooms they are going to have in their tiny house, and what things in each room. They divide the rooms between students.

Homework

Each student draws the plan for their allocated rooms.

Lesson 3

In class

In their pairs, students share room designs. Students plan how to share their design with the class and write a script for this.

Homework

Students practise their script.

Lessons 4 onwards

In class

Two or three pairs share their tiny house design with the class. It usually works best to have only a few students present in any one lesson to maximise interest of the other students. Get two or three watching students to give positive comments or ask questions to the presenting students.

HOW TO TEACH WITH READERS

The benefits

Readers are books based on well-known stories which are designed for language learners. They allow learners to read at a level appropriate for them, whether that is A1 or C1. Stories include modern classics, contemporary fictions, shorts stories and plays. Readers allow learners to read extensively, in contrast to the intensive reading usually done in class. There are questions which help learners to check their comprehension as they read. There is also a wordlist and additional teacher support materials to help teachers create interesting lessons based around readers. Readers come with or without an audio CD.

There are many benefits to students using readers in the English language classroom.

1 Authenticity

Although readers are simplified for different levels of learners, the stories remain authentic as they are based on existing books or films.

2 Skills development

No matter what their level, students can develop all four skills. Students predominantly develop reading skills but they can also develop their listening skills through the use of the audio CD. They can develop speaking and writing skills through classroom or homework tasks and activities.

3 Language input

Students receive language input at a level appropriate to them. They consolidate their existing knowledge of language by seeing it in action. They can also develop their vocabularies by seeing new language. Extra practice materials in the books can help students to notice new vocabulary.

4 Development of autonomy

Students can be encouraged to make decisions about their learning by selecting the book they want to read, deciding when to read it, how often to read it, what kind of vocabulary to note down etc. When reading takes place outside the classroom learners develop independence.

5 Motivation

When readers have the right book, they are motivated to spend time developing their language skills, whether that is in or outside the classroom. Learners can enjoy using their English skills to experience another time and place, or see the world from a different perspective. The sense of accomplishment when finishing a book in English can help to recognise their progress in English, as well as motivate them to continue their studies.

How to exploit Readers

There are many ways that readers can be exploited in class. Here are a few of those ideas:

- Students read and summarise a chapter for another student in the class.
- Students note down useful vocabulary and teach it to another student.
- Students write a social media feed from the perspective of one of the characters in the book.
- Students role play an interview with one of the characters in the book.
- Students make predictions about what will happen as they read.
- Students write the dialogue for and act out the scene from a book.
- Students write a review of the book.
- Students write a comparison of the book and the film.

Selecting Readers

There are benefits and drawbacks to asking a class to read the same book and encouraging students to choose a book for themselves. With the former, the class can participate more easily in activities based on that book as everyone is reading the same thing. The teacher can create wonderful lessons that encourage analysis, discussion and creation based on that book However, encouraging students to select a book of their choice may result in more motivation to read that book, as not everyone in the class will have the same interests.

Pearson readers can be found at *https://readers.english.com/*. On this page you can find access to the catalogue of books as well as sample teaching resources which accompany readers.

Level 1 books are those appropriate for A1 level learners. *Six Sketches* by Leslie Dunkling may be appropriate for the core of the class. *Twenty Thousand Leagues Under the Sea* by Jules Verne is a classic science-fiction story which is likely to stretch those learners who are already at a solid A1 level.

Pearson English Readers
Six Sketches
Leslie Dunkling

Pearson English Readers
Twenty Thousand Leagues Under the Sea
Jules Verne

The only
source of
knowledge
is **experience**.

Everything else
is just information.

–Albert Einstein

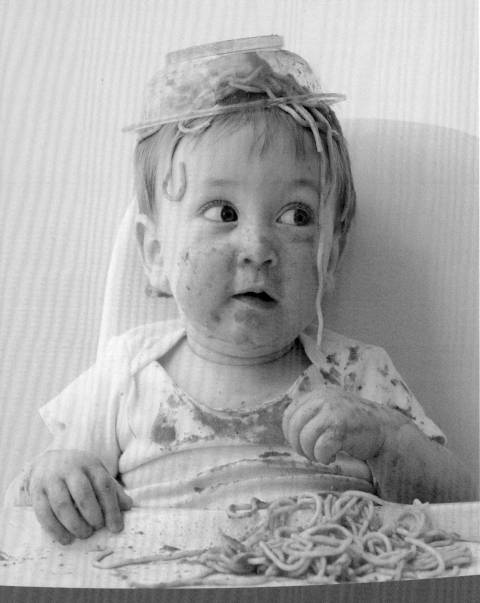

Starter: Welcome to my world

READING
read short texts about Sam and his family

GRAMMAR
use *to be* to talk about you and your family

LISTENING
listen for topics in a video call

SPEAKING
talk about your favourite things

WRITING
write sentences about yourself, your family and your classmates

Lead-in SB p6

Bring a prop to pass around for this game, such as a soft ball, or scrunched piece of paper. If your class layout allows, organise students into a circle.

Write on the board in two separate speech bubbles: *Hi, I'm Kate. Hi Kate!* (Use the name you wish students to call you.) Say the first bubble slowly so students can hear your name and repeat a few times if the students don't already know you. Then point to the second bubble and indicate to students to say *Hi Kate!* If necessary, repeat a couple of times until everyone is participating.

Erase your name from the bubbles, and pass the prop to a student, and point to the first bubble, and indicate for the students to say their own name, e.g. *Hi, I'm Azra*, then indicate to the class to say *Hi Azra*. The student passes the prop to another student, and the game repeats until everyone has had a turn.

Once students get the hang of the game, try to keep a pacey rhythm. If you have a small class, students could have more than one turn.

PAGE 6

To start

Share a few pictures of yourself when you were younger and get students to guess how old you are in the photo, e.g. *Five? Six?*

Invite students to electronically share with you, or bring in, a photo of themselves when they were younger for the next class. Make an electronic/photocopied collage of the photos with numbers and have other students guess who is in each photo. Weaker students could just give the number and a name, e.g. *picture three – Ana.* Stronger students could make sentences, e.g. *Is picture three Ana? Picture five is Mateo!*

1 Focus students' attention on the picture on the left of page 6 and start by asking: *What can you see in the picture?* (a baby/child, spaghetti). Say: *This is Sam. How old is Sam?*

Possible answer:
He's two.

---

explore **language**

Magnify the numbers on your projector if using, or list them vertically on the board. Add a '0', before the list, and say: *Zero.*

watch out for ⓘ

The *th* /θ/ sound in *three* may be unfamiliar to some students. Demonstrate how the tongue must be placed between your lips to make that sound.

2 S.1 Play the recording for students to listen first, and as you do, indicate on the board where you are up to. Then play the recording for students to listen and repeat. If the numbers are new to students, drill the number sequence in different ways, appropriate for your class, e.g. whispering along with the recording, using a baby's voice, clapping in between the numbers. Then, on the board, point to different numbers for students to say what they are.

extra 💬⁺

Write up on the board the words for one to twelve in random order, e.g. *two, five, one, twelve, three, four, seven, three, six, nine, eight, eleven.* Ask students to list the numbers 1–12 in their notebooks and write the correct word next to each. Alternatively, make a photocopied sheet with the numbers written out of order. Students cut up and put the numbers in the correct order.

extra: project ✏

Cut up numbers written in English from one – twelve. Place these around the room. Put students into small groups and each group must find numbers one to twelve and order them. To avoid chaos, only one student from each group gets up and finds a number and brings it back. Then the next student and so on.

---

alternative ⤴

For students who are already familiar with the number sequence, ask them to add numbers up to twelve. This is to practise number recognition when the numbers are out of sequence. For example, say *two and seven* (*nine*), *eight and four* (*twelve*). Then ask students to test each other in pairs, and see how many they can do it a minute.

Me and my family

3 S.2 Put students into pairs. Read each question, including the number, and ask students to tell their partner their guess.

extra: mixed-ability classes 🔀

If necessary, give a few possibilities for each, e.g. *Question One: How old is Sam now?* (*Five? Nine? Ten? Twelve?*) Allow a moment for students to guess in pairs. *Question Two: What's his favourite colour?* (*Red? Blue? Yellow?*) Point to something of each of the colours as you say the words. Then give students a moment to guess in pairs. *Question Three: Is spaghetti his favourite food now?* (*Yes? No?*) Give students a moment to guess in pairs.

Play the recording for students to check. Then read the questions one more time and elicit a choral answer to each from the class.

1 (He's) twelve.   **2** (It's) blue.   **3** Yes, (it is).

4 S.3 Give students a couple of minutes to read the quiz. Clarify unknown vocabulary by drawing or miming while repeating the word. Then play the recording again and ask students to underline Sam's answers. Go through the answers by repeating the number and question to elicit the answer, e.g. *One: What's Sam's favourite colour?* (*It's D – blue*).

1 D blue   **2 B** dog   **3 A** Italian food (spaghetti)
4 C photography   **5 A** football

extra 💬⁺

Use each question in the quiz as a springboard to elicit other colours, animals etc that students know, and write these on the board. Leave these displayed for reference during Ex 6–7.

Possible answers

colours: blue, green, red, yellow, pink, purple, black, white, brown
animals: bird, fish, duck, cow, pig, sheep
food: Turkish food, Spanish food, pizza, ice cream
hobbies: reading, TV, cooking, shopping
sports: tennis, cycling

PAGE 6 (Continued)

5 Ask students to answer the quiz questions. Circulate, providing any vocabulary required. Then, invite each student to tell the class one thing that their partner said.

Possible answers
Name and age: Adam, 10
1 green
2 D Other (bird)
3 C Mexican food
4 A Music
5 D Other (tennis)
<u>Reporting to the class</u>
Adam's favourite colour is green.
Adam's favourite animal is a bird.
Adam's favourite food is Mexican food.
Adam's favourite hobby is music.
Adam's favourite sport is tennis.

To finish

Draw a picture of one of the words from the lesson on the board (e.g. *swimming*), and while you are doing it, have students guess the word. Then, put students into groups of three or four. Students take turns to draw a word from the lesson, while the other students guess the word.

Presentation tool:	Starter Unit
Workbook / Online Practice:	p4
Grammar reference:	SB p114
Audioscript:	SB p144
Extra Practice App	

PAGE 7

To start

Show some photos of your family or draw your family on the board (real or invented). Write or share people's names, and try to elicit words in English for each family member's relationship with you (e.g. mother/mum, brother, parents, etc.). Write these on the board, and chorally drill them.

6 Direct students to Ex 1, read the rubric aloud, and ask students to find Sam's brother (D). Students match the words with the people in the photo then check the answers as a class.

A dad / father
B grandmother / grandma
C sister
D brother
E mum / mother
F grandfather / grandad

7 Give students a couple of minutes to read the post and find the names of each person then check as a class. Get students to work in pairs and take turns to say something about a person in the picture, e.g. *This is Sam's mum, Carmen.*

Sam's mum, Carmen
Sam's dad, Joe
Sam's brother Oscar
Sam's sister, Molly
Sam's grandfather, Ed
Sam's grandmother, Jill

explore **grammar**   ↳ SB p114 ▱

Point out the box, and review the pronouns: *I, you, he, she, it, we, they* by saying them aloud, and demonstrating with your hands, e.g. pointing to yourself for *I*. Then say *my* and point to some of your things as you say them, e.g. *my book, my bag, my chair, this is my mother.* Read the example aloud.

Do the same with the other possessive adjectives, e.g. say to a student: *Your name is Ben.* Then say to the class: *His name is Ben. Your name is Hana. Her name is Hana. Their names are Hana and Ben. Our school's name is … Its name is … .*

Turn to page 114, and go through the notes, then ask students to complete Ex 3 on page 115. Check as a class.

watch out for   ⓘ

Point out that *you* and *your* cover second person singular and plural, and are used with people you know well and people you don't know. The third person singular possessive adjectives *her / his / its* follow the gender of the possessor not the thing possessed.

8 Read the first sentence aloud as an example and elicit the missing word (*my*). Students complete the rest individually or in pairs, then check as a class.

1 My **2** Her **3** His **4** Their

explore **language**

Go through the box. Read out some numbers and ask students to write down the number they hear, e.g. say *sixty-two* and students write down *62*. Write them on the board for students to check. To challenge stronger students, try the reverse: you write up a numeral, e.g. *39*, and they have to whisper it to a partner or call it out (*thirty-nine*).

watch out for

Point out that numbers 13–19 have their own pattern, ending in -*teen*. Elicit the numbers … thirteen, fourteen, fifteen, sixteen, seventeen, eighteen, nineteen. Check students know the irregular <u>thir</u>teen and <u>fif</u>teen. Check students can differentiate the sounds of 13 and 30, 15 and 50, and 19 and 90 by calling out the numbers and asking students to write what they hear.

extra

Ask students to draw up a four by four grid and put in different numbers from one to one hundred in each square. Call out numbers, and students cross off the numbers they hear. The first to get four in a row horizontally, vertically or diagonally calls out 'Bingo!', and is the winner.

9 ◀)) S.4 Play the recording for students to listen and repeat. Then ask students to refer back to the text in Ex 2 and write down sentences showing each person's age, like the example: *Carmen is 37.*

Joe is 40.
Molly is 6.
Oscar is 5.
Ed is 59.
Jill is 62.

explore **grammar**   ↳ SB p114

Read through the box with the class, and as you go through the examples, ask students to notice the pronunciation of the contracted forms. Refer students to page 114, go through the notes and chorally drill the short forms. Ask students to complete Ex 4–6 on page 115, then check as a class.

watch out for

It's (short form of *it is*) and *its* (possessive adjective) sound the same, but are used differently. Only the short form of *it is* has an apostrophe.

10 Go through the grammar box. Tell students that the text is about some of Sam's other relatives. Give students a few minutes to read and complete the text. Ask students to compare their answers. Point out that this exercise is similar to the A1 Movers Reading and Writing Part 4 and A1 Key for Schools Reading and Writing Part 7 exam tasks. In both A1 Movers and A1 Key for Schools, the options are more varied (i.e. not just forms of the verb *to be*) and students will be presented with three possible options for each gap.

1 aren't (*aren't* is the short negative form *of to be*. This must be negative because the next part of the sentence says they are from Manchester (so not London).

2 is (subject is *my uncle's name* = it)

3 is (subject is *she*. Dad's sister is an aunt.)

4 are (subject is *the boys* = they)

5 am (subject is *I*)

6 is (subject *he*)

7 are (positive, because very close in the previous sentence = good friends)

8 isn't (*Tom* is a singular subject (he), and negative because he is not old, he's five.)

9 are (The subject is *Tom and Joel* so we use the *they* form of *to be*.)

extra: fast finishers

Ask fast finishers to try writing some positive sentences to go with each negative sentence in Ex 6 on page 115, e.g. *I'm eleven. Vassili and Kosta are friends.*

11 ◀)) S.5 Play the recording for students to check their answers. Write them on the board as well for weaker students. Ask some questions to test students' comprehension, e.g. *Who is fifteen?* (*Joel*). *What is Sam's uncle's name?* (*Andy*). *How old is Tom?* (*five*).

Possible answers

This is Sam's aunt, Jane.
This is Sam's cousin, Joel.
This is Sam's cousin, Tom.

extra: fast finishers

Students say a sentence about themselves or a person they know, for their partner to guess true or false, e.g. *My sister is two. Our dog's name is Max. My aunt is from London.*

To finish

Ask students to draw some of their family members or find some photos online (if they have access to mobile devices), then write at least one sentence about the person/people. Encourage stronger students to write more, and to see what other details they could write about, such as favourite hobby. Invite students to share about the family members they have drawn in small groups, e.g. *This is my cousin, Sarah. She is sixteen.*

Presentation tool:	Starter Unit
Workbook / Online Practice:	p5
Grammar reference:	SB p114
Audioscript:	SB p144
Extra Practice App	

PAGE 8

To start

Using the alphabet in Ex 1, ask students to count aloud in English the number of letters in the English alphabet to see how many there are (26). Ask students to work in pairs to review the alphabet and place a tick underneath any letters they already know the names of in English.

1 🔊 S.6 Play the recording for students to listen and notice the pronunciation. Then, play the recording again for students to listen and repeat.

> ### extra
> Choose a word from the unit so far, e.g. *eight*. Say it out loud, and students write the letters they hear, e.g. *E-I-G-H-T*. Then write the word on the board for students to check. Do two more examples with the class, e.g. *grandma, hobby*. Put students into pairs and ask them to choose words from the unit to spell out for their partner, who writes down the letters they hear. Circulate, listening to pronunciation of the letters and remodelling as required.

> ### watch out for ①
> Pay special attention to students' pronunciation of the letters, especially *i* and *e*. Other letters to watch for include the other vowels and the consonants *g, h,j, w, x y, z*.

2 Direct students to the picture of Sam's friends. Go through the words in the box, eliciting or communicating the meanings with sound/action, e.g. you could say *birthdays* then hum the first line of the *Happy Birthday* song. Then, re-read the list in the box and ask students to indicate what Sam and his friends are going to talk about.

> They talk about name and age, birthdays, hometown and favourite things.

3 🔊 S.7 Play the recording, then elicit which things were talked about.

4 🔊 S.8 Play the recording for students to write down the letters they hear, then write the answer on the board for students to check.

> A–L–Y–O–N–A (Alyona), I–N–E–S–S–A (Inessa)

5 For the class, spell out your first name and family name, or an invented name or the name of a celebrity, for them to write down, e.g. Say: *My first name is Taylor (T-A-Y-L-O-R) Taylor, and my family name is SWIFT (S-W-I-F-T) Swift.* Then put students into pairs to spell out their names to each other. If students are preparing for an exam, point out that students will be required to write down names or words that are spelled out (A1 Movers Listening Part 2 and A1 Key for Schools Parts 4 and 5 exam tasks).

> **Possible answers**
> My first name's Jason. J–A–S–O–N. Jason. My family name is Brown. B–R–O–W–N. Brown.

> ### extra: fast finishers 🏃
> For extra practice, students could choose the name of a famous person they like, and spell that name for their partner or spell out a family member's name.

> ## explore **grammar** → SB p114 ☑
> Go through the grammar box with the class. Ask a few students the example question: *Are you eleven?* (*Yes, I am* or *No, I am not.*). Then share the following examples: *Is your brother's name Harry? Yes, it is. | No, it isn't. Are your parents at home? Yes, they are. | No, they aren't.*
>
> Go through the Grammar reference on page 114 and ask the students to complete Ex 7 on page 115. After checking the answers as a class, invite students to ask and answer the questions in pairs. Circulate, listening to check that students are using relevant short answer replies.

> ### watch out for ①
> Students may need you to re-model the pronunciation of the short forms, especially *isn't* and *aren't*.

6 After going through the grammar box, write on the board: *… Sam eleven now?* Elicit whether the question should be completed with *Is* or *Are* and why. (*Is* because *Sam* (*he*) is singular.) Students complete the remaining questions. Check these as a class, then put students into pairs to ask and answer the questions.

> **1** Is **2** Are **3** Are **4** Is

7 🔊 S.9 Play the recording for students to hear the months of the year. Then give them time to practise before playing the recording again to listen and repeat.

> ### extra: whole class 👥
> Call out months of the year in random order and ask students to stand up and sit down when their birthday month is called. Gradually get faster.

8 🔊 S.10 Play the recording for students to match the names with the birthdays. Check the answers as a class. Point out that we use ordinal numbers to show the order of things, especially dates. We usually add *-th* to the end of a number to make an ordinal number. For ordinal numbers that end in 1, 2 or 3 we say, *first, second* and *third*.

> **1** B **2** G **3** C **4** A **5** F **6** E

> ### watch out for ①
> Point out to students that we write: 1st January, but we say: *The first of* January.

> ## explore **grammar** → SB p114 ☑
> Read through the explore grammar box with the class. Demonstrate 's for things people have by pointing to your Teacher's Book and say *Teacher's Book*. Write *Teachers Book* on the board, then make a point of adding the apostrophe, underlining the 's. Then point to other books in the class and say *Eve's book, Max's book*, etc. Write one of these on the board, emphasising the apostrophe. Refer students to the Grammar reference Ex 2 on page 115 to complete, then write the answers on the board for students to check.

watch out for

With most names, 's is not pronounced as a separated syllable. However, names that end in the sounds /s/, /ʃ/ or /dʒ/, such as Jess, Josh or Raj, then 's becomes a separate syllable, pronounced as /əz/. Introduce this information if required, depending on the names of students in your class.

9 Put students into pairs to ask questions about their birthdays.

extra: digital

Before class, search for a suitable alphabet or months song for your class, e.g. by searching YouTube for 'British English months of the year song'. Play the song to your class and invite students to listen and join in.

Fun footer

Ask students the question in the footer, if necessary clarifying the word *unusual* (different to what is usual or normal). Try to elicit the answer before sharing it. (February usually has 28 days. It is only every fourth year that February has 29 days. We call this a leap year.)

To finish

Distribute small pieces of paper for students to write their name and their birthday, e.g. *My name is Kevin. My birthday is 23 February.* Students could decorate if time allows. Combine these into a birthday table or poster to display in the classroom.

extra: critical thinking

If space allows, challenge students to order themselves in a line from the earliest to latest birthday in the year as fast as possible using only English. If you hear anyone speaking in other languages, they need to sit down and start again.

Presentation tool:	Starter Unit
Workbook / Online Practice:	p6
Grammar reference:	SB p114
Audioscript:	SB p144
Extra Practice App	

PAGE 9

To start

Students keep their books closed. Quickly revise the alphabet pronunciation from the previous lesson by saying the alphabet through with the class, using an alphabet song or replaying audio S.6 for students to listen and repeat.

Draw gaps on the board that correspond to the English name of the country you are in.

e.g. If you are in Poland, write _ _ _ _ _ _ .

Elicit guesses as to the letters in the word from the class, writing in correct guesses (and re-modelling correct pronunciation of letters as required), until students have completed the word. Repeat the game with a few other country names from page 9, e.g. Mexico, Australia, the USA.

10 Focus students' attention on the picture and elicit and chorally drill the word *map*. Work with students to find their country on the map and say the name(s) in English. Some students may identify with more than one country, and it may be important to them to acknowledge this.

Possible answers

My country's name is the Czech Republic.
My country is Argentina.
My countries are Peru and Britain.

11 Do the task as a class. Elicit what people students know in other countries and ask students to find the countries on the map. Give an example, e.g. *My brother lives Canada*, and direct students' attention to Canada on the map.

Possible answers

My aunt lives in France.
My friends are in Japan.

12 Direct students to the task. Do 1, 2 and 3 together, then instruct them to work individually. Monitor to provide encouragement. When students finish, put them into pairs and ask them to check their answers with their partner. Conduct class feedback, chorally drilling each country and checking understanding with the class.

1 Russia **2** Britain **3** the USA **4** Spain **5** Poland
6 Mexico   Turkey **8** China **9** Nigeria **10** Australia

13 Direct students to the task. Look at the first two sentences with the class. Put students into pairs to complete the exercise. Conduct whole class feedback.

1 Turkey **2** Mexico **3** USA **4** Spain **5** Poland **6** Britain
7 China **8** Nigeria **9** Russia **10** Australia

background

Britain may be used to refer to the physical island of Great Britain (where England, Wales, and Scotland are), or to the political country (officially *the United Kingdom of Great Britain and Northern Ireland*), which is made up of England, Wales, Scotland and Northern Ireland.

PAGE 9 (Continued)

14 Go through the words for nationality with the class, chorally drilling. Point out the example sentence, *Inessa's Spanish*, and elicit what the *'s* refers to here (short form of *is*). Check as a class, making sure students used the plural form *are* for the sentences about more than one person (*Alyona and Inessa*, and *Sam and Molly*).

Elif is Turkish.
Diego is Mexican.
Millie is American.
Alyona and Inessa are Spanish.
Stefan is Polish.
Sam and Molly are British.
Ju is Chinese.
Olu is Nigerian.
Anna is Russian.
Ryan is Australian.

> **alternative**
>
> If you are short on time for Ex 14, ask half the class to write sentences about the top row of people, and the other half to write sentences about the bottom row of people. Then conduct whole class feedback.

15 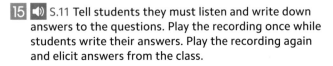 S.11 Tell students they must listen and write down answers to the questions. Play the recording once while students write their answers. Play the recording again and elicit answers from the class.

1 Anna is from Russia.
2 Elif is from Turkey.
3 Stefan is from Poland.
4 Jus is from China.
5 Olu is from Nigeria.
6 Ryan is from Australia.
7 Milie is from the USA.
8 Sam and Molly are from Britain.
9 Alyona and Inessa and from Spain.
10 Diego is from Mexico.

> **extra:** whole class
>
> Write the following questions on the board:
>
> *1 Where are you from?*
> *2 What's your favourite country?*
>
> Chorally drill the first question, then give your own answer, for example, say: *I'm from Russia.*
>
> Chorally drill the second question, then answer it, using the following model: *I like Britain, I like Mexico, but Russia is my favourite!* To support weaker students, write up your answers on the board so that they can use it as a prompt.
>
> Organise students into pairs to ask and answer the questions, or ask students to move around the classroom, asking and answering the questions of their classmates.

> **game** on
>
> Write on the board the following prompts for students to use if they need to (encourage more advanced students to avoid using them): *Yes, she/he is./No, she/he isn't./Yes, they are./No, they aren't.*
>
> Demonstrate the game as a class first. Ask everyone to close their books, and ask: *Are Sam and Molly from Britain?* Elicit the answer. (No, they aren't.) *Are Sam and Molly from Britain?* (Yes, they are.) Put students into pairs to play the game and tell them to ask three questions before swapping roles. (The person asking the question is allowed to look at the book.)

> **alternative**
>
> Put students into groups of three for the game. One student asks a question, and the other two race to answer correctly. The fastest person to answer asks the next question.

To finish

Challenge students to make a word grid. Write *Australian* on the board, then add the word *American* vertically down from the *A* of *Australian*. Then add the word *Brazilian* sharing the second *A* of *American*. Say: *How fast can you make a connected grid with all the nationalities in the lesson?* For more of a challenge, students could try it with the country names.

Presentation tool:	Starter Unit
Workbook / Online Practice:	p7
Grammar reference:	SB p114
Audioscript:	SB p144
Extra Practice App	

UNIT CHECK SB p10

This Unit check reviews numbers, family, months, countries and nationalities, possessive adjectives, possessive s and present simple of *to be*.

Practice

1 1 based 2 challenge 3 speak our minds
4 follow the crowd 5 issue 6 make up 7 reveals
8 stand out

2 **3** 🔊 9.12 and 9.13 1 addictive 2 patient 3 foolish
4 obsessed 5 suspicious 6 faulty 7 confidential
8 ambitious

1 Check students understand the word *important*, then share with the class your own answers (real or imagined) to 1–5. Write these on the board for students to refer to. Give some simple and some detailed answers to show your mixed-ability students a range to aim for, for example, by linking some of your examples with *because*.

Possible answers
1 Twenty-one, I'm twenty-one.
2 October, my birthday is in October.
3 The third. My birthday is on the third of October.
4 My important person is Sophie because she is my sister.
5 My important nationality is Nigerian because my grandfather is from Nigeria.

2 Elicit where to put *American* and *Australian* in the table (second column) then ask students to complete the remainder of the table independently. Go through the answers with the class. If students know any other nationalities with the endings, invite them to share for adding to the table, e.g. *Irish, Colombian, Portuguese*.

-ish: British, English, Polish, Spanish, Turkish
-an / -ian: American, Australian, Mexican, Nigerian, Russian
-ese: Chinese

3 🔊 S.12 Play the recording while students write the words they hear. Ask students to compare their answers in pairs, then play the recording again. Organise students into groups of four to rewrite the sentences. Give each group a different coloured board pen to come and write their answers on the board, and see which group got the sentences exactly right.

1 My grandmother is from Brazil. She's seventy. Her name's Marina.
2 My cousin is Spanish. His birthday is in March. He's ten.

GRAMMAR FILE SB p115

1 1 Those are the cat's toys. 2 My sister's pens are in her bag.
3 My cousin's name is Ross.

2 Sentences 2, 3, 5 and 7 have possessive 's.

3 1 Our 2 Her 3 Their 4 His 5 My 6 your

4 1 are 2 is 3 is 4 is 5 are 6 are

5 1 A 2 C 3 E 4 D 5 B

6 Students' own answers.

7 1 Are 2 Is 3 Are 4 Is 5 Is

Presentation tool:	Starter Unit, Unit check
Grammar reference:	SB p114
Audioscript:	SB p144
Extra Practice App	

Come in

1

VOCABULARY 1
things in a room, prepositions of place

READING
topic: a birthday party – story
skill: using photos to understand a text
task: sentence completion

GRAMMAR
there is/there are (+ some/any)
have got

VOCABULARY 2
the home

LISTENING
topic: homes around the world
skill: choosing the correct picture
task: multiple choice (pictures)

SPEAKING
topic: phone conversations
skill: using appropriate levels of formality
task: make a phone call

WRITING
topic: favourite things
skill: using capital letters
task: make a personal profile

SWITCH ON
video: tiny house tour
project: tiny house presentation

Lead-in SB p11

As students enter the classroom, make a point of saying *come in* which is the unit title.

Magnify the quote on the Presentation tool, if using, or write the quote on the board for students to read. Check they understand the words: *room*, *special* and *world*.

1 Direct students to the photo and ask them to work in pairs to find the words in the box in the photo.

> **extra:** whole class
>
> As an extension, ask students to find out what colour each thing is, e.g. white bed, orange chair. Ask: *What else can you see in the room?* e.g. mat, book, clock, picture, bin, flags.

2 Students give their opinion of the room in the photo by selecting one of the emjois (great, OK, boring). Conduct whole class feedback and find out how many students chose the same emojis. Elicit reasons for their answers.

> **Possible answer**
> I think the room is great because it has the colour blue. Blue is my favourite colour.

> **extra**
>
> Ask students to work in pairs and talk about their own bedroom at home. Give an example, e.g. *My bedroom is white and yellow. Yellow is my favourite colour. There is a bed, a lamp, a table and a window in my bedroom.* Encourage them to use the words in the list in Ex 1 and to talk about colours.

VOCABULARY 1 SB p12

To start

Write on the board the following anagrams of colours: *dre, nrege, leub, worbn, granoe, clakb, lewoly, wheti, regy.* Point to the first word, cross out the *r* and write it somewhere else on the board. Ask students: *What colour is this?* (Red.) Then cross out *e* and write *e* next to *r.* Cross out the *d* and write it next to *re* to make *red.* Put students into pairs to solve the other anagrams and write down the other colours listed (green, blue, brown, orange, black, yellow, white, grey). If students find this too hard, supply them with the first letter of each colour. Drill the colours chorally, indicating something of each colour if possible, paying special attention to the correct pronunciation of orange /ˈɒrəndʒ/.

If students are preparing for the Pre A1 Starters exam, point out that they will have a spelling task (Reading and Writing Part 3), which involves unscrambling letters to spell words. They will be given pictures for each scrambled word.

Power up

1 Ask: *Do you like your bedroom? Why?* Less confident students may respond to first part of question alone with *Yes/No.* Encourage more confident students to give reasons, e.g. Yes, because it's green / big / nice / my room!

Drill the words in the box, pointing out the *bed covers* and *mat* in the picture on page 11, and pointing to curtains, wall, floor in the classroom. checking students know how to say curtains /ˈkɜːtnz/ correctly. Direct students to the question: *What colour are these things in your room?* and ask: *What colour are your curtains?* Elicit some responses, e.g. (Blue. / My curtains are blue. / I don't have curtains.). Ask: *What colour is your mat?* (e.g. Brown and white. / My mat is brown and white. / I don't have a mat.) Get two stronger students to write up these two questions on the board, aided by the rest of the class. Put students into pairs to ask their partners what colour the things are.

Possible answers
My bed covers are blue and purple. My curtains are green. My floor is grey. I don't have a mat. My walls are white.

> **extra:** fast finishers
> Encourage fast finishers to ask about other items, using the list in Ex 2 for ideas.

things in a room

2 Direct students to the list of things. Ask: *Where is the bin?* And get students to find it in the photos, the write the letter next to the word. Ask students to match the remaining things with the photos then compare their answers in pairs. Don't check the answers at this point as they will be checked in Ex 3.

A lamp	**B** desk	**C** pictures	**D** cushions	**E** TV
F shelf (shelves)	**G** noticeboard	**H** clock	**I** mirror	
J bin	**K** laptop	**L** wardrobe		

3 1.1 Play the recording for students to check their answers to Ex 2. Play the track again, pausing the recording for students to repeat the words.

A lamp	**B** desk	**C** pictures	**D** cushions	**E** TV
F shelf (shelves)	**G** noticeboard	**H** clock	**I** mirror	
J bin	**K** laptop	**L** wardrobe		

4 Students make a list of things in their room from Ex 2. They will need the list for Ex 5 and Ex 7.

Possible answer
bin, desk, lamp, mirror, pictures, shelves

5 Go through the instructions and example. In pairs, students take turns to tell their partner about an item in their room and what colour it is (using their list from Ex 4).

Possible answer
My bin is grey.
My desk is brown.
My lamp is red.
My mirror is white.
My pictures are blue, green, red and yellow.
My shelves are black.

prepositions of place

6 To demonstrate and drill the prepositions in Ex 6, use a prop appropriate for your cohort, such as a teddy bear, a ball, or a pen, with a box. For example, hold the prop above a box, and say *above, the ball is above the box* and chorally drill *above.* Move the ball in relation to the box and repeat with the other prepositions. Direct students to the artwork in Ex 6, and ask students to write a sentence with each, while you circulate to provide assistance. Go through the answers with the class.

> **extra:** project
> Students make a poster showing the prepositions of place in panels similar to the artwork listed using their own interests, e.g. a football and a school bag, or a dog and a bed. Each picture should be labelled with the preposition. Alternatively, for a shorter activity, divide the prepositions amongst the class, and ask each student to prepare a picture demonstrating one preposition. Display these in the classroom.
>
> **1** The cat is in the bag.
> **2** The cat is on the chair.
> **3** The cat is under the chair.
> **4** The cat is next to the chair.
> **5** The cat is above the chair. / The cat is on the shelf.
> **6** The cat is behind the bag.
> **7** The cat is in front of the bag.
> **8** The cat is near the chair.
> **9** The cat is between the bag and the chair.
> **10** The orange cat is opposite the grey cat.

VOCABULARY 1 (Continued)

7 Ask a student to give you their list, and demonstrate asking some questions about items on it, e.g. *Where's your lamp?* (It's on the desk.) Students do the activity in pairs.

Possible answer

A: Where's your TV?   **B:** It's on the table.
B: Where are your pictures?
A: On the wall and on the shelves.
A: Where is your laptop?   **B:** It's in my bag.

---

extra: whole class

Get one student at a time to go up to the board and write a word at a time to make a sentence about something in the classroom.

e.g. Student 1 – The
Student 2 – board
Student 3 – is
Student 4 – behind
Student 5 – the
Student 6 – teacher's
Student 7 – desk.

Then, get students to sit in groups in circles. Each student starts with a piece of paper and writes the first word of a sentence, then passes it to the next student who has to write the next word, and so on. When the sentences are complete, ask students to read them out to the group.

---

game on

Ask students to read the example, and underline the structure *Is it a … on … a … ?* on the Presentation tool, if using, or write up the prompt on the board.

Demonstrate the game. On the board, very quickly and roughly draw a TV on a shelf. Ask: *What's in my picture?* and elicit guesses using the structure. Students then play with a partner, and then play again with a new partner.

Fun footer

Read the fun footer with the class. If you have the facilities, show a picture of Buckingham Palace. Ask them to guess how many bathrooms there are (seventy-eight).

To finish

Play this game with the whole class. Call out sentences for students to draw in 20 seconds, e.g. *Draw a cat on a bed.* Then ask students to show their partner to check they have drawn the correct preposition. If students have coloured pencils or pens each, add a colour element, e.g. *Draw a blue bag next to a brown chair.* Students could say their own sentence for a partner to draw.

Presentation tool:	Unit 1, Vocabulary 1
Workbook / Online Practice:	p8
Grammar reference:	SB p116
Extra Practice App	

READING SB p13

To start

Write up the following puzzles on the board and put students in small groups to solve them. Students should write the answer on a piece of paper and race it to you. The first group to get all correct wins.

1 J F M A M J J   2 M T W T F S S   3 O T T F F S S

1 January, February, March, April, May, June, July
2 Monday, Tuesday, Wednesday, Thursday, Friday, Saturday, Sunday
3 one, two, three, four, five, six, seven

Power up

1 Direct students to the pictures and ask them to work in pairs to see how many things they can name in the room using the words from the previous lesson, e.g. *lamp, door, mat, bin*. Point to the *box* in the picture B, and the *key* in picture C, and see if students know these words (or teach them). Demonstrate two sentence forms students can use to make sentences about the room, e.g. *This is a key. The key is yellow.* Students work in pairs and take turns making sentences.

Possible answer

This is a mat. The mat is grey. This is a table. The table is brown. The walls are grey. This is a picture.

skill tip

Read the tip with the class. Point out that students can this is a useful strategy when reading books and in the exam if they take one. Tell students it is best to look at the pictures first to work out what the story is about before reading the text.

2 Go through the instructions with the class. Then give students time to read the story and answer the questions. Clarify unknown vocabulary as necessary, e.g. escape, special, secret, instructions, lock (verb). If students haven't guessed where they are, tell them that it is an escape room – a special room which is a puzzle and you have to solve clues to escape.

1 There are three children.   **2** Joanna (Jo), Kate and Ben
3 They're in an escape room.

---

exam task: A1 Movers Reading and Writing Part 5

In the A1 Movers Reading and Writing Part 5 exam task, there are two examples and seven items. The text is a continuous narrative.

3 Direct students to the instructions and the example. Students complete the sentences individually then compare in pairs before checking as a class.

1 (birthday) party (Ben and Kate are at her **birthday party**. *HAPPY BIRTHDAY, Jo!* The party is in an Escape Room.)
2 the bin (Jo: *There's a message in* **the bin**.)
3 box (Ben: *Here's the* **box** *– look!*)
4 a key (*The* **key** *is for the box under the bed.*)
5 on (Ben: *Under the mat* **on** *the floor.*)
6 door/secret door/escape door (Kate: *Yes, there is a* **door**! *It's the escape door!*)

Sum up

4 Go through the instructions as a class, then direct students to the first word *birthday*. Ask students to find it in the text (line 1) and elicit the object it goes with *party*. Ask students to complete 2–5 by finding the words in the text. Conduct whole class feedback.

1 birthday **party** **2** secret **door** **3** big **puzzle game**
4 special **room** **5** red **picture**

Speak up

5 Elicit some responses to the first question, encouraging stronger students to give a reason. Then ask students to ask and answer the questions in pairs. Elicit some other fun party ideas.

Possible answers

Yes. / No.
Yes because I like puzzles. / I like escape rooms. / There are friends at the party.
Pizza parties are fun. / Parties at the swimming pool are fun. / I like parties at home.

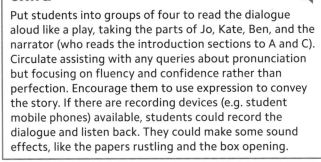

extra

Put students into groups of four to read the dialogue aloud like a play, taking the parts of Jo, Kate, Ben, and the narrator (who reads the introduction sections to A and C). Circulate assisting with any queries about pronunciation but focusing on fluency and confidence rather than perfection. Encourage them to use expression to convey the story. If there are recording devices (e.g. student mobile phones) available, students could record the dialogue and listen back. They could make some sound effects, like the papers rustling and the box opening.

Fun footer

Read the fun footer aloud. Ask: *Are there escape rooms in this country? Have you been to an escape room?*

To finish

In front of the class, make a show of writing a secret note on a piece of paper, (e.g. *Well done!*), and folding it up so that the message cannot be seen. Ask for three volunteers to be the secret agents and indicate for them to briefly wait outside the classroom. With the remaining students, negotiate a hiding place for the secret note with the class to hide the note, e.g. behind the curtain. Invite the secret agents back into the class. The secret agents stand at the front of the class, and take turns to guess where the secret note is hidden, using prepositions, e.g. *Is it in the cupboard? Is it on the TV? Is it under Sam's chair?* Indicate the class should chorally respond *yes* or *no*. The first secret agent to guess the place correctly, is allowed to retrieve the note and read it. If after three guesses each, the secret agents have not guessed correctly, then the class is the winner. Repeat with other students as the secret agents if time allows.

Presentation tool:	Unit 1, Reading
Workbook / Online Practice:	p9
Photocopiable activity:	1A
Grammar reference:	SB p116
Extra Practice App	

GRAMMAR SB p14

To start

Tell the students that you are going to give them a puzzle to solve and they should listen carefully. Read the puzzle twice. There are ducks in front of two ducks. There are two ducks behind two ducks. There are two ducks in between two ducks. How many ducks are there? Ask students to whisper to a partner what they think the answer is, then elicit guesses. (Answer: There are four.)

alternative

You may want to download the Grammar Presentation for this lesson from the Teacher Resources area of Pearson English Portal. This presentation has been created specifically for this lesson and is fully editable for teachers.

explore **grammar** ↳ SB p116

1 Direct students to the first sentence and elicit the correct alternative ('s) and why (there is only one desk). Go through the answers with the class, and as you do, elicit a reason for each answer. Ask students to underline the words *a*, *any* and *some* in sentences 1–4, and see if students can work out a rule of why each word has been used in each case (*a* is used after *is / isn't*, *any* is used after *aren't*, and *some* is used after *are*). For more detailed notes, refer students to page 116 and go through the notes with the class in the left column. Try to add some examples from your own classroom.

extra: fast finishers

Write up these two additional items for Ex 1 on the board for fast finishers.

There's / are some boxes under the bed in Ed's room.
There isn't / aren't a laptop in May's room.
(answers: 3 are 4 isn't)

1 There's (desk is singular)
2 isn't (bin is singular)
3 aren't (pictures are plural)
4 There are (cushions are plural)

watch out for

Check students are clear that *some* is used in positive sentences and *any* is used with negative sentences and questions.

2 ▶ ◀») 1.3 Give students a moment to read the sentences, then play the recording. Elicit the answers, then play the recording again for students to notice the pronunciation, especially of *isn't* and *cushions*. Give students a moment to practise reading the sentences aloud, focusing on pronunciation.

We hear sentences 2, 3 and 5.
2 There is a bed next to the window.
3 There isn't an iPad on my desk.
5 There are lots of cushions on the end of my bed.

GRAMMAR (Continued)

3 1.4 Play the recording for students to listen and notice the pronunciation of the highlighted words and letters. Elicit what they noticed (e.g. *are* is unstressed, pronounced (/ə/), and the *'s* is pronounced /z/ and *There's* is one syllable). Play it again for students to listen and repeat.

4 Read through the instructions with the class. Put students into pairs for the activity and ask them to decide who will write about each picture. Circulate while students write their questions, checking the questions are correct.

alternative

Organise students into pairs then assign each pair either picture A or B. Students in a pair work together to write three questions about their assigned picture, but both students need to write out theirown copy of the question. Then organise students into new pairs of one student who has prepared question for picture A and one for B, to ask and answer the question.

Possible answer

Questions about picture A

Is there a dog on the chair?

Are there any books on the shelves?

Are there any drinks on the table?

5 Students keep the same pairs as Ex 4 and ask and answer their questions. Ask each pair to share one of their questions and answers for the class (or if you have a very large class, ask a few students to do so).

Possible answer

Questions about picture A

A: Is there a dog on the chair?

B: No, there isn't. There's a cat on the chair!

A: Are there any books on the shelves?

B: No, there aren't.

A: Are there any drinks on the table?

B: Yes, there are.

exam task: A1 Movers Speaking Part 1

In the A1 Movers Speaking Part 1 exam task, the pictures are a little less cluttered, so each difference is very clear and easy to spot. Above-level language is never required to describe any of the differences. The interaction here is between two students, which is useful in the classroom, but in the A1 Movers exam the interaction is between one candidate and an examiner.

6 **e** Make sure students understand *differences*. Read the example, and elicit a way to complete the sentence, e.g. … *it's behind the chair.* In pairs, students should take turns to describe differences. Elicit some differences from the class and write them on the board (if there are errors, acknowledge the part that is correct, and remodel correct version, e.g. Student: *There are popcorn on the table.* Teacher: *There is popcorn on the table.*)

Possible answers

In picture A there are some computer games on the shelves, next to the TV. But in picture B the games are on the floor.

In picture A there's a lamp next to the TV, but in picture B it's behind the chair.

In picture A there's popcorn on the table, but in picture B it's on the floor.

In picture A there is a grey cat on the chair, but in picture B the grey cat is under the table.

The order of answers doesn't matter. Your sentences can be different, as long as you find four things and explain what you think about each one. E.g. you could say *This cat is happy. But now it isn't happy. The popcorn is on the table, but now it isn't on the table. This thing* (if you can't remember the name) *is next to the TV, but now it's near/ behind/next to the chair.*

Speak up

7 Direct students to the instructions. Ask a few students the example question and some similar questions, e.g. *Are there books in your bedroom? Is there a TV in your room?* Ask students to write two similar questions while you monitor for accuracy. Students ask and answer the questions in pairs.

Possible answers

A: Are there posters in your bedroom?

B: Yes, there are.

A: Is there a laptop in your bedroom?

B: No, there isn't.

To finish

Finish with another puzzle, e.g. *In a house, there are two fathers and two sons. How many people are there in the house?* (Three: a grandfather, father, and son. The father is also a son.)

Presentation tool:	Unit 1, Grammar
Workbook / Online Practice:	p10
Grammar reference:	SB p116
Audioscript:	SB p144
Extra Practice App	

VOCABULARY 2 SB p15

To start

On the board, write: *b ... s ... c ... p ...* Get students to guess the things in your bedroom based on the first letters of each word on the board (bed, shelves, clock, poster) and write them up. Next, tell the students to write the first letter of four things in their bedroom. Put students in pairs to guess their partner's four things.

the home

1 🔊 1.5 Focus students' attention on the picture of Joe's apartment. Indicate for students to point to the relevant space in the apartment as they hear it. Play the recording, indicating for students to repeat after Joe.

1 Welcome to my home. These are the stairs.
2 This is the living room.
3 This is the kitchen.   4 Here's the dining room.
5 And here's the bedroom.   6 That's the bathroom.
7 This is the balcony   8 That's the garden.
9 And that's the garage.

2 Say: *Where is Joe's bed?* Indicate for students to point to the bed, and say: *The bed is in the bedroom.* Put students in pairs to say where they can see each of the things. Conduct whole class feedback.

The bed is in the bedroom.
The chairs are in the dining room.
The light is in the living room.
The picture is in the bedroom.
The TV is in the living room. / The TV is under the light.
The window is in the bathroom.

3 Go through the example with the class and demonstrate that students can form new questions by substituting *windows* with other objects.

explore **language**

Read the box aloud, and ask the question indicating you mean in Joe's apartment. Ask the class some questions using *How many ... ?* e.g. *How many students are in our class? How many doors | windows | lights are there in our classroom?*

watch out for ①

Make sure students only use plural nouns with *how many*, e.g. ~~How many light is there?~~ *How many lights are there?*

Possible answer

A: How many chairs are there?
B: There are four chairs. How many cats are there?
A: There aren't any cats. Is there a TV?
B: Yes, there is.

exam task: A1 Movers Reading and Writing Part 6 ↪ p15

Read the exam tip with the class. In the A1 Movers Reading and Writing Part 6 exam task there would be two examples, and the gap in question 2 would be at the end of the sentence. There would not be animals all around the house as in the illustration, and the rubric would be 'Look and read and write'.

4 🅔 Point out that for sentences 1 and 2, students only need a few words. For 3 and 4, students should make sure that they use the same grammar in the answer as in the question, e.g. *Are there ... ? Yes, there are.* For questions 5 and 6, students need to write a full sentence with a verb (*is/are*). It can be a short sentence but they shouldn't use the same sentences from questions 1–4!

Students complete the exercise then compare in pairs. Conduct whole class feedback.

Possible answers

1 on the balcony
2 Model answer: The man and (the) woman
3 The two dogs are in the bathroom. / There are two (dogs in the bathroom).
4 Two children are upstairs. / There are two (children upstairs).
5 & 6 Model answers: The people are happy. The house is small. There's a garden and it's very green. There are brothers and sisters in the house.
(These sentences move from simple/correct to more complex.)
1 and 2: You only need a few words.

game on

Go through the instructions. Demonstrate the game by choosing one of the homes and inviting students to ask you *Yes/No* questions about it to work out which one., e.g. *Are there children in the house? Is there a TV? Is the house yellow?* Then put students into teams of 3–4 and organise the teams to play each other.

alternative ⇅

Find pictures of two or three new home interiors on the internet to show on your projector/IWB for the game.

To finish

Write a number on the board, and see if students can work out the question using *how many*. Encourage students to help each other generate questions if necessary, e.g. write the number 7 (*How many days in a week? | How many windows are there in the classroom? How many pens are there on the table?*). Do a few numbers, then students could try the game in pairs if time allows.

Presentation tool:	Unit 1, Vocabulary 2
Workbook / Online Practice:	p11
Grammar reference:	SB p116
Audioscript:	SB p144
Extra Practice App	

LISTENING SB p16

To start

Write on the board some scrambled sentences about your home and ask students to work in pairs to work out the correct order. Alternatively, if you have time, you could write the words on slips of paper for students to re-order (a different colour for each sentence). Elicit the order and write the correct sentences on the board as a prompt for Ex 2.

e.g. 1 a apartment it's big (*It's a big apartment.*)
　　2 are there bedrooms three (*There are three bedrooms.*)
　　3 a balcony there isn't (*There isn't a balcony.*)

Power up

1 Put students into pairs to describe their home. Encourage students to talk about the items listed but some students may choose to describe other aspects of their home as well.

Possible answers

It's a house. There isn't a balcony. There's a brown door. There's a nice garden. There are two bedrooms, a small bathroom and a living room. There are big windows.

Listen up

2 Direct students to the photos. Elicit some sentences about the first picture. If students are likely to have problems making sentences, write up three possible structures on the board: *There's a small | big house | apartment. It's blue | yellow … The door is grey | green.* Put students into pairs to describe the photos. Conduct whole class feedback.

Houses: 1 A　**1** C　**3** A　**3** B　**3** C　**5** B
Apartments: 1 B　**5** A　**5** C

---

exam task: A1 Movers Listening Part 4

In the A1 Movers Listening Part 4 exam task, there is an example, and the items would not have a common theme. In Ex 3 there is one because this is the topic of the unit.

3 **e** 🔊 1.6 Direct students to the first row of pictures in Ex 2. Explain that students will hear people describing their homes. They then have to choose which home is described.Play the first conversation, then pause for students to tick the picture. Then tell students they will hear four more conversations, and to tick the related picture in each row. Play the rest of the recording. Elicit the answers. Check students understand the meaning of *sunny, roof, lift* using questions, e.g. sunny: *Is it light or dark? Is it cold or warm?* Roof: *Is this at the bottom of the house? Is it at the top? What is it for?* Lift: *What is it for?*

---

1 B (it's got orange walls and a sunny balcony)
2 A (it has a balcony , no lift – the cat likes the balcony)
3 A (it's got a garden)
4 A (it's got white walls, kitchen and dining room downstairs, this is the living room)
5 C (it hasn't got a garden, it's got stairs outside)

---

explore grammar　➥ SB p116

Read through the box with the class and go over the positive, negative and question forms, focusing on the pronunciation of contracted forms..

alternative

Get students to find and highlight examples of *have got* in the audioscript on page 144. Get students to notice the different forms (negative, positive, questions) and how it is used. Get them to explain to you (using L1 if appropriate).

watch out for ⓘ

Point out that *it's* can be a short form of *it is* or *it has*, e.g. *It's got a sunny balcony* = it has. *It's a small apartment* = it is.

For more detailed notes and examples, refer students to the Grammar reference on page 116. Direct students to Ex 4–5 on page 117 and do the first one of each on the board with the class as an example. Students complete the remainder of the exercises then check as a class.

extra

Students move around the class, asking and answering the questions in Ex 5 on page 117 with different partners. You could encourage stronger students to try not to look down at their book.

4 Direct students to the table and ask students to work out which are Nina and Luke's homes. Ask students to write sentences about the homes using *has got/hasn't got*. Circulate, monitoring for accuracy. Fast finishers could draw up a similar table for another home, then either swap with another fast finisher to guess which home it was, or share for the class to guess.

Luke's house has got a garden and big windows. It hasn't got orange walls or a red balcony.

Nina's apartment hasn't got a garden or big windows. It has got orange walls and a red balcony.

---

5 Go through the instructions and example with the class then give students time to ask and answer in pairs. Ask a few pairs to share one of their question and answers.

Possible answers

Has Nina's apartment got big windows?
No, it hasn't.
Has Luke's home got a garden?
Yes, it has.

To finish

Introduce the idea of a dream home. Tell students about your dream home, e.g. say *My dream home is a very nice house in California with a swimming pool. It has got ten bedrooms and three bathrooms. I have got three dogs in my big garden.* Ask students to draw a picture of their dream home, and present to a partner / group / the class (depending on class size).

Presentation tool:	Unit 1, Listening
Workbook / Online Practice:	p12
Photocopiable activity:	1B
Grammar reference:	SB p116
Audioscript:	SB p144
Extra Practice App	

SPEAKING SB p17

To start

Say a phone number, pronouncing each number individually, but chunking the numbers and pausing between chunks, e.g. *zero-seven-four three-six-two-five-nine-four* and indicate for students to write down the numbers they hear. Say it at normal speed – then slow – then normal speed. If possible, use an actual relevant number, e.g. your school's phone number.

Power up

1 Put students into pairs to practice the conversation. Remind them to focus on the chunking of numbers and pausing between chunks. Circulate to provide pronunciation assistance as required.

2 Direct students to the instructions. Tell students that they can use a real or imagined number. Get students to sit back to back to have this conversation and to note down the numbers. This helps focus on the listening skill and also avoids students looking and immediately correcting their partner.

Possible answer
A: What's your mobile number?
B: It's 034 764 341.
A: (*Student A writes down the number and shows the number*) Is that right?
B: No, this number is wrong. It's 034 76<u>5</u> 341.

3 🔊 1.7 Get students thinking about the situation before completing the exercise by drawing a plant pot next to a wall with a key in it. Label *plant pot* and *spare key*. Ask: *Why might there be a key in the plant pot?* Get students to complete the conversation individually. Then students could compare their answers in pairs. Play the recording for students to check their answers.

   1 Where are you?
   2 Have you got your key?
   3 Where's the spare key?
   4 Is it in the plant pot next to the wall?

Speak up

4 🔊 1.8 Play the recording for students to write down the words they hear. Check answers as a class.

   1 Hello **2** Hi **3** Thanks **4** Bye

5 Chorally drill the phrases in the useful language box. Put students into groups of three to practise the conversation. If students want to, they can change the names of the characters to suit them, e.g. Mum can become Dad/Mr Reeves.

SPEAKING (Continued)

Speaking extra

6 Chorally drill the words in the skill tip box using some different manners – happy, sad, angry, bored, etc. Put students into pairs to roleplay the phone calls. If students are able to, they could roleplay the phone call without notes. Weaker students/classes may like to write their own script and then practise it. Give students the opportunity to perform their phone call for the class.

Possible answer

A: Hi. It's Molly here.

B: Hi Molly. It's Cara. Have you got my mobile?

A: Your mobile? No, sorry, I haven't got it but is it in your coat?

B: Oh yes ... it is! Thanks Molly.

A: That's okay, bye.

7 Students swap pairs and think of different things and people for the conversation in Ex 6. They then practise the conversation. Ask a few pairs to model their conversations for the class.

Possible answer

A: Hi. It's Brenden here.

B: Hi Brenden. It's Tom. Have you got my pen?

A: Your pen? No, sorry, I haven't got it, but is it in your bag?

B: Oh yes ... it is! Thanks Brenden.

A: That's okay, bye.

To finish

Write up on the board *bye, goodbye, see you later, see you tomorrow, see you next week*. Ask students to say goodbye with one of the phrases to at least three other students before leaving the class. Then say goodbye everyone and indicate for them to say *goodbye [your name]*. Repeat with the other phrases. If possible, stand at the door of the classroom so that each student can practice saying goodbye to you individually as they leave.

Presentation tool:	Unit 1, Speaking
Workbook / Online Practice:	p13
Photocopiable activity:	1C
Grammar reference:	SB p116
Speaking file:	SB p134

WRITING SB p18–19

To start

Write a sentence on the board about a holiday you have been without capitals. Tell the students to work in pairs to talk about how many capital letters are needed and where they should be. Invite students to the board to make the changes.

i went to london in june with my friend mary. (Answer: 4 capital letters: I went to London in June with my friend Mary.)

Power up

1 Direct students to the words in the box. If you can, bring in real objects, e.g. a birthday card, a cinema ticket. Otherwise, use the pictures on page 18 or pictures from the internet to show these items. Check they understand the new words and chorally drill them.

Possible answer

I've got some books. I've got some cinema tickets and photos. I've got a poster. I haven't got any postcards or birthday cards.

2 Focus students' attention on Jorge's noticeboard. Ask them to find the things in the box and then elicit which of the things start with capital letters (all of them).

Possible answer

a city: Sydney

a country: Canada

a film: Ocean Warrior

some names: Jake, Marina, Isabella

3 Direct students to find the answers to the questions by looking at the noticeboard. Elicit the answers. Background note: polar bears live within the Arctic Circle, so they come from the northern parts of other countries, too, e.g. Norway, Russia, Alaska (part of the USA) and Greenland.

1 Isabella 2 Ocean Warrior 3 07977 405637
4 Canada 5 twelve 6 Marina

---

alternative

Display Jorge's noticeboard on your projector. Put a copy of the questions from Ex 3 outside the classroom and tell students to close their books. Put students into groups of 4. One person from each group runs outside to read the question and runs back to repeat the question from memory to their group. If they forget the question they have to run back outside. The group listens to the question then finds the answer to the question on the projected noticeboard. When they have written down the answer the next person in the group runs outside to read and memorise question 2 and so on.

---

extra

Ask students to find and highlight instances of the words *about, of* or *from* on Jorge's noticeboard.

---

4 Direct students to the first sentences as an example and elicit the correct preposition. Students complete the remaining sentences then check as a class.

1 from 2 of 3 about 4 about 5 of 6 from

In the Flyers Reading and Writing Part 3 exam task there would be ten words in the box and the title question would be after the text. 'I' would always be capitalised.

5 e Go through the task instructions and the example with the class, pointing out how *tickets* is crossed out, and recommend that students cross out as they use words to keep track. Students complete the task individually before comparing in pairs, then checking as a class.

1 My (capital letter to start a sentence, *My* not *your* because the profile is Emma's and she is talking about her interests.)

2 fantastic (*fantastic* means *very good*. It can't be *favourite* because *favourite* usually comes after a possessive adjective like *my*. It cannot be *blue* because *blue* must fit gap (3) which is about colour.)

3 blue (*blue* is the only colour on the list.)

4 favourite (*favourite* is an adjective meaning the one someone likes best.)

5 Spain (After *I'm from* we need a place. Spain is the only place on the list.)

C All about my favourite sport (C is the best title because the whole profile is related to her favourite sport. She mentions her favourite football players and colour, but it is not the overall topic.)

Plan on

6 Ask students to choose three or four things to bring for their profile to discuss in the next class. Even if they can't bring actual items, students should decide on 3–4 answers to talk about.

Possible answer
Things for my profile
1 birthday card – from grandma
2 photo – me and Mary
3 postcard – from Italy
4 pool ticket
5 menu – pizza restaurant

Write on

Go through the useful language box, and use examples from your own things. For example, hold up some books, and say *here are some of my books. This is my cinema ticket. That's my photo. My favourite postcard is from my friend Mary in London.*

7 Students can choose to layout their profile like Jorge's or Emma's or in their own way. They could handwrite or type if computers are available. Circulate, providing assistance.

Possible answer
Here is a photo of me and my friend Mary.
This is a special birthday card from my grandma.
This is a postcard from my friend. It's from Italy.
My favourite sport is swimming. Here is my pool ticket.
That's a picture of my home. Look at my cat on the balcony!

Improve it

8 Remind students to check capital letters against the list in the skill tip. Get students to check a partner's work for capital letters.

skill tip

Go through the skill tip with the class. Elicit or highlight any differences from students' other language(s).

To finish

Put students into small groups to share their profiles. Encourage students to ask questions about each other's profiles like the questions in Ex 6.

Presentation tool:	Unit 1, Writing
Workbook / Online Practice:	p14
Grammar reference:	SB p116
Writing file:	SB p134

SWITCH ON SB p20

Tiny house tour

1 Put students into pairs to think of five rooms in a house and write their list. Check as a class.

Possible answers
bathroom, bedroom, dining room, kitchen, living room

---

extra: whole class

Show some pictures of *tiny houses* on your projector/ interactive whiteboard if you can. Elicit that *tiny* means very small. Ask: *What rooms would you expect a tiny house to have?* Introduce the word *loft* for an open upstairs area.

Tell students that they're going to watch a video about Annabel O'Neill, who built her own tiny house on wheels.

---

2 ▶ Ask students to think about how their house is different to Annabel's as they watch the video clip for the first time. Give some examples of things that might be different, e.g. What rooms are in the home? What things are in the home? What colour are the things? Who lives there? Give them the option to take notes if they want to. Then ask students to discuss differences they noticed. Conduct whole class feedback.

Possible answers
Annabel lives in a house. I live in an apartment.
Annabel's house has four rooms, but my house has six rooms.
Annabel's clothes are on shelves, but my clothes are in drawers.
Annabel's house is yellow, but my house is white.
One person lives in Annabel's house, but five people live in my house.

3 ▶ Get students to read the list before you play the clip again and check students understand *knives* and *shower* (perhaps get a student to draw or mime these words). Get students to tick the things Annabel talks about while they listen. Elicit the answers.

knives, clothes, stairs, windows

4 ▶ Play the clip for students to watch again and decide if the statements 1–5 are true or false. Elicit answers from the class.

1 T   **2** F   **3** T   **4** F   **5** F

---

extra: mixed-ability classes

Get stronger students to listen for more information on the things Annabel talks about and share it afterwards.

---

5 This is a grammar rather than a listening exercise. Put students into pairs to complete the sentences using the correct form of *to be*. Remind students to look at whether the noun before the verb is plural or singular to decide between *are / is*. Elicit the answers.

1 is   **2** are   **3** is   **4** is

Project

6 Put students into pairs. Break down the task for students by writing the following steps on the board for students to follow.

1 Make a list of rooms.
2 Make a list of furniture and things.
3 Draw your house.
4 Practise talking about your house.
5 Present your house to the class.

For steps 1–2, remind students that they can look back through the unit for words, or use the wordlist on page 20. Students could draw their houses in cross section or in bird's-eye view. Give students large pieces of paper to draw their house, or alternatively, students could make a digital drawing on a computer or tablet.

Suggest that students divide the rooms and do two rooms each. Before students practise talking about the house, play the clip one more time for students to remind themselves of the sorts of things Annabel says.

Get students to take turns to show their pictures and tell the class about their tiny house. Alternatively, students could write the sentences and display with their picture around the classroom (or in your class online area).

---

alternative

1 Ask students to think about what it would be like to live in a tiny house. Put students into small groups. Ask them to make two lists about living in a tiny house: the good things and the bad things. Some of the discussion can be in L1, but encourage students to use English words where possible, and assist them with presenting their lists, using as much English as possible.

2 Extend the project by asking students to write a description of each room (before the presentation stage).

Presentation tool: Unit 1, Switch on

Switch on videoscript: TB p139

UNIT CHECK SB p21

This Unit check covers things in a room, prepositions of place, *there is/there are* and *have got*.

Practice

1 Run this as a challenge. Put students into pairs and give them one minute to look at the wordlist and write out as many words that they can see that match task 1 (that they can see right now). After the minute is up, ask the pair with the highest number of items written down to read out their list, and other pairs may raise their hand if they don't believe an item can be seen, or if there are additional items to add. Repeat the same process for (2) and (3).

Possible answers
1 bin, clock, cupboard, noticeboard, pictures, laptop, shelves, desk, books, box, chair, desk, door, floor, light, object, posters, wall, window
2 balcony, downstairs, garage, garden, lift, stairs, upstairs
3 pictures, laptop, birthday card, cinema / concert / sports tickets, books, box, computer game, key, mobile, photo, postcard

2 Students write their sentences individually while you circulate, helping as needed. Students then share their sentences in pairs.

---

alternative

Tell students that they may make the sentences in Ex 2 true or false. Put students into pairs to share their sentences and say whether their partner's sentences are true or false.

Possible answers
Dan's desk is in front of my desk.
There are posters on the wall.
There is a clock above the noticeboard.

---

3 1.9 Play the recording and ask students to write down the sentences they hear. Play the recording again. Then elicit the sentences and write them on the board.

1 There's a desk in front of the window.
2 There are two pictures on the wall.
3 Is there a bathroom upstairs?
4 Are there ten chairs? No, there aren't.

4 🔊 1.10 Play the recording twice for students to write down the questions. Put students into pairs to compare, and ask and answer. Conduct whole class feedback.

Possible answers
1 Has (your teacher got a laptop in the classroom?) Yes, he has.
2 Has (your friend got a black school bag?) No, she hasn't.
3 Have (you got a brother or a sister?) Yes, I have got two brothers and one sister.
4 Have (you got a blue pen in your bag?) No, I haven't.

GRAMMAR FILE SB p117

1 1 There is a TV on the table.
2 There are three lamps in the room.
3 There isn't a pen in my bag.
4 There aren't any students in the classroom.
5 Is there a poster on the wall?
6 Are there any bags under the desk?
7 Are there any shelves on the wall?
8 Are there two keys in my bag?

2 1 There are   2 There is/There's   3 There isn't
4 There aren't   5 Is there, there is   6 Are there, there are
7 Are there, there aren't   8 Is there, there isn't

3 1 a   2 is/'s   3 are   4 aren't

4 1 has got ('s got)   2 have got ('ve got)   3 have got ('ve got)
4 has got   5 has got ('s got)   6 have got ('ve got)
7 have got ('ve got)   8 has got

5 1 Have you got a   2 Have you got a   3 Have you got any
4 Have you got an   5 Have you got any   6 have you got

6 Student's own answers.

Presentation tool:	Unit 1, Unit check
Workbook / Online Practice:	p15
Grammar reference:	SB p116
Audioscript:	SB p144

What a week!

2

VOCABULARY 1
everyday activities

READING
topic: a different school day
skill: looking at the questions before you read
task: multiple-choice cloze

GRAMMAR
present simple: positive and negative
present simple: questions and short answers

VOCABULARY 2
free time activities

LISTENING
topic: going to school
skill: writing numbers
task: gap fill

SPEAKING
topic: a school timetable
skill: answering questions about you
task: answer questions about your day

WRITING
topic: favourite days
skill: using punctuation
task: write interview questions

SWITCH ON
video: Kung Fu School
project: perfect school day

Lead-in SB p21

1 Read the quote and say: *Do you like the classroom in this photo?* Ask more confident students to explain why/why not. Ask students to find the teacher and students in the photo.

Possible answers
Here is the teacher. (*the woman on the right*)
Here are the students. (*the children sitting on chairs*)

2 Students tick the items they can see. Conduct whole class feedback.

chair, pencil, paper, laptop

---

extra: whole class

Ask students to circle the items in Ex 2 which they can see in your classroom. Take the opportunity to teach / revise words for any other commonly used objects in your own classroom, e.g. interactive whiteboard, computer, notebook, etc.

---

3 Get students to work in pairs to make at least two sentences about what is similar and different about the classrooms.

Possible answers
Similar: There is a teacher. There are pencils.
Different: This classroom is outside, but our classroom is inside. There aren't any tables in this classroom.

---

extra

Ask students to work individually and design their perfect classroom. They can choose to include items from the list in Ex 2 or use other items. They draw a sketch of their classroom and then share it with a partner. Encourage pairs to discuss their perfect classroom and give reasons why they chose the various items to include. Elicit ideas from around the class during feedback.

VOCABULARY 1 SB p22

To start

On the board, write some anagrams of days of the week for students to solve (tell students the spaces don't matter). Remind students to use capital letters to start each day of the week. Students who finish quickly could put the days in order and add the missing days. Elicit the answers and write them on the board.

weedy sand (Wednesday), *dynamo* (Monday), *sea duty* (Tuesday), *rash duty* (Thursday), *a rust day* (Saturday)

Power up

1 🔊 2.1 Play the recording twice for students to listen and repeat. Ask: *what days are the weekend? Does the week start on Sunday or Monday in your country?* Direct students to the questions and examples. Remind students that with the date we usually say *the* before the ordinal number although it is not written, e.g. We say *Tuesday the 18th of October.*

Put students into pairs to ask and answer the questions. Elicit the date and some answers to question 2. Encourage some students to give reasons for their favourite day if they have enough language, e.g. *because we have pizza for dinner; because it's my dance class.*

Possible answers
Today is Wednesday (the) 3rd of March.
My favourite day is Saturday because it's football.

everyday activities

2 Direct students to the instructions and elicit which is the first picture (*I get up*). Write this on the board. Ask students to write down the sequence in order and then compare their answers in pairs. The answers will be checked in Ex 3.

1 C I get up.   2 B I have a shower.
3 H I get dressed.   4 E I have breakfast.   5 I I go to school.
6 A I meet my friends.   7 G I watch TV.
8 J I do my homework.   9 D I play computer games.
10 F I go to bed.

3 🔊 2.2 Play the recording for students to check their answers. Play the recording again for students to listen and repeat.

1 C I get up.   2 B I have a shower.   3 H I get dressed.
4 E I have breakfast.   5 I I go to school.
6 A I meet my friends.   7 G I watch TV.
8 J I do my homework.   9 D I play computer games.
10 F I go to bed.

4 Ask students to choose a day of the week to describe. Encourage students to write several sentences for each time of day. Put students into small groups to share about their day.

Possible answers
On Monday in the morning, I get up. I get dressed. I have breakfast. I go to school. I have history and science.
In the afternoon, I have lunch. I have PE. I go home.
In the evening, I have dinner, I watch TV and I go to bed.

explore **language**

Point out that students need to learn which expressions have or do not have an article, e.g. *have lunch* (no article), *have a shower* (article *a*). Write the two columns (Have/Have a) on the board.

Ask students to close their books. Call out the words and ask students to take turns writing them on the board in the correct column. Provide guidance as they go along. At the end, students copy the columns and words and come up with rules, e.g. *have* + meals, *have* + school subjects.

watch out for ①

Check students' pronunciation of breakfast. /ˈbrekfəst/ and the syllabic stress in *history*, *science* and *geography*.

game on

Go through the instructions and tell students that part of the game is responding as quickly as you can. Ask a student to give you a time of day and respond quickly as a demonstration. Point out that each student should be asked each time of day but that students can repeat one time of day more than once. Put students into pairs to play.

Possible answer
A: The evening
B: In the evening, I do homework and I go to bed. The afternoon.
A: In the afternoon, I have history. I play computer games. The morning.
B: In the morning, I get up. I have a shower. The evening.
A: In the evening, I have dinner. I go to bed. The afternoon
B: In the afternoon, I have music. I have fun. The morning.
A: In the morning, I have breakfast. I go to school.

Fun footer

Read the footer. Teach *sun* and *moon* if necessary. Ask if it is the same in students' languages and whether they notice any similarities between the days of the week in their language and in English. Students could work in small groups to rename the days of the week in a fun way according to what they do on that day e.g. Sleepday, Pizzaday, SnapChatday …

To finish

Write on the board: *What's your favourite time of day?* and give students an example, e.g. *My favourite time of the day is the afternoon because I have lunch and I have English class.* Put students into small groups to ask the question and share their favourite time of day (with a reason if they can).

Presentation tool:	Unit 2, Vocabulary 1
Workbook / Online Practice:	p16
Photocopiable activity:	2A
Grammar reference:	SB p118
Audioscript:	SB p145
Extra Practice App	

READING SB p23

To start

Write the numbers from Ex 1 on the board in individual circles or boxes: 16, 450, 1,500, 7.30, 4.00. Ask students to work in pairs to see which ones they can say. Conduct whole class feedback and drill correct pronunciation, e.g. six**teen** / four hundred and fif**ty** / one **th**ousand five **h**undred / seven **th**irty / four o'clock.

Write on the board *Wales* and *South Korea*. Ask if students know where these countries are in the world and if you have the facilities, ask students to find them on a map. Introduce the words *Welsh, Korean* to describe nationalities of these countries.

Power up

> ### background: school swap ℹ
>
> The article in this lesson follows three Welsh students who did a school swap to South Korea. The BBC made a two-part documentary on the students' experience called *School Swap: Korean Style* which you may be able to find and view online.

1 Ask students: *What is the title of the article? What can you see in the photos?* Direct students to the instructions and ask them to match each one to the notes (without reading the article yet.) They will check their answers in Ex 2.

Possible answer
1 4.00 **2** 7.30 **3** 450 **4** 1,500 **5** 16

2 Ask students to read the article to check their answers. Go through the answers as a class.

1 4.00 **2** 7.30 **3** 450 **4** 1,500 **5** 16

skill tip

Read through the skill box with the class. Write another item on the board *or = used between choices*. Ask students to find and underline an example of *and, but* and *or* in the article.

> ### exam task: A1 Movers Reading and Writing Part 4
>
> In the A1 Movers Reading and Writing Part 4 exam task there would be five items and one example, and the items would test a range of words, e.g. prepositions, verbs, adverbs. Words in one item would not be repeated in other items. Also, the keys would not appear elsewhere in the text used in a similar way. This exercise is practising grammar points in the unit, hence the repetition.

3 e Focus students' attention on the first gap and direct students to the list of options in Ex 3.1. Elicit the correct answer (*from*) and tell students to copy it into the gap. Students complete the exercise then compare in pairs before checking as a class.

1 C (*from* used before a place someone was born or lives)
2 C (*and* adds a similar thing)
3 A (*have* is part of the verb *have got*)
4 B (*up* is part of the verb/action *get up*)
5 A (we use *have* before a meal, e.g. breakfast, lunch, dinner)
6 C (we use the possessive adjective *his* for something belonging to a boy or man)

> ### extra: fast finishers
>
> Fast finishers could try and explain in pairs why the other options can't be correct. Then at the class feedback stage, they could then be involved in giving feedback to the weaker students and explaining why the other options aren't right.

Sum up

4 Elicit some possible ways that the first sentence can be completed. Students write the sentences. Elicit some ideas for each one.

Possible answers
1 from Wales/the UK/Britain/the same school.
2 from South Korea/in the same school.
3 phones in class (and talk in class)
4 10/ten (o'clock)

Speak up

5 Draw a Venn diagram on the board. Label the left section *Our school*, the right section *Schools in South Korea*, and explain that the intersecting area is for things that are the same in both schools. Elicit an item for each area. Put students into groups of three to four. Ask them to work together to talk about similarities and differences and record their ideas on a Venn diagram (if possible on a large piece of paper). Ask each group to explain a few similarities or differences to the class. Ask: *Do you like your school or the Korean school?* Elicit some opinions.

Possible answer (feedback stage)
Korean schools have got uniforms but my school hasn't got a uniform.
Students talk in lessons at my school. But in Korea, the class is quiet.
Schools in Korea are big but my school is small.
In Korea, students give their phones to the teacher. At my school, it is the same.
There is homework in Korean schools and at my school.

Fun footer

Read the footer aloud. Students also clean classrooms and schools in some other countries like Japan. Students usually clean the floor, the tables and sometimes even the bathrooms!

To finish

In pairs, ask students to find at least three things that are different about themselves and one thing that is the same. Ask each pair to share a difference with the class using *but*, e.g. *I have one brother but Jack has three brothers. Sarah gets up at 6.00 but I get up at 7.00. I have got a cat but Toby has a dog.*

Presentation tool:	Unit 2, Reading
Workbook / Online Practice:	p17
Grammar reference:	SB p118
Extra Practice App	

GRAMMAR SB p24

To start

Call out sentences about daily activities and ask students should stand up if it is true for them. e.g. T – *Who gets up early in the morning?*

(Students who get up early stand up)

T – Looking around the room – *Diego and Anna get up early in the morning but Juan gets up late.*

(Students sit down.)

T – *Who goes swimming every week?*

T – *Joana goes swimming every week but Julia doesn't.*

Other possible questions

Who plays computer games? Who comes to school on the weekend? Who plays football? Who goes swimming every week?

alternative

You may want to download the Grammar Presentation for this lesson from the Teacher Resources area of Pearson English Portal. This presentation has been created specifically for this lesson and is fully editable for teachers.

1 Students complete the exercise then compare in pairs before checking as a class.

> **1** get   **2** starts   **3** play   **4** don't

explore **grammar**   → SB p118

Go through the box with the class. For B, give another example of the spelling change after he/she/it *School finish_es_ at 10:00 at night!* Refer students to the Grammar reference on page 118 and go through the notes in the left column. Ask students to complete Ex 1–3 on page 119, then compare in pairs before checking as a class. Alternatively, set the grammar practice activities for homework which fast finishers may complete during the class.

extra: *fast finishers*

Write up the additional items for fast finishers to complete.

My brother **don't / doesn't** do his homework in his room. (doesn't)

My friend and I **meet / meets** near the school. (meet)

2 Note that the Switch On video for this unit is about Tian Tian and the Kung Fu School. Consider showing the first minute of the video (up to the point after Tian Tian is introduced) to introduce the idea of the Kung Fu School. Direct students to the picture and title of the article. Read the first part aloud until you get to the first gap but read the text in the sentence after the gap. Elicit the correct answer (*loves*) and why (TianTian is *she*. The *she* form of present simple adds *-s*)

> **1** loves   **2** get up   **3** finishes   **4** do   **5** don't go
> **6** don't study   **7** talk   **8** live

3 Elicit corrections for the first sentences as an example, making it a negative sentence.

> **1** It doesn't start at 8.00. (It starts at 5.00.)
> **2** It doesn't finish in the afternoon. (It finishes in the evening.)
> **3** She doesn't go home after school. (She sleeps at school.)
> **4** She doesn't watch TV in the evening. (She watches TV on her free day.)
> **5** Her parents don't see her on Sunday. (They live far away.)

watch out for

In the negative form, the auxiliary verb takes the it/he/she form so the main verb does not need -s, e.g. TianTian's school day doesn't start~~s~~ at 8.00.

extra: fast finishers

Fast finishers write a correct positive sentence to follow each negative sentence using information from the article. See possible answers in brackets above.

4 🔊 2.4 Give students a moment to read the words and sentences. Play the recording for students to notice the pronunciation. Play again for students to listen and repeat.

extra

Write up the words *plays, gets, likes, starts, finishes* on the board, and ask students to decide in pairs how each one is pronounced i.e. which ending type it takes *-s, -z, or -iz.*

-s (likes, starts, gets)
-z (plays)
-iz (finishes)

5 🔊 2.5 Play the recording for students to choose the sentence they hear from each pair. Then ask students to tick the sentences which are true for them then compare their answers in pairs.

> **1** B I don't get up early on Saturday.
> **2** A My friend does her homework in the morning.
> **3** B My friends don't play football.
> **4** B My friend doesn't like English lessons.

6 Write the phrase *every day* on the board. Give an example of something you do every day, e.g. *I go for a run every day.* Go through the instructions and examples. Point out that these are sentences using *I* so there is no -*s* on the verb. Write up some other useful prompts: *on/at the weekend, on Tuesday, every morning.* Circulate while students write their sentences.

Possible answers

I play games every day.
I get up every morning!
I don't go to school on the weekend.
I watch TV on Tuesdays.

GRAMMAR (Continued)

Speak up

7 Put students into pairs to share their sentences. Ask each student to share something their partner said, following the example. Make sure students focus on using an -s ending for third person.

Possible answers
Anna plays games every day.
Jack gets up every morning.
Martha doesn't go to school on the weekend.
Toby watches TV on Tuesdays.

Fun footer

Students read the fun footer. As a joke, say: *Here's another famous kung fu actor* and show a picture or a short clip of *Kung Fu Panda.*

To finish

Play the same game as the warmer but this time, invite some students to take a turn to call out a sentence.

---
alternative

Fruit salad. If space allows, ask students to make a circle with everyone sitting on a chair. One student does not have a chair and stands in the middle. Call out questions and students for whom the answer is 'me' must stand up and find a new chair and the student in the middle tries to sit down. When students understand the game, you could ask the person in the middle to call out the question.

Presentation tool:	Unit 2, Grammar
Workbook / Online Practice:	p18
Grammar reference:	SB p118
Extra Practice App	

VOCABULARY 2 SB p25

To start

Write *free time activities* in the centre of a diagram on the board. Tell the class about two free time activities you like, if necessary miming to demonstrate, e.g. *In my free time, I like singing and reading.* Add *singing* and *reading* to the diagram. Ask: *What free time activities do you like?* Get students to write their ideas on the diagram. Alternatively, have students brainstorm their ideas in an online collaborative tool (e.g. a Google doc) and have it displayed on your projector or Presentation tool. Ask students to explain or mime any unusual ideas.

free time activities

1 Ask students to match the activities. As you go through the answers, drill the pronunciation of the words.

---
1 volleyball **2** football **3** computer games
4 card games **5** the drums **6** the guitar
7 singing lessons **8** swimming lessons **9** have fun
10 have a party **11** the beach **12** the cinema
---

2 Get students to close their books. Draw a three-column table on the board with the column headings: *play, have, go to.* Elicit where *volleyball* would fit and write it in the column *play.* Ask students to draw the same table and work in pairs to write the activities from Ex 1 in the relevant columns. Check as a class.

---
play: volleyball, football, computer games, card games, the guitar, the drums
have: a party, fun, swimming lessons, singing lessons
go to: the beach, the cinema
---

3 2.6 Direct students to the timetable. Tell students they are going to listen to Ivan talking about his week. Tell students to include the relevant verb when they complete the list. Play the recording twice then elicit responses.

---
1 Monday: (play) computer games
2 Tuesday: (go to) swimming lessons
3 Wednesday: (play) computer games
4 Thursday: (play) football
5 Friday: (play) computer games
6 Saturday: (play) the drums
7 Sunday: (go to) the cinema
---

explore **language**

Go through the language box with the class. If using the Presentation tool, underline the preposition in each example for emphasis. Have students highlight examples of *in, at* and *on* in different colours in Ivan's blog in Ex 4, e.g. in = green: in January, in the spring, in November; at = yellow: at 1 p.m.; on = blue: on Russia Day.

---
watch out for

To talk about times of day generally, we use *in the*, e.g. <u>in the</u> morning, <u>in the</u> afternoon, <u>in the</u> evening. When talking about the time of day on a specific day of the week, we use *on*, e.g. <u>on</u> Monday morning, <u>on</u> Saturday afternoon.
---

4 Check students understand *blog* (a webpage where someone often writes their ideas and opinions). Give students time to complete the blog individually. Go through the answers. Elicit the meaning of *have a picnic* /ˈpɪknɪk/ and tell students to add *have a picnic* and *have a holiday* to the table they drew in Ex 2.

1 in **2** in **3** in **4** at **5** In **6** on

> **extra:** fast finishers
>
> Ask students to find the two seasons mentioned in Ivan's blog (*spring, summer*) and see if they know the other seasons. Write them on the board (*autumn, winter*). Ask students to divide a page into four rectangles. In each rectangle, students write the name of a season and a picture. Students add the preposition *in* as a visual reminder of *in a season* and *in a month*. They add the months of the year or a sentence about what they like to do in each season.

Speak up

5 Some students may benefit from time to think about their answers or write notes before speaking. Put students into small groups to share what they like to do.

> **Possible answer**
>
> My school holidays are in August. I go to the beach with my friends and we have a picnic. I have swimming lessons. I don't get up early because I don't have school!

> **alternative** ⇕
>
> Get students to say three things that they do in their holidays – two true and one lie. Their partner has to guess which thing is the lie.

> **game** on
>
> Go through the instructions. Put students into pairs. Tell students to write down six activities without showing their partner. Then, play the game.

Fun footer

Ask students to read the footer. Elicit how the numbers are said. Help students work out how many days they spend in school in a year. Use *how many*, e.g. *How many days of school are there in a week?* (5) *How many weeks are there in a term?* (10) *How many days are there in a term?* (50) *How many terms are in a year?* (4) *So, how many school days are in a year?* (200)

To finish

Students close their books. Act out one of the free time activities in the lesson, e.g. *play the guitar*. Students guess what it is, including the verb. Invite volunteers to act out one of the other free time activities from the lesson.

Presentation tool:	Unit 2, Vocabulary 2
Workbook / Online Practice:	p19
Grammar reference:	SB p118
Audioscript:	SB p145
Extra Practice App	

LISTENING SB p26

To start

Tell students that you're going to draw a picture of some of the words they'll need to know for this lesson and they need to guess what it is. Draw a bike, one line at a time, e.g. start with one circle, then add one handle bar, etc. eliciting a guess of what it might be after each addition. When students guess it correctly, get a student to come and write the word *bike* on the board with the class to help them spell out the letters. Then do the same with the following words, or invite students (two at a time) to come and draw them (you can give them the word in L1 if necessary).

Suggested words: *bus, shower, car, children, canoe.*

Power up

1 Ask students to work through the quiz and circle their own answers. Provide vocabulary as required. Students may add their own additional items to the quiz if needed, e.g. train, scooter; 50 minutes; music. Point out that 0–15 minutes is said *zero to fifteen minutes.* Drill the questions. Ask students to move around the classroom asking and answering the questions to see who else has the same answers.

> **Possible answer**
>
> (Quiz stage)
> **1** walking
> **2** 15–30 minutes
> **3** English
> (Sharing answers stage)
> **A:** How do you travel to school?
> **B:** Bike. You?
> **A:** Walking. How long is your journey to school?
> **B:** 15–30 minutes.
> **A:** Me too!

Listen up

2 🔊 2.7 Before doing the listening exercise, direct students to the photo. Generate some interest by asking: *What can you see in the photo? Where do you think they live? Where are they going?* Read the questions aloud with the class then play the recording. Elicit the answers.

Questions 1, 2 and 5

LISTENING (Continued)

exam task: A1 Movers Listening Part 2

In the A1 Movers Listening Part 2 exam task there would be an example, and the key is repeated. This exercise is good practice because only hearing the key once makes the task a little harder. In the A2 Flyers exam, the key is not repeated. The recording is heard twice in each exam.

3 **e** 🔊 2.8 Read the exam tip with the class. Then give students a moment to read the notebook page in Ex 3 before you play the recording. Encourage them to predict the kind of word they will need for each. Ask: *which of the answers is a number?* (1, 3). Play the recording twice. Elicit the answers and give the tips below. Write the correct answers up on the board for students to check their spelling.

1 seven/7 (you can write numbers with letters or just the number)
2 Mateo (the letters are spelled out by the speaker; you should have each letter correct)
3 six/6 (you can write numbers with letters or numbers)
4 talk (to friends) (the verb is the important word here – your writing and spelling should be easy to understand)
5 geography (your writing and spelling should be easy to understand)

explore **grammar**   → SB p118 ☑

Go through the box then work with the class to construct a visual chart on the board like the one on Student's Book page 118. Refer them to the Grammar reference on page 118 to check. Set Ex 4–6 on page 119 for students to complete in class or for homework.

watch out for   ⓘ

Some students may not understand *infinitive*. Tell them it is the basic form of a verb, e.g. go/walk/like.

4 🔊 2.9 Play the recording for students to notice the pronunciation of *Do you* (weak form of *do*) then play it again for students to repeat.

1 Do you walk to school?
2 Do you meet your friends?
3 Do you like your journey?

5 Ask students to write out the questions in the correct order. Remind students to start the question with a capital letter and add a question mark at the end. Drill the pronunciation of the questions focusing on the pronunciation of *Do you* as in Ex 4.

1 Do you go to school with your friends?
2 Do you have a shower before school?
3 Do you do your homework before your lessons?
4 Does your teacher go to school on the bus?

extra: fast finishers

Write up these additional items for fast finishers.

5 your lessons / like / you / do / ?
6 your school / does / a special bus / have / ?

Answers
5 Do you like your lessons?
6 Does your school have a special bus?

6 Students ask and answer in pairs. Encourage students to respond with a short answer, e.g. *Yes, I do / No, I don't.* If you are going to do the extra exercise, tell students to make a note of their partner's answers.

Possible answer
1 A: Do you go to school with your friends?   B: No, I don't.
2 Do you have a shower before school?   B: Yes, I do.
3 Do you do your homework before your lessons?
   B: No, I don't.
4 Does your teacher go to school on the bus?
   B: Yes, she does.

extra: mixed-ability classes

When you conduct feedback, ask weaker students a question about themselves, and challenge stronger students by asking something about their partner. They will need to use *does*, e.g. A: *Does Anna go to school with her friends?* B: *Yes, she does.*

Fun footer

Pre-teach *happy* and *sad* by drawing faces on the board. Ask students to read the footer. Ask: *Do you like the joke?*

To finish

Choose a pattern of things for your 'grandmother' to like without telling the class, e.g. She only likes words with an e in them. Say: *My grandma likes science, but she doesn't like maths. My grandmother likes bikes, but she doesn't like cars.*

Students take turns to ask questions about what she likes using *Does she like … ?* As they guess the pattern, students don't reveal it, instead just asking questions using words she does like. You can repeat the game with a different pattern, e.g. A: Does she like English? B: Yes, she does. But she doesn't like art.

Presentation tool:	Unit 2, Listening
Workbook / Online Practice:	p20
Photocopiable activity:	2C
Grammar reference:	SB p118
Audioscript:	SB p145
Extra Practice App	

SPEAKING SB p27

To start

Demonstrate the activity by mouthing silently *I have breakfast* without actually saying the words. Students have to work out what you are 'saying'. Repeat with two other everyday actions e.g. *I get dressed. I come to school by bus.* Ask students to write down three things they do every weekday, without showing anyone. Put students into small groups and ask them to take turns to mouth their sentences for their team mates to guess.

Power up

1 Students complete the sentences.

> **Possible answer**
> I go to school at eight o'clock.
> I go home at three fifteen.
> I do my homework at four thirty.
> I go to bed at nine thirty.

explore **language**

Direct students to the clock faces on page 27 and drill the times in the explore language box chorally. Ask students to ask a few of their classmates the question in the language box.

> **watch out** for ⓘ
> Remind students to include the apostrophe in *o'clock.* The apostrophe indicates that it is a shortened form of *of the clock* (a very old phrase that we don't use anymore.)

Speak up

2 Put students into new pairs. Write the question stem on the board: *What time do you … ?* Students ask and answer questions about their day using the prompts from Ex 1 or their own ideas. Tell them to take notes. Then, ask each student to share something about their partner's day.In the feedback, check that students are using the third person *s*, and remind students of correct pronunciation of the *s* if necessary.

> **Possible answer**
> (Ask and answer stage)
> **A:** What time do you go to school?
> **B:** Seven thirty.
> **A:** What time do you go home?
> **B:** I go home at three o'clock.
> **A:** What time do you have dinner?
> **B:** I have dinner at six thirty.
>
> (Feedback stage)
> Isabel goes to school at seven thirty. She goes home at three o'clock. She has dinner at six thirty.

3 Focus students' attention on the picture of Gabriel's timetable. Ask: *What time does he start school? What times does he finish school? How many subjects does he have each day? How many days can you see?* Then put students into pairs to complete the sentences.

> **1** seven forty-five/7.45
> **2** ten/10 o'clock
> **3** Monday (morning) and Tuesday (morning)
> **4** Tuesday
> **5** ten fifteen/10.15 on Monday
> **6** eleven/11 o'clock

4 🔊 2.10 Read the exam tip with the class then students work with the same partner to practise the conversation.

> **Possible answer**
> **A:** Do you have English on Wednesday?
> **B:** Yes, I do. I have English on Wednesday and Friday.
> **A:** What time does your English lesson start
> **B:** It starts at ten thirty.
> **A:** Do you have history in the morning of in the afternoon?
> **B:** I have history in the morning.

> **extra:** mixed-ability classes
> Give students the option to practise reading the dialogue without changing anything, changing some of the words or all of the words.

5 **e** Write the first question for the class on the board as an example. Circulate while students write the questions individually. Then students ask and answer with a partner.

> **Possible answers**
> **A:** What time do you have lunch? **B:** At twelve/12 o'clock. (We use *at* + time.)
> **A:** Do you like music? **B:** Yes, I do./No, I don't. (The main verb *do* comes after the subject in the short answer.)
> **A:** What time does your art lesson end? **B:** At three thirty/3.30. (We use *at* + time.)
> **A:** Do you have geography on Tuesday? **B:** Yes, I do./No, I don't. (The main verb *do* comes after the subject in the short answer.)

> **exam** task: A2 Key for Schools Speaking Part 1
> For students preparing for the A2 Key for Schools, point out that Ex 4–6 are useful preparation for Speaking Part 1, where they may be asked about their school or studies. In the A1 Movers Speaking Part 4 exam task, students will be asked about themselves and this may include questions about school.

Speaking extra

6 Students work in pairs and take turns to make questions for their partner using one of the prompts.

> **Possible answers**
> Do you like maths? Yes, I do.
> What time do you go home? I go home at 2.45.
> Do you have history on Thursday? No, I don't. I have history on Monday and Tuesday.

SPEAKING (Continued)

7 Ask students to turn to page 143 and complete the questionnaire individually. Then put students into new pairs to ask and answer the questions.

Possible answers

1

1 I arrive at school at eight thirty.
2 **A** My favourite lesson is English.
  B It starts at ten and finishes at eleven.
3 No, I don't.
4 Yes, I do.
5 My English teacher.
6 Yes, I do. I like Fridays because I play volleyball.

2

1 Sasha arrives at school at eight fifteen
2 **A** Sasha's favourite lesson is maths.
  B It starts at eleven and finishes at twelve.
3 No, she doesn't.
4 Yes, she does.
5 Her maths teacher.
6 Yes, she does because she watches TV.

---

extra: whole class

Write dream day on the board and tell students about your dream day, e.g. *It's a Saturday. I'm in Paris. I get up at ten o'clock. At 10.30, I have a nice breakfast on a balcony. At 11.30, I go for a nice walk near the Eiffel Tower. At 12.30, I have lunch with my friends. Then at 2.00, we go to the cinema. We have dinner at six o'clock then we go to a concert. It starts at 8.30 and finishes at 10.00. What a dream day!*

Organise students into pairs and ask them to plan their dream day. Tell them to make notes of at least five activities with times. Then organise students into new pairs to talk about their days and see who has the best dream day.

To finish

Draw a clock on the board or use an internet clock. Change the time, and have students write it down in English. Elicit the answer. Then students work in pairs and take turns to draw the time. Their partner should say it in English.

Presentation tool:	Unit 2, Speaking
Workbook / Online Practice:	p21
Photocopiable activity:	2B
Grammar reference:	SB p118
Speaking file:	SB p135
Pairwork file:	SB p143

WRITING SB p28

To start

Write on the board:

- *computer games vs board games*
- *singing lessons vs swimming lessons*
- *drums vs dance*
- *weekends vs weekdays*

Elicit what *vs* means. Explain that it is short for *versus* and can mean *or*. Ask: *which days are the weekend?* (Saturday, Sunday) and *Which days are weekdays?* (*Monday, Tuesday, Wednesday, Thursday, Friday.*) Put students in pairs to talk about which they like best from each pair. Then elicit a show of hands for each one.

Power up

1 Put students into pairs to ask and answer the questions. Elicit some answers.

Possible answers

I like weekends. I play volleyball. I have guitar lessons. I don't have school.

I like weekdays because I have school with my friends. We have fun every day. And on Wednesdayafternoons, I have guitar lessons.

2 Direct students to the pictures. Ask students to talk in pairs about each picture. Give students a few minutes to read the article and complete the phrases.

at the weekend
on school days

explore **language**

Go through the box with the class. Write a few other examples on the board and elicit the full form, e.g. *aren't, isn't, there's* (are not, is not, there is).

---

watch out for

Remind students that apostrophes are also used to show possession and there is no 'full form' for these, as the apostrophe isn't replacing a missing letter. In the article there are two examples of *'s* for possession: *Nur Amirah Syahira's videos, her uncle's garage.*

Make sure students don't confuse closed quotes around speech with apostrophes.

---

3 Tell students that they can choose either text A or B. Elicit examples and possible full forms.

A

Monday's, Monday is
we've, we have
it's (x 2), it is
We're, we are

B

don't (x2), do not
it's, it is
doesn't, does not
Syahira's, hers
uncle's, his

Plan on

4 Ask students to read the interview. Elicit the problem.

The interview is missing apostrophes.

5 Tell students to rewrite the conversation rather than just adding the apostrophe. This is to practise copying accurately which is a skill they will use if they are sitting an exam.

Carla:	Hi, Joe. I'm twelve and I'm from Spain. How old are you? Where are you from?
Joe:	I'm thirteen. I'm from Paris in France.
Carla:	Do you like films?
Joe:	Yes, I do. I go to the cinema with my friends on Saturday.
Carla:	Do you like weekends?
Joe:	Of course. I love weekends. I don't like Mondays.

Write on

6 Go through the task and the skill tips. Point out that students can adapt Carla's questions in Ex 4. This could be done in pairs.

Model answer

Hi, I'm Ana. I'm eleven and I'm from Chile.

How old are you?

Where are you from?

What's your favourite day?

Do you like sports?

7 Students swap interview questions with a partner and write answers to their partner's questions.

Possible answers

I'm twelve years old.

I'm from Brazil.

Yes, I like swimming and football.

Improve it

8 Put students into pairs to check for accuracy.

skill tip

Go through the box. For each point, get students to find an example in Carla's interview.

To finish

Invite students to interview you using their questions. Invite one question from each student. If you don't want to reveal something like your age, just use an invented answer, e.g. say *I'm twenty-one/I'm ninety-four.*

Presentation tool:	Unit 2, Writing
Workbook / Online Practice:	p22
Photocopiable activity:	2C
Grammar reference:	SB p118
Writing file:	SB p135

SWITCH ON SB p29

Kung Fu School

1 Put students into pairs. Give students one minute to write down as many school subjects as they can. After the task, the students can write them on the board, or you may elicit their answers and write them on the board.

Possible answers

art, English, geography, history, maths, music, science, sport

---

extra: whole class

Tell students that they are going to watch a video about the Kung Fu School they read about on page 24. Write the following words on the board, and get students to share in pairs any meanings they know. Elicit the meanings (students could draw, mime or explain in L1) and teach any words that students don't know, e.g. *actor/actress, kung fu training, run, jump, kick, library, medal, sword.*

---

2 ▶ Tell students that they are going to watch a video clip about the Kung Fu School they read about on page 24. Ask students to watch the clip and to think of two differences between this school and theirs. Give students 2–3 minutes to discuss with their partner, depending on the level of the class. Elicit some ideas.

Possible answers

The Kung Fu school is in China, but my school isn't.
They fight at school, but we don't fight.
The Kung Fu school starts at 5 a.m., but my school starts at 9 a.m.

3 ▶ Ask students to read the sentences individually. Tell them they will watch the clip again and must decide if each sentence is true or false. Play the clip. Ask students to check their answers in pairs then ask students for their answers. If the answer is false, ask students to explain what the correct answer is, if possible, depending on the level of the class.

Possible answers

1 True
2 False (She loves reading.)
3 False (She wants to be a kung fu actress.)
4 True

Project

4 Ask students to think about their perfect school day and the timetable. Elicit one or two ideas: *In your perfect school day, what time does school start? What activities do you do?* If it is a quieter or lower level class, give them your answers to these questions as a model, e.g. *My perfect school day starts at 10 a.m. I play tennis for two hours. I study English for one hour.*

Set students time to complete the task and allocate one minute per group to present their perfect school day. If the presentation is in a later class, students could bring in props to support their presentation (e.g. a tennis racket for playing tennis) or create some digital slides for homework. Once each pair has presented, elicit some reasons students like the day.

5 Ask students to vote for the best school day. A simple way to do this is for students to close their eyes and raise their hands to vote (no peeking!). That way, you don't need to reveal the numbers (e.g. if some pairs got no votes) and you can make sure students don't vote for their own. Encourage the class to give reasons for their choice.

---

alternative

For a longer project, students could develop an idea for a new school on a theme that matches their interests. You could encourage students to be creative and come up with a new type of school that is either serious (e.g. a football academy or science school), fantasy (e.g. a wizard school, a fairy school), or funny (e.g. a party school, a chocolate school). Students could design an advertising brochure (or web page) for the school which includes a description of the school (i.e. where it is, who it is for, what the theme is), and a sample week timetable.

Presentation tool: Unit 2, Switch on

Switch on videoscript: TB p139

UNIT CHECK SB p30

This Unit check covers days of the week, everyday activities, free time activities and present simple.

Practice

1 Ask students to find at least five things in each category. Check as a class.

> ### alternative
>
> If you have an interactive whiteboard, display the wordlist and make it a race. Choose a category from Ex 1 and put on a timer for a minute. A student from each team takes it in turn to run to the board and circle a word from the category as fast as possible. When the timer runs out, the teams who are not in the process of running to the board win.
>
> ---
>
> **Possible answers**
> **1** I do my homework, I go to bed, I have a shower, I meet my friends, I watch TV, I have swimming lessons.
> **2** a lesson, a shower, a bath, breakfast, lunch, dinner, history, maths, singing lessons, swimming lessons, fun, a party.
> **3** art, geography, history, maths, science, sport

2 Students could work individually or in pairs to write their sentences. Monitor for accuracy especially present simple verb forms and prepositions.

> **Possible answers**
> There are 20/twenty students in my English class.
> We have art on Friday.
> My school starts at 8.00.

3 🔊 2.11 Get students to think about what kind of word is missing from the gap before listening. Point out that Ex 3 and 4 revise the present simple forms, free time activities and time of day.

> **1** singing   **2** bed   **3** volleyball   **4** the guitar

4 🔊 2.12 Play the recording twice for students to write the sentences. Invite a student to write each sentence on the board and others to correct if required.

> **1** We have maths lessons on Tuesday morning.
> **2** My art teacher likes Friday afternoons.
> **3** My friend watches TV in her English lessons.
> **4** I don't like Sunday evenings.

GRAMMAR FILE SB p119

1 **1** goes   **2** meet   **3** has   **4** play   **5** watches   **6** studies

2 **1** My brother doesn't go to a different school from me.
2 My friend and I don't meet in town at the weekend.
3 Our dog doesn't have a shower after a walk.
4 My cousins don't play football with us.
5 My grandma doesn't watch TV with her cat.
6 My sister doesn't study music in Italy.

3 **1** We get up early in the morning on school days.
2 We don't go to school on Sunday.
3 Our mum goes to work at 8.30.
4 Dad has lunch at work on weekdays.
5 Our sister does not like art lessons.
6 Our grandfather watches TV all the time!

4 **1** Does   **2** Do   **3** Does   **4** Do   **5** Does   **6** does

5 **1** C   **2** B   **3** B   **4** A   **5** C

6 **1** Do you get up
2 Do your parents work
3 Do you and your friends play
4 Does your best friend come
5 Do you do your homework
6 Does your teacher help

7 Students' own answers.

Presentation tool:	Unit 2, Unit check
Workbook / Online Practice:	pp23–25
Audioscript:	SB p145
Grammar reference:	SB p118

Animal magic

3

VOCABULARY 1
animals

READING
topic: what are armadillos like?
skill: choosing a word for a gap
task: gapped text with picture cues

GRAMMAR
adverbs of frequency
present simple: question words

VOCABULARY 2
the world around us

LISTENING
topic: an Australian nature reserve
skill: reading questions before you listen
task: matching

SPEAKING
topic: similarities and differences between animals
skill: saying what you think and why
task: picture sets

WRITING
topic: fairy penguins
skill: using *and*, *but*
task: write a description of an animal

SWITCH ON
video: panda protection
project: animal sanctuaries

Lead-in
Begin by asking: *What is a pet? Is it good to have a pet? Why/why not? What animals make good pets? What animals make bad pets?*

1 Draw students' attention to the photo of the dog. Do they like the photo and/or think it's funny? Put students into pairs to discuss whether or not the animals are good pets, then conduct whole class feedback.

Possible answers
A duck is a good pet for a farm.
An elephant isn't a good pet. It's too big.
A horse is a good pet because you can ride it.
A mouse is a good pet. It's small.
A rabbit is a good pet because it's small.

2 Invite students to tell their partner about a pet they have got, or one they would like. Students who have pets could bring in photos of their pets. Elicit responses from around the class, and discuss any unusual or interesting pets.

extra: digital
Students could research and choose funny animal videos to show in class. Get students to name the animal in each video. Get students to vote on the funniest video. If you have a private online space for your class, the videos could be shared and voted for homework.

VOCABULARY 1 SB p32

To start

Get students to work in small groups to write an A–Z of animals. See how many letters they can think of an animal for in five minutes. The group with the most is the winner.

To extend the activity, get students to put their names on the lists and collect the lists. At the end of the unit, get students back into the same groups, and see how many more animals they can add to their lists.

Power up

1 Direct students to the pictures and drill the animal words chorally. Ask questions to the class. (*Which of these animals are big? Which are small?*) Get students to write out the list of animals in order, from biggest to smallest. If students are preparing for an exam, point out that in some of the exam activities require words to be copied accurately, so this is good practice.

1 elephant   2 hippo   3 sheep   4 bird/parrot   5 spider

animals

2 Tell students to look at the animals on the poster. Ask them to write a list with letters A–L on a separate piece of paper and write the animal names from the box next to each letter. The answers will be checked in Ex 3.

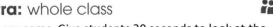

> **extra:** whole class 👥
>
> Memory game. Give students 30 seconds to look at the pictures. Get students to close their books and, in pairs, try to remember what the animals were. They write them down on a piece of paper.

3 🔊 3.1 Play the recording for students to check their answers in Ex 2. Play it a second time for students to notice the pronunciation, then ask students to practise saying the animal names.

A parrot   B frog   C bee   D monkey   E polar bear
F panda   G whale   H penguin   I armadillo
J kangaroo   K dolphin   L lion

4 Revise the letters A–L by asking students to chant them chorally (pay special attention to e/i, g/j). Direct students to the example, then ask: *What's J?* (It's a kangaroo.).

Possible answers
A: What's F?
B: It's a panda. What's E?
A: A polar bear. What's K?
B: It's a dolphin. What's I?
A: It's an armadillo.

5 🔊 3.2 Tell students they are going to hear some animal sounds. Play the recording for students to guess the correct animal. Play the recording again, and elicit the answer after each sound.

1 C   2 A   3 B   4 C

> **extra:** whole class 👥
>
> Get students to work in groups and take turns to make the sound of an animal from the poster in Ex 2. Students may have to get a bit creative if an animal doesn't have a well-known sound. Get the other students in the group to guess which animal it is. Invite each group to choose one of the animal sounds to make together for the class to guess.

> **extra** 💬+
>
> Write the actions on the board: *walk, jump, run, jump, climb, run, fly*. Ask if anyone knows these words, and get them to mime one to the class for other students to guess. Ask students to see if they can match any of the words to the photos of animals in the poster in Ex 2.

animal actions

6 🔊 3.3 Ask students to stand up on the spot. Play the recording and demonstrate miming the action on the recording. Play the recording again, for students to repeat the word while miming.

A walk
B jump
C swim
D climb
E run
F fly

7 Ask the class to look at the list of animals in Ex 2 and guess quickly which animal can do the most actions from the table (students could write their guess down). Draw up the table on the board with the six actions at the top of each column. Choose another animal from the poster in Ex 2, e.g. armadillo, and demonstrate by going through the columns systematically. Ask: *Does an armadillo walk?* (Yes, it does.) Write *armadillo* in the walk column. *Does an armadillo jump?* (No, it doesn't.) Put a dash (–) in the *jump* column. Continue through the remaining columns for armadillo. In pairs, students add other animals to the column. Depending on speed of work, some students may get through more animals than others, but encourage each pair to check at least four animals. Then, ask students to use the chart to see if their prediction of the animal that could do the most actions was correct.

Suggested answers
walk: lion, penguin, monkey, armadillo, panda
jump: lion, penguin, monkey, kangaroo, frog
swim: penguin, monkey, blue whale, dolphin, frog
climb: lion, monkey, panda
run: lion
fly: parrot, bee
Parrots fly, but they don't swim.
A penguin walks, jumps and swims, but it doesn't fly.

VOCABULARY 1 (Continued)

> ### extra: digital
> Students may be surprised to learn that penguins can jump. If you have the internet, look for (or ask students to look for) a video of penguins jumping out of the water to show the class.

8 If students are preparing for the A1 Movers exam, point out that this is useful practice for Reading and Writing Part 1. In Part 1 students have to match words with their definitions. The words are under pictures representing their meaning. Students read a definition then match it to the correct picture. Give an example description for students to guess, e.g. say: *This animal isn't very big. It climbs trees.* (Answer = monkey.) Students complete the exercise then compare in pairs before checking as a class.

1 bee **2** panda **3** kangaroo **4** whale

> ### game on
> Some students may want to write their word down on paper, to help with spelling backwards.

> ### extra: mixed-ability classes
> Give students the option to choose whether their partner should spell a word forwards or backwards for them. Students can also write down the words to help with spelling them aloud.

> ### alternative
> In preparation, make some sets of different coloured papers that spell animals, e.g. on green paper, write the letters that spell monkey: on the first piece – *m*; second piece – *o*; third piece – *n*, etc. On blue paper, write the letters that spell *dolphin*, etc. Make as many letters as there are students in your class.
>
> Randomly distribute the papers. Students need to form groups based on the colour of the paper, then hold their paper in front of them and make a line so they can spell the word. The first team to spell their animal correctly wins the round. Collect and redistribute the papers to play again.

To finish

Students work in pairs to choose an animal and write their own clues like the ones in Ex 8 on post-it notes or a piece of paper with the answer on the back. Alternatively, the clue could be written on an envelope and the answer inside. Get students to stick / place them around the classroom. Students walk around with their partner, guessing each one.

Presentation tool:	Unit 3, Vocabulary 1
Workbook / Online Practice:	p26
Grammar reference:	SB p120
Audioscript:	SB p145
Extra Practice App	

READING SB p33

To start

Ask: *What animals live in your garden or near your home?* Even if students live in an urban area, there may be some, e.g. insects, mice, birds. If there are any animals that are a part of students' daily lives/local area, but not included in the unit, take the opportunity to teach them here.

Before students open their books, show a small clip of an armadillo (e.g. from National Geographic), but try not to show the word. See if students know what it animal it is. Elicit anything they know about *armadillos*. Teach: *hard shell, curl up in a ball, dig.*

Power up

1 Direct students to the photo of Flavio and the titles. Elicit predictions about what the post is about. Then give students one minute to scan the post to answer: *Who? What? Where?* the text is about. Point out that if students are taking an exam, they should get in the habit of quickly scanning texts (and looking at pictures and any titles) to see what they are about before they read.

> He's from Brazil and his post is about an armadillo. The armadillo's name is Maddy and it lives in his garden.

2 Give students one minute to find the information. Help students by telling them there are three foods and two hobbies to find. Check the answers as a class.

1 insects/spiders, fruit, frogs, mice
2 digging, swimming

> ### exam task: A1 Movers Reading and Writing Part 3 ➡ p33
> In the A1 Movers Reading and Writing Part 3 exam task, there would be one example and five gapped items, and the title question as in Ex 4 here.
>
> **3** **e** Before students complete the post, read through the exam tip. Get the class to look at the words before and after the gaps and to guess the missing word without focusing on the words already given. Elicit ideas and write up the students' suggestions on the board for each gap.
>
> Encourage students to mark the words that they put in a gap (e.g. by ticking them), so that they can track which ones they have used. Ask students to compare their answers in pairs, then, as you check as a class, get students to explain why they have chosen a particular word. Look back at the predictions and see if any were correct.
>
> **1** garden (a place where an animal can live)
> **2** sleep (a daily activity)
> **3** sun (the hot sun)
> **4** morning (a time of day)
> **5** frogs (small animals; not monkeys because they're not small)
> **6** water (something you can swim in, and stay 'under')

4 Point out that *the best title* means the title that best describes what the post is about as a whole. Ask students to select the best title then check as a class.

> Maddy the armadillo (This title describes best what the whole text is about.)
>
> (*Maddy's big adventure* isn't the best title because the post describes Maddy and her regular activities rather than talking about one story/adventure that happened to her. It isn't *Maddy's favourite pet* because Maddy is an animal)

Sum up

5 Tell students to close their books. Ask them to say three things about armadillos to a partner. Encourage them to use whole sentences. Elicit some of these or ask students to come and write one of their sentences on the board.

Possible answers
Armadillos love warm places.
Armadillos live in South and Central America.
Armadillos dig and swim.
Armadillos aren't pets. They are wild animals.
Armadillos are small and brown with a hard shell.
Armadillos live under the ground.

Speak up

6 In pairs, students think of similarities and differences. Conduct whole class feedback

Possible answers
Armadillos swim and people swim.
Armadillos are wild animals, but people aren't wild animals.
Armadillos have a hard shell, but people don't have hard shells.

Fun footer

Ask students to read the fun footer. Get students to draw what they imagine a pink fairy armadillo looks like on paper or on a drawing app on their phone. Have a competition for the funniest and most realistic drawing. If you have the internet, show some pictures of giant armadillos and pink fairy armadillos. Teach *fairy* (a small imaginary creature with magic powers, which looks like a very small person).

To finish

Write the adjectives from the post on the board: *special, small, brown, warm, hot, early, interesting, funny, wild.* Students work in pairs to think of something else that is each of those things, e.g. *What is special? My grandmother, my dad, my pet dog, a birthday party. What is small? A mobile, a key, a mouse, a frog.* Conduct whole class feedback.

Presentation tool:	Unit 3, Reading
Workbook / Online Practice:	p27
Grammar reference:	SB p120
Extra Practice App	

GRAMMAR SB p34

To start

Write on the board the following gapped sentences:

Big armadillos can eat small animals like frogs and mice, but Maddy … eats them.
She … eats fruit.
She … digs in our garden.

Ask students to look back at the post on page 33 Ex 2 and complete the sentences. (never, sometimes, often). Elicit the answers. Point out that the words *never, sometimes, often* are examples of adverbs of frequency which we use to talk about how often something happens.

> ### alternative
>
> You may want to download the Grammar Presentation for this lesson from the Teacher Resources area of Pearson English Portal. This presentation has been created specifically for this lesson and is fully editable for teachers.

> ### explore grammar ➥ SB p120
>
> **1** Encourage students to use the percentages in the chart in Ex 1 as a guide rather than an exact science.
>
> Students write the adverbs in the correct place. Ask students to compare their answers in pairs then check as a class. Point out that the phrase we use to ask about frequency is: *How often*, e.g. *How often do you play football?*
>
> sometimes, often, usually

> ### watch out for
>
> As you review B in the explore grammar box, point out that we can use *don't / doesn't* with the adverbs *always, usually* and *often.*
>
> *don't always* means *usually* (70%)
>
> *don't often / don't usually* means *almost never* (10%)
>
> We don't use *don't / doesn't* with the adjectives *sometimes* or *never.*

2 🔊 3.5 Look at Question 1 with the class and elicit where *always* goes (I *always* go …) referring back to explore grammar box point A. Ask students to copy and complete the sentences with the adverbs in the correct place. Check the answers as a class. Tell students that they are going to hear two people being interviewed in a public place, i.e. *a vox pop*, about their daily routines. Play the recording twice for students to select which sentences from this exercise they hear in the recording. Check as a class.

1 I always go on my phone.
2 I often play football.
3 I am usually late for school.
4 I never have a bath.
5 I sometimes watch TV.
We hear sentences 1, 2, 4 and 5

GRAMMAR (Continued)

3 Elicit some of the other things the speakers said in the recording which weren't mentioned in Ex 2. Then put students into pairs to write similar sentences. During the activity, invite each pair to write one of their sentences on the board. Go through the sentences on the board as a class, eliciting any corrections if the adverbs of frequency are not placed in accordance with the explore grammar box points.

---

extra: mixed-ability classes

Weaker students could rewrite the sentences in Ex 2 so that they are true for them, replacing the adverbs of frequency as necessary, e.g. *I usually go on my phone. I sometimes play football.*

Possible answers
I always make my bed.
I usually do my homework at night, but sometimes I do it before school.
On/At the weekends, I often go to the park with my friends.
I never have Nutella at my house, but I love Nutella!

---

extra: whole class

In small groups, students record a vox pop of their group members talking about some of their regular activities using the adverbs of frequency. Play them in class or ask students to upload them to a private shared location online. You could ask each group to choose a topic or allocate a certain topic to each group, e.g. swimming.

A: I love swimming, I always go to the pool every week.
B: I sometimes go to the pool with my friends.
C: Swimming is my favourite sport. I usually go on Mondays.
D: I never go swimming!

---

4 🔊 3.6 Show some wildlife photos if you can, e.g. by searching online for 'amazing wildlife photos'. Elicit or teach *wildlife* then ask how you get photos of wildlife, leading to the term *wildlife photographer*. Ask students to read the interview with Amy, a wildlife photographer, and predict which adverb of frequency will go in each gap. Then play the recording for students to complete the interview.

1 often **2** usually **3** always **4** sometimes **5** often
6 usually

5 Direct students to the photo at the bottom of the page and elicit what kind of animal it is (monkey). Ask: *What is it eating?* Elicit *crisps*. Elicit guesses to the following questions: *What do monkeys usually eat? Where do monkeys usually live?* Give students a minute to read the text to check their ideas. Students complete the text with the phrases.

If students are preparing for an exam, point out that this is useful practice of a gapped text task (e.g. A1 Movers Reading and Writing, Part 3).

1 often live **2** usually sleep **3** always get up
4 sometimes take **5** are never **6** usually learn
7 often jump

Speak up

6 As an example, share a few sentences about your own family members or friends using the words and phrases in the box. Give students time to make notes or write their sentences before saying them. Encourage stronger students to make more complex sentences and include at least one example of points A–C from the explore grammar box.

Possible answers
My brother never eats meat.
My grandmother's usually at my house in the afternoons.
My friend Mary doesn't often visit me so her visits are very special.

To finish

Students work in pairs to write a crazy question starting with *How often do you … ,* e.g. *How often do you eat insects for dinner? How often do you sleep in the swimming pool?* Invite each pair to share their question with the class and the question which generates the most laughter from the class wins. Students walk around the room asking different people their crazy questions. The responder has to try to answer without laughing.

Presentation tool:	Unit 3, Grammar
Workbook / Online Practice:	p28
Photocopiable activity:	3A
Grammar reference:	SB p120
Audioscript:	SB p145
Extra Practice App	

VOCABULARY 2 SB p35

To start

If possible, before class find some photos of each place (or some of the places) in Ex 1, e.g. *cave*, *lake*, *desert*, etc. Make a slide presentation. Show the first slide and see if students know what it is, e.g. a cave. Chorally drill *cave*. Repeat through the whole slide deck. Continue through a few times for students to say the words.

alternative

Record the presentation as a short video with you saying the word for each place against the slide. Upload this to your private online space for students to watch before class. As an extension, students could make their own similar presentations / videos.

If you don't have technology at your school, draw four gaps for each letter of the word *cave*, e.g. _ _ _ _ and have students guess the letters that go in each gap until they guess the word. Invite students to draw a picture of a cave (explaining to their classmates if necessary what it is). Repeat with some of the other words from Ex 1.

the world around us

 Ask students to match the words with the letters in the picture. Students compare their answers in pairs then check as a class. Chorally drill the words in the box.

extra

Get the class to make up some (culturally appropriate) actions for each place in Ex 1, e.g. for *cave*, students could crouch down as if they are going to enter a small cave. For *lake*, students could make a horizontal circle with their arms in front of them. Once the actions are established, get students to stand up. Call out the word and have students do the action, then reverse it so that you do the action and students do the word. As students get the hang of it, increase the speed. You can also invite students to call out words or do actions for the class to respond to.

A sea   B desert   C river   D jungle   E forest   F lake
G mountain   H cave

 Ask: *Is a lake water or land?* (water). Add *lake* to the column *water*. Students complete the table then check as a class.

land: (cave), desert, forest, jungle, mountain
water: (cave), lake, river, sea

explore language

Go through the explore language box, checking students understand the words. Point out that the Earth has a capital letter when it refers to the planet and that earth meaning *land* / *ground* isn't capitalised.

watch out for ⓘ

Point out the capital in the Earth.

---

3 Direct students to the example speech bubbles. Look at the first animal with the class. Ask: *Do bats live in the sea?* Elicit a response, e.g. *No, they don't. I think they usually live in caves but they sometimes live in the forest.* (Or a simpler, but acceptable answer might be: *No, they live in caves.*)

Possible answer

A: Do bats live in the desert?
B: I think they usually live in caves. They sometimes live in forests. Do dolphins live in the sea?
A: Yes, they do. They sometimes live in rivers too. Do fish live in the mountains?
A: No, they don't. Fish live in rivers, lakes and the sea. Do snakes live in the sea?
B: Snakes sometimes live in the sea but they usually live in the jungle or the desert. Do camels live in caves?
A: No, they don't. Camels usually live in the desert. Do mountain goats live in the mountains?
B: Yes, they live in the mountains. Do brown bears live in the jungle?
A: I think they usually live in the forest or in the mountains. Do crocodiles live in the mountains?
B: No, crocodiles never live in the mountains. They usually live in rivers. They sometimes live in the sea.

 3.7 Point out that there may be more than one possible answer for the places these animals live, e.g. fish live in the sea, lakes and rivers. Students should choose the appropriate place based on the first letter given in the exercise. Play the recording for students to check their answers.

1 forest   **2** sea   **3** desert   **4** jungle   **5** cave
6 mountain   **7** river

Speak up

5 Students work in pairs to think of some wild animals in their country and talk about where they live and what they do. If students have devices, they could do some brief research about the wild animals and tell their partner.

Possible answer

There are snakes here. They usually live in the forest. They often live near rivers or lakes.

game on

Go through the instructions and examples with the class. Ask students to close their books, but write another example on the board for students to use as a prompt, e.g.

A: It sometimes lives in the sea.
B: Is it a fish?
A: Yes, it is. / No, it isn't.

VOCABULARY 2 (Continued)

Fun footer

Read the first part of the footer aloud. Ask students to think about the water and write down a guess of how much of the Earth's water is in the sea (ninety-seven percent). Read the second part of the footer aloud then say: *But how many animals do you know that live in the sea?* See how many students can name (e.g. fish, shark, whale, dolphin).

To finish

Choose an animal from the unit so far. Students see if they can work out what it is from only *Yes / No* answers, e.g. *Does it live in a desert? Is it brown? Does it live underground? Does it swim? Is it an armadillo?* Divide the class into two teams. Give team A the opportunity to ask the first question. If the answer is *Yes*, the team can ask another question to a different student. If the answer is *No*, the other team gets to ask the next question. The team who guesses the animal correctly gets a point. You can play to three or five points. If time allows, students play the game in groups of three.

Presentation tool:	Unit 3, Vocabulary 2
Workbook / Online Practice:	p29
Photocopiable activity:	3B
Grammar reference:	SB p120
Extra Practice App	

LISTENING SB p36

To start

Write: *go on holiday* on the board. Elicit the meaning (when you travel to another place for fun). Ask: *Where do you go on holiday?* In addition to the names of cities or areas, elicit types of places, e.g. *the beach, the mountains, the sea.* Write these on the board. Then ask *where is your dream holiday?* (If necessary, remind students that *dream* means *imagined, perfect.*)

Power up

1 Put students into pairs to name the animals. Elicit which one is a *koala* and the other animal names.

> **A** whale **B** kangaroo **C** shark **D** snake **E** parrot
> **F** koala **G** dolphins
> Photo F is a koala.

2 Elicit which country these animals live in (Australia). If possible, show students where Australia is on a map. If you use an online map, work out how far away Australia is from your country in hours. Ask students to work in pairs to decide which animals are dangerous and put a tick next to them. The answers will be checked in Ex 3.

> **extra:** whole class
>
> Ask students to talk about animal lives in more detail, as they did in Ex 3 on page 35, using the places for the world around us and adjectives or frequency, e.g. *A: Where does a crocodile live? B: I think a crocodile usually lives in a river, but it sometimes lives in the sea or in a lake.*

Listen up

3 3.8 Play the recording of Lily and Dan's holiday. Elicit the answers to Ex 2.

> These animals all live in Australia.
> Sharks and snakes are often dangerous.
> Kangaroos are sometimes dangerous – when they kick.

> **exam** task: **A1 Movers Listening Part 3**
>
> In the A1 Movers Listening Part 3 exam task, there is one example and five items. Also, there are eight pictures to choose from, not seven.
>
> **4** 3.9 Read the exam tip and get students to read the question in Ex 4 (highlight key words: *animal, each person, like*) and options 1–6. Point out that in this exercise, the information in the recording comes in the same order as the options, but it will not be in the same order in the exam.
>
> Make sure students know that they should write the letter of the animal's photo next to the person's name. Play the recording. If a number of students have not heard the answers, play it again. Check the answers as a class.

1 (Lily) B (kangaroo) (*I know there are kangaroos in Australia. They're my favourite animal.*)

2 (Grandma) F (koala) (*I love koalas.*)

3 (Dad) G (dolphin) (*It's your favourite animal, Dad!*)

4 (Mum) D (snake) (*I like them. They're very interesting animals.*)

5 (Dan) E (ground parrot) (*Aww! I like it a lot. It's very funny!*)

6 (Grandad) C (sharks) (*I like sharks … I want to see one!*)

extra: mixed-ability classes

To help weaker students understand the exercise, play the first part of the recording and pause it after Lily says: *I know there are kangaroos in Australia. They're my favourite animal.* Direct students to question 1 (Lily) and elicit what animal she likes (kangaroo). Get students to write *kangaroo* in the gap. Then play the remainder of the recording for students to complete the rest of the task.

explore **grammar**   → SB p120

Refer students to the Grammar reference on page 120. Go through the table and examples with the class. Ask students to complete Ex 4–6 on page 121 in class or set for homework. Students could ask and answer the questions in Ex 6 in pairs.

watch out for

Check students remember to use *does* in the third person singular.

5 🔊 3.10 Play the recording for students to listen first, focusing on how *do* you is pronounced in the questions /dju/. Ask students to practise saying the questions by themselves, then play the recording for students to listen and repeat as a class.

6 Students choose the best words to complete the sentences, then check as a class.

1 How 2 Where 3 What 4 Who 5 When 6 Why

7 Put students into pairs to ask and answer the questions in Ex 6.

alternative

Write the possible answers on the board out of order and ask students to match the answers with the questions in Ex 6.

Possible answers

1 L–I–L–Y, Lily.

2 Barcelona.

3 I like to meet my friends and play basketball.

4 Mary.

5 Usually at night. Sometimes I do it before school.

6 They are funny and cute.

To finish

Ask students to close their books. Give them two minutes to write down five question words, three animals from Australia and one thing they learned in the lesson. Put students into new pairs to share their answers.

Presentation tool:	Unit 3, Listening
Workbook / Online Practice:	p30
Grammar reference:	SB p120
Audioscript:	SB p145
Extra Practice App	

SPEAKING SB p37

To start

Whisper one of the following words from the unit to a student: *lake, forest, river, sea.* That student quickly whispers it to the next student, who whispers it to the next, etc. The last student to hear the word gets to write it on the board or say it aloud. Then whisper the next word to a student in the middle of the class so it goes around the room in a different order and the last student is different.

When students have the four words, introduce the phrase *odd one out* by asking: *Which place is different from the other places? Which place is the odd one out?* Ask students to whisper in pairs then elicit their ideas and reasons, e.g. *The forest is different because it is land. Lakes, sea, rivers are water.*

Power up

1 Ask a student to read the questions in the example and use the possible answers to respond. Put students into pairs to play.

Possible answers

A: Where does it live?
B: In the desert.
A: What does it eat?
B: I don't know!
A: Has it got four legs?
B: Yes, it has.
A: Is it a camel?
B: Yes, it is!

Speak up

2 🔊 **3.11** If possible, show some pictures (e.g. from the internet) of a zoo, wildlife park and farm, and ask students to match them to the words. Tell students they will hear a conversation between two students discussing which photo is different or *the odd one out*. Play the recording for students to answer the questions. Elicit the answers. Then ask: *What do you think? Which is the odd one out? Why?*

1 A (zoo), C (farm)
2 The giraffe because it doesn't live on a farm.
3 The sheep because it's white and the chicken because it flies.

3 For students preparing for A1 Movers, point out that this exercise is a reduced form of the Reading and Writing Part 2 task where students choose what speaker 2 says in a conversation. Students select the best answer then compare in pairs before checking as a class.

1 A **2** B **3** A

skill tip

Read the skill tip and ask a student to read the example. Write on the board the two parts of the example: *I think …* (saying what you think) *because …* (give a reason). Point out that there is often more than one possible answer. Point out in Ex 3, question 1 part A, the speaker uses an alternative introduction to saying what you think (*Maybe it's …*). Keep these on the board for students to refer back to in Ex 4.

---

exam task: A1 Movers Speaking Part 3

In the A1 Movers Part 3 Speaking exam task, the items all relate to different lexical sets. There are four sets, not three. Having all the items about animals here matches the topic of the unit and practises language learnt.

4 **e** Reassure students that there are no extra marks for giving one specific answer in the speaking exam – there is no *one* correct answer. The important thing is for the students to comment on each set of photos and give a reason for each choice. In pairs, students talk about each set of photos.

Possible answers

1 C (panda) I think the panda is the odd one out because it's black and white. The other animals are brown.
2 D (bat) Maybe it's the bat because it flies. The other animals don't fly.
3 B (fish) I think it's the fish because it's very small, but the other animals are big.

Speaking extra

5 If time allows, students could find or draw illustrations for their 'odd one out' question, take a photo and present it to the class on a projector or document camera. Alternatively, or if time is short, students could just write down the names of animals.

---

alternative

This could be set for homework and the students could present their 'odd one out' animals at the beginning of the next class (or for a group if you have a large class).

If you have a private class online space, create a forum where students can post their 'odd one out' question, and other students can reply below with a sentence about which one they think is the odd one out and a reason.

Fun footer

Ask students to read the joke, and if students don't understand it, see if a student can explain it to the class. (*Eye* sounds like *i*. The word *fish* without an *i* is *fsh*.) See if students can come up with any other similar jokes using animals from this unit … , e.g *What do you call a bird without an eye?* (*brd*).

To finish

Do some more practice of 'odd one out' while revising vocabulary from previous units. Write up sets of words and get students to work in pairs to decide which is the odd one out in each set. Encourage students to think of more than one possibility. Elicit ideas and reasons, e.g.

1 football, basketball, swimming, reading (e.g. Swimming is the odd one out because it is in water. The other activities are on land. / Reading because the other activities are sports.)
2 Australia, the USA, London, China (e.g. London because it is a city, but the others are countries. / China is different because people speak Chinese. In the other places, people speak English.)

Presentation tool:	Unit 3, Speaking
Workbook / Online Practice:	p31
Photocopiable activity:	3C
Grammar reference:	SB p120
Speaking file:	SB p136
Audioscript:	SB p146

WRITING SB p38

To start

If they prepared them for homework, get students to share their animal odd one outs from Ex 5 on p37. Alternatively, this is a good time to revise the animal A–Z (from *To start* Vocabulary 1) and see how many new animals students can add to their lists.

Power up

1 Ask students to cover the text at this stage and only look at the photos (or display it on the IWB if using a digital text). Direct students to the photos and elicit what students can see (penguins) and what they know about them. If students aren't sure what they know, help the discussion along with some more specific questions that students can answer from the photos or guess, e.g. *Are the penguins big or small? Where do they live? What do they eat? Do they swim? Do they fly?* If it doesn't come up in discussion, pre-teach the word *nest*.

Possible answer

Penguins swim. They eat fish. They live in cold places. They jump. They don't fly.

2 Direct students to the title *Fairy penguins.* Ask: *Do you remember another animal with fairy in its name?* (Pink fairy armadillos in the fun footer on page 33.) If you have the technology available, consider showing a short clip of fairy penguins (search for 'penguin parade Australia'). Give students two minutes to read the text and find out how they are different.

They are different because they are very small.

explore **language**

3 Ask students to highlight or underline *and* and *but* in the article. Go through the explore language box with the class.

Fairy penguins

Fairy penguins live in Australia. They are different from other penguins because they are very small. They are only thirty-three centimetres tall. Other penguins live in very cold places **but** not fairy penguins. They don't like the cold. They make their nests under the ground, near the sea. The baby penguins, called chicks, live in the nests. The father usually looks after the chicks when they are young. The mother goes out **and** finds food. She swims all day, **but** she comes back to the nest at night to feed her chicks.

WRITING (Continued)

4 Students complete the exercise individually then compare in pairs before checking as a class.

---

watch out for

In this exercise, students shouldn't begin sentences with *and* or *but*. If they do, say that it is okay to do that sometimes, especially in informal texts, but the purpose of this exercise is to practise linking two ideas within a sentence.

1 Fairy penguins live on land, **but** their food is in the sea.
2 Penguin chicks stay in their nests **and** they wait for their food.
3 Penguins live in cold countries **and** they live in some hot countries, too.
4 Penguins eat fish, **but** they don't eat meat.

---

extra: fast finishers

Ask students to choose one of the previous texts from this unit, either *A post from Brazil* on page 33 or *Monkey life* on page 34. Students highlight or underline the words *and* and *but* and see how many there are. Then ask them to choose one example of *and* or *but* to share with the class which they think is a clear example for linking similar or different ideas.

A post from Brazil: 4 buts, 7 ands
Monkey life: 2 buts, 4 ands

Fun footer

Read the fun footer as a class and ask students: *What do you call a very large group of penguins?* (a colony). Show a clip of a big group of penguins, either real or a colony of dancing penguins from the film *Happy Feet*.

Plan on

skill tip

Read the skill tip with the class. Ask: *How does a plan help you write?* (e.g. A plan helps you organise your ideas and make sure you include everything you need to).

5 Ask students to complete the notes using the information in the article. Check as a class.

1 Australia
2 Their nests are near the sea.
3 The father looks after the chicks.
4 The mother finds food.

6 Go through the information about whales. Point out that in this plan, the notes are not full sentences, which is fine for a plan. Ask students to decide on an animal they would like to write about. Students may want to do extra research online or in books to find good information. This could be done in class on student devices, for homework, or in the school library.

---

extra

This is practice for A1 Movers Listening, Part 2 [Note-taking]. After going through the whale notes, but before students do their own research, read the model answer from Ex 7 below, aloud twice, and see if students can fill in notes in the table in Ex 6. Check as a class. (They will then need to do their own plan on a separate piece of paper.)

Possible answer
Kangaroo
Where does it live? in Australia, in the desert
How big are they? some small, some two metres tall
What colour are they? brown or grey
What do you know about them? They jump; usually eat plants and occasionally insects; babies are very small; mothers carry babies in their pouches.

Write on

7 Students could find a picture on the internet or from a book or draw a picture. Circulate while students write their paragraph to help as required.

Model answer
Kangaroos live in Australia in the desert. Some kangaroos are small, but some kangaroos are two metres tall! They are usually brown and sometimes grey. Kangaroos don't walk but they jump. They usually eat plants, but occasionally eat insects.

Improve it

8 Tell students to re-read their work and see if they can add one more sentence or join two sentences with *and* or *but*. Remind students to check for full stops and capital letters to begin sentences, countries, etc.

Baby kangaroos are very small and mothers carry babies in their pouches.

---

extra: digital

Get students to work in pairs to check each other's work before they show you, then ask them to publish it on the computer or by writing it out neatly for display in the classroom.

To finish

Read the model answer in Ex 7 but substitute the word kangaroo for fairies, e.g. say *Fairies live in Australia in the desert. Some fairies are small, but some fairies are two metres tall! They are usually brown and sometimes grey. Fairies don't walk but they jump. They usually eat plants, but occasionally eat insects.*

Then say: *They're not fairies, they're …* (and elicit) *kangaroos.*

Organise students into new groups with people they haven't been working with for this lesson. Tell students to read their descriptions but substitute the animal name with fairy/fairies and get other group members to guess the animal. Alternatively, choose another word instead of fairies that may interest your class, e.g. *Pokemon, ghosts,* etc.

Presentation tool:	Unit 3, Writing
Workbook / Online Practice:	p32
Grammar reference:	SB p120
Writing file:	SB p136

SWITCH ON SB p39
Panda protection

1 As a model, choose an animal from the unit (e.g. parrot) and get students to ask questions to guess what it is and if it is common or endangered. Check students' understanding of *endangered* and review if necessary. Put students into pairs to think of an animal in their country and three ways to protect animals. To wrap up, do one more example with the class and choose *panda* as your animal.

2 ▶ Ask students to talk in pairs about what they already know about pandas. Invite a couple of students to the board as writers, and elicit what students know about pandas, with the student writers writing up the ideas in a spidergram. If students are reluctant, you may need to use questions like: *What colour are pandas? What can pandas do? Where do pandas live?* It doesn't matter whether the facts are correct at this stage; get students to write up all their ideas. Direct students to the question and point out that it looks simple, but there is more than one answer on the video clip. Play the clip. After the clip, elicit the answer. Ask students to tell a partner at least one thing they learned from the clip. Conduct whole class feedback, eliciting things students learned or found surprising.

Possible answer

These pandas live in a sanctuary. When they are big, they move to the mountains. Then they live in the mountain forests of China.

3 ▶ Play the clip again for students to put the things in the correct order.

1 a baby panda drinks milk
2 a panda mum cleans a baby panda
3 baby pandas go to sleep
4 a panda eats a carrot
5 a panda exercises

4 Brainstorm possible question starters on the board first, e.g. *Do, What, When, Why, Who, Where.* Put students into pairs to write three questions about the panda sanctuary. Monitor, checking question forms. Then combine pairs into groups of four to ask and answer the questions. You may need to play the clip again for students to see the answers.

Possible answers

What do the baby pandas drink? (They drink milk.)
Do you like pandas? (Yes.)
How much does the baby panda weigh? (1.3 kilos.)
Who do the pandas play with? (People and other pandas.)

---

extra: mixed-ability classes

Write the questions in the possible answer above with the words out of order. Get students to order the questions then ask and answer in pairs. Stronger students can write some of their own questions.

SWITCH ON (Continued)

Project

5 Start with a class discussion about what kinds of animal sanctuaries there are, and show some pictures if you can. Divide students into groups of 4–6 students. Assign a student to act as a leader in each group to help facilitate a discussion on what sort of animal sanctuary they are going to research. You could suggest they brainstorm options then vote. (If you think this is too open for your students, choose four options for each group to choose from.)

Within the group, get the students to form pairs or groups of three. The group should assign an aspect of the research to each pair. Provide a list of questions for the group to assign 1–2 to each pair, e.g. *Why are the animals in the sanctuary? What do they eat? What do they do? Where do they live? Who cares for the animals? Do they go into the wild again?*

Students could do the research for homework or during class time. For a longer term project, students research out of class then spend the last half an hour of the next lesson sharing what they've discovered.

Planning the presentations could be done over a period of two or three classes, using the last half an hour of each class. Students decide how they are going to present their information, e.g. digital slides, posters, oral presentation. With the final presentations, allocate one or two groups to present at the beginning of each lesson to avoid the presentation section going on too long in any one lesson. Encourage questions from the watching students at the end of each presentation.

---

alternative

1 As an extension, students could write 30 words or more (individually) about the sanctuary they researched.
2 Students work in pairs and choose a geographical area in their country to research, e.g. a specific beach, lake, cave or mountain. What kinds of animals live there? Are they big or small? What do they eat? Are there problems with the animals? Give groups a choice of how to present their information: a poster, an oral presentation or a short audio recording. This could also be a short or long project as per the example above.

Presentation tool:	Unit 3, Switch on
Switch on videoscript:	TB p139

UNIT CHECK SB p40

This Unit check covers vocabulary related to animals, the world around us and actions. It also covers adverbs of frequency and present simple questions.

Practice

1 Write each of the following categories on four pieces of paper: *farm animals, zoo animals, places you can go to, actions people can do.* Divide the class into four groups and give each group one piece of paper. Give them a minute to write as many words from the wordlist that fit the category as possible on the sheet. Then, have the groups pass the sheet to the next group. In the next minute, the students must read the items that have been put in and see if they can add any more. They can add other words that are outside the wordlist if they know them.Continue until the original brainstorm gets passed back to the first group to read. Display the ideas in the classroom.

Possible answers
1 goat, chicken, chicks, cow, dog, horse, sheep, rabbit, fish, duck, bee zoo animals: armadillo, bat, frog, fish, kangaroo, lion, monkey, panda, parrot, penguin, polar bear, bear, camel, crocodile, snake, elephant, giraffe, hippo, koala, tiger, shark
2 cave, desert, forest, jungle, lake, land, mountains, river, sea, farm, national park, pool, the moon, nest
3 climb, fly, jump, run, swim, walk

2 Share a few true sentences about you and animals. If students need support, consider writing up the possible answers for students to adapt to their own situation.

Possible answers
My favourite animal is a panda.
I like blue whales, but I don't like sharks.
There are birds in my garden.

3 3.12 Tell students they are going to hear some sentences about animals. Play the recording twice for students to write what they hear. Invite some students to write up a sentence (or some words from a sentence) to check.

1 Tigers sometimes swim in the river.
2 I often watch videos about animals.
3 Lions don't often climb trees.
3 We usually go to see monkeys at the wildlife park.

---

extra: mixed-ability classes

For weaker students, you could tell them the number of words in each sentence so they know if they have missed any words.

---

4 3.13 Give students time to complete the questions. Play the recording for students to check. Play it again for students to listen and notice the pronunciation of *do* or *do you*. Students write down their own answers to the questions. Put students into pairs to ask and answer the questions.

1 Do you 2 What do you 3 Why do you 4 How many
1 I go to the zoo every year.
2 There are kangaroos, crocodiles and koalas in Australia. Some animals are dangerous.
3 I like English lessons because we talk about different things and we play games.
4 I usually watch TV for ten hours a week.

REVIEW: UNITS 1–3 SB p41

Vocabulary

1 1 climb 2 have fun 3 cupboard 4 polar bear
5 swim 6 cave 7 guitar 8 garden

2 1 B 2 C 3 A 4 A 5 C 6 B

3 natural world: desert, lake, mountains, jungle, cave
home: bathroom, garage, lift, downstairs, kitchen

4 🔊 R1.1
1 school 2 monkeys 3 parrots 4 jungle 5 lions
6 apartment 7 balcony 8 meet

5 **e** In the A1 Movers Reading and Writing Part 1 task
there are eight pictures to choose from, and they are
always nouns.

1 get dressed 2 stairs 3 fly 4 go to bed 5 jump

Grammar

1 1 are 2 aren't 3 have 4 hasn't 5 is 6 has

2 1 's/is 2 lives 3 like 4 doesn't eat 5 eats
6 play 7 love 8 doesn't like

3 🔊 R1.2
1 Where, in the kitchen
2 When, in the evening
3 Who, my mum
4 What, computer games
5 How long, twenty minutes

4 1 F 2 A 3 E 4 D 5 C 6 B

5 **e** The rubric in the A1 Movers Reading and Writing
Part 6 task is 'Look and read and write.' and there are
two examples.

1 the polar bear
2 blue and yellow
3 (They're) next to the elephants
4 (They like) football
5/6 Possible answers
The monkeys are brown.
The polar bear is near a pond.

6 **Model answer**
Grace is a koala from Australia. She isn't grey, she's purple!
Grace is two years old and she lives in a big blue tree. She
sleeps every day! Her friend is Hugo the green koala.

GRAMMAR FILE SB 121

1 1 Penguins always eat fish.
2 Sharks never sleep.
3 I sometimes play with my pet goat.
4 Bats usually like fruit.
5 Lions often sleep for sixteen hours a day.

2 Student's own answers.

3 Student's own answers.

4 1 When do lions sleep?
2 How often do you go to the zoo?
3 What time does the zoo open?
4 Where do armadillos live?
5 What do you know about desert animals?

5 1 C 2 A 3 A 4 C

6 1 Where/When 2 Why 3 Who 4 How 5 What

7 Students' own answers.

Presentation tool:	Unit 3, Unit check
Workbook / Online Practice:	p33
Grammar reference:	SB p120
Audioscript:	SB p146

Let's explore

4

VOCABULARY 1
buildings and places in town

READING
topic: real-world adventure game
skill: choosing an answer
task: multiple-choice cloze

GRAMMAR
imperatives
must/mustn't
can/can't (ability)
object pronouns

VOCABULARY 2
vehicles

LISTENING
topic: a game app
skill: finding things in a picture
task: gap fill

SPEAKING
topic: visiting a new place
skill: finding your way around
task: ask for help

WRITING
topic: notes, lists and messages
skill: identifying information to include
task: write a message

SWITCH ON
video: school journeys
project: video diary

Lead-in

Point out the unit title *Let's explore*. Check students understand *explore* (to get outside and find out about interesting things), which is on the 2018 handbook wordlist for A1 Movers.

Read the quote with the class and check students understand *adventure*.

1 Put students into pairs to look at the photo and answer the question. Conduct whole class feedback, and elicit reasons why students think the people are where they are, e.g. *I think they are in a park because it looks like there are lots of trees.*

> **Possible answer**
> I think they are in a forest. / Maybe it's a park.

2 Ask students to share with the class some interesting places they have visited on a day out. Get students to discuss the things they saw or did or their day out in pairs. Remind them to use at least one of the adjectives from the list in their answer.

> **Possible answer**
> I go to the beach. It's beautiful. We often swim and walk. We sometimes eat ice cream.

---

extra: digital

Ask students to quickly find a photo on their mobile phone of an interesting place they have been. It can be a photo they took or one from the internet.

Conduct a class mingle where students walk around the room and try to find another person or people in the class with the same interesting place.

Then split the class into four groups. Students take turns telling showing their photo to the group and saying the name of their interesting place.

VOCABULARY 1 SB p44

To start

Write on the board *buildings and places in town* and elicit words students know for these. Write the words on the board. Use questions beginning with *Where*, e.g. *Where can people buy food?* (shop / market / supermarket / café), *Where can people catch the bus?* (bus stop / bus station). *Where can people go if they are very ill?* (hospital). *Where can children go to play?* (park / playground). *Where can people watch a film?* (cinema). *Where can people play sports?* (sports centre / park). *Where can people go for a swim?* (swimming pool).

Power up

1 Direct students to the buildings and places listed in Ex 1. Chorally drill the words. Read through the question and the example. Point out the capital letters for the street name *Mountain Road*. If students don't know the street name, they could say what it is near, e.g. *There's a bus stop near the school*. Both *in* and *on* can be used to talk about the street. *In* is more common in British English, while *on* is more common in American English.

> **Possible answers**
> There's a playground on Brown Street.
> There are shops in Lake Road.

> **extra:** digital 🛜
> Show an online map of the area around the school on your projector or get students to look up the streets on an online map on their mobile device.

buildings and places in town

2 4.1 Direct students to the map and ask them to find the bank. Tell students that they will hear a list of places on the recording and they should listen and point to each one as they hear it. Play the recording again (pausing if necessary) for students to write down the number and place. Write up the numbers 1–12 on the board. While students compare their answers in pairs, ask six students to come and write up two answers each of their choice.

> **1** hospital **2** sports centre **3** supermarket **4** bank
> **5** shopping centre **6** swimming pool **7** cinema **8** café
> **9** square **10** bus station **11** bridge **12** park **13** museum

> **extra:** whole class 👥
> Ask students to work in pairs to review their list of places from Ex 2 and tick the places which are buildings.

3 Revise *opposite*, *near* and *next to*. Ask students to read the text and choose the correct word. Check as a class.

> **extra:** fast finishers 🏃
> Students write sentences with preposition options about other places on the map which are **opposite, next to or near** one another, e.g. *The bank is next to / opposite the shopping centre*. Students could swap sentences in pairs or write a sentence on the board for their classmates to read and select the correct option.
>
> **1** museum **2** hospital **3** square **4** café
> **5** bus station / shopping centre

4 4.2 Tell students that they are going to hear three short conversations. Write on the board:

1 the bus number _ _ _ _ _ _
2 the second speaker is at the _ _ _ _ _ _
3 the bus stop is in _ _ _ _ _ _

Play the recording twice for students to write down the word or number then write the answers on the board for students to check.

For students preparing for A1 Movers or A2 Flyers exams, point out that this is useful practice for Listening Part 2 [Note-taking], where they will need to write a word or number next to five short prompts. There is sometimes a question that involves writing a word which is spelt out in the conversation.

> **1** S3 **2** Odeon **3** Queen Street

5 Check students understand the words *city*, *town* and *village*. To provide context, give or elicit some examples of local cities, towns and villages to demonstrate the difference between the words. Chorally drill the pronunciation, paying special attention to *village* /ˈvɪlɪdʒ/. Put students into pairs to work through the activities. Then conduct whole class feedback.

> **Possible answers**
> **1** We live in a city. / I live in a village.
> **2** River Road. R–I–V–E–R. Smith / Street. S–M–I–T–H.
> **3** There is a supermarket in / River Road. Its name is Fresh World, F–R–E–S–H W–O–R–L–D.
> There is a small shop opposite our school. Its name is Sam's. S–A–M–apostrophe–S.

> **game** on
> Read the instructions then time students for a minute while they list as many places as they can. Ask the pair with the most places to read their list to the class.

To finish

Write the following lists in two columns on the board. Ask students to match a word from the first column with a word from the second column to make a name of a place.

1 sports, internet, swimming, bus, bus, shopping
2 café, pool, station, centre, centre, stop

Check as a class. Then ask students to ask and answer the following questions in pairs: *Which place is your favourite? How often do you go to each place?*

Answers: sports centre, internet café, swimming pool, bus station, bus stop, shopping centre.

Presentation tool:	Unit 4, Vocabulary 1
Workbook / Online Practice:	p34
Grammar reference:	SB p122
Audioscript:	SB p146
Extra Practice App	

READING SB p45

To start

Before class, draw or print sets of *a medal, a gold egg, a silver cup* (trophy) on different colours of paper, i.e. a medal, egg and cup on green paper, a medal, egg and cup on red paper, etc. You will need a set for each small group.

In class, write *treasure hunt* on the board and elicit what it is (a game where you have to find something).

Divide the class into teams of three to four. One person from each team leaves the room. The other members of the team have to hide their teams' medal, gold egg, trophy around the room. The team member then comes back in the room to look for their items with their team members helping them by shouting instructions using prepositions from the previous lesson like *next to the chair, opposite the teacher's desk*, etc. The first team to collect all their items is the winner.

Power up

1 Tell students to cover the main text with a piece of paper and just look at the title, the first three lines and the photo. Ask if anyone has played a treasure hunt game like this before, e.g. *Pokemon Go*. Tell students to answer the questions individually then compare their answers in pairs before checking as a class.

> **1** a phone with a game app on it
> **2** Treasure Hunt
> **3** you explore your town and find treasure

> **background:** AR games
>
> The Treasure Hunt game in the article is an example of an augmented reality (AR) game like *Pokemon Go*. In AR, computer-generated information, images etc are combined with things in the real world or images of real things. In the image on Student's Book page 45, the player looking at the screen sees the street they are in with a cup super-imposed which the player can collect for points.

Read on

> **exam** task: **A1 Movers Reading and Writing Part 4**
>
> In the A1 Movers Reading and Writing Part 4 exam task, there is one example and five items. No key would be given away elsewhere in the text.

2 **e** Go through the exam tip and demonstrate *crossing out* on the board. Ask students to read the text and choose the correct answer for each gap. Review the answers as a class and elicit why each option is correct and the others are incorrect.

Check students understand the following words or phrases: *press, button, screen, download.* Use a smartphone or a picture of one to demonstrate the words.

each: students may recognise this from their coursebook exercises.
join: say it means to become part of a group or team.
walk into someone/thing: you can demonstrate this!

1 C (How = Question word asking for instructions. *Who / What* fit grammatically, but the paragraph following the question explains *how* to play not *who / what* to play.)

2 B (are = Second person, verb *to be* to go with pronoun *you*. *Am / is* don't go with pronoun *you*. *Am* goes with the pronoun *I*, and *is* goes with *he / she / it*.)

3 A (do = First person question form, to go with pronoun *I*. *Does* goes with third person singular not *I*. *Don't* doesn't make sense because the instructions explain what to do.)

4 C (to = Set phrase, we use *to* in the phrase *next to*. When talking about position, we don't say *next on* or *next of*.)

5 A (your = Instructions (*have fun and enjoy* are addressed to second person, you). It isn't *her new* game or *their new* game.)

Sum up

3 Students use the text to order the instructions. Check as a class. Remind students that they should always tell their family where they are if doing this sort of treasure hunt.

> **1** Download the free app.
> **2** Explore your town.
> **3** When you see some treasure, press the 'X' button.
> **4** Take a photo.
> **5** When you have ten things, join a team.
> **6** Have fun!

> **alternative**
>
> Ask students to divide a piece of paper into six rectangles and number them 1–6. Students copy the instructions in the correct order and draw a picture for each one.

Speak up

4 Get the class brainstorming together first. Put two columns on the board – a tick for good things, and a cross for bad. Ask the class for a couple of examples of good and bad things about their town. Then put students into pairs to brainstorm more ideas, then combine the pairs into groups of four to compare their ideas and make sentences. If you think your students need it, this is a good chance to review *there is/there are*, and *but/and* for adding different or similar ideas. Conduct whole class feedback.

Possible answers

There is a park and a playground near my home.
There is a swimming pool, but there aren't any sports centres.
There is a nice shopping centre, but it isn't near our school.

Fun footer

Ask students to read the fun footer. Ask: *Do you play games on a mobile phone? What is your favourite game or app? How often do you play?* If games are popular in your class, make a class chart with the most popular games, with the number of ticks to represent each person in the class who plays the game.

To finish

Students work in pairs to create a treasure hunt for another team. They make a list of five objects around the classroom. This could also be played outside in the school grounds, if appropriate. Collect the lists and distribute each one to a new pair. Pairs race to find the objects and write down a sentence about the location.

Sample list: 1 red pencil   2 a light   3 keys
4 blue schoolbag   5 picture of a cat

Sample answer: 1 It's on Anna's desk.
2 It's above the teacher's desk.   3 They are on the shelf.
4 It's near Charlie's chair.   5 It's on the poster near the door.

Presentation tool:	Unit 4, Reading
Workbook / Online Practice:	p35
Grammar reference:	SB p122
Extra Practice App	

GRAMMAR SB p46

To start

Give students some instructions as imperatives, demonstrating as required, e.g. *Stand up. Sit down. Stand up. Jump. Walk (on the spot). Run (on the spot). Stop. Sit down. Open your book. Close your book.* Get faster as students get to know the instructions.

---

alternative

You may want to download the Grammar Presentation for this lesson from the Teacher Resources area of Pearson English Portal. This presentation has been created specifically for this lesson and is fully editable for teachers.

---

explore **grammar** → SB p122

1 Refer students to the notes on imperatives on page 122 and go through them with the class. Ask students to complete Ex 1 on page 123.

1 D (Find all the treasure.)
2 C (Walk around the streets.)
3 B (Don't fall in a river!)
4 A (Don't worry!)

---

watch out for

The *please* goes at the beginning or the end of the sentence, e.g. Please take a photo. Take a photo please. NOT Take please a photo.

---

2 ◀)) 4.4 Students will need a pen and a piece of paper for this exercise. Play the recording for students to follow the instructions. Ask some students to read their sentences for the class.

Possible answers
George
is at the
supermarket.

3 ◀)) 4.5 Play the recording and encourage students to notice the voice going up to ask politely. Play the recording again for students to listen and repeat.

Write your name here.
Write your name here, please.
Buy some apples at the supermarket.
Please buy some apples at the supermarket.

GRAMMAR (Continued)

---

exam task: A1 Movers Reading and Writing Part 2

In the A1 Movers Reading and Writing Part 2 exam task, there is a continuous dialogue between two people and there are three options per item. There is one example and six items.

4 Tell students that the highlighted words are for the next exercise, but point out that just because a word (e.g the highlighted word) from the first speaker is repeated doesn't mean it's the correct answer. After students have done the exercise, go through the answers as a class.

1 B   2 B   3 A

---

5 Give an example of how the highlighted words in conversation 1 in Ex 4 could be changed, e.g. *Write your age here please.* Circulate while students practise the conversations, encouraging students to use polite (upward) intonation for the requests to be polite.

Possible answers
A: Write your phone number here, please.
B: OK. Of course.
A: Please buy some pizza at the supermarket.
B: Of course. Do you want bananas, too?
A: Meet me near the playground after school.
B: Great. See you there.

---

explore grammar ↳ SB p122

Refer students to the Grammar reference on *must/mustn't* on page 122 and go through them with the class. Set Ex 2 and Ex 6 on page 123 in class or for homework.

---

6 Ask students to look at the signs (A–G). They work individually to match the sentences (1–4) with the signs and then compare their answers with a partner. Ask them to practise saying the sentences and make sure they know to place emphasis on *must/mustn't*.

1 A   2 F   3 B   4 D

---

watch out for   ⓘ

Make sure students understand that *mustn't* / *must not* means that it is necessary not to do something (rather than meaning something isn't necessary).

---

extra: fast finishers   🏃

Students decide what the other signs mean and write a sentence to go with each one using an imperative or *must / mustn't*.

Speak up

7 Put students into small groups for this exercise. In their group, ask students to decide if they are going to be an extra strict teacher or a really soft teacher. Then they should brainstorm some possible instructions and decide on three to write down. Circulate, checking for accurate use of imperative and *must/mustn't*.

Possible answer
(extra strict teacher)
Please read five books for homework.
Sit down, please.
Don't talk to your friends.

---

alternative

Ask each group to secretly choose one of the places or buildings from the Vocabulary lesson on page 44, e.g. *bank, museum, school, playground, swimming pool, bridge.* Students brainstorm a list of instructions for that place then write down three. Each group reads their three instructions to the class and their classmates must guess which place it is. If it is too hard to guess, the group could give a choice of three, e.g. *Are these instructions for in a shop, at a park or at a hospital?*

To finish

This is a version of the classic game *Simon says* to help students remember to use *please* to make imperatives more polite. Tell students that you will play a game where they will get some instructions like in the *to start* exercise but that they should only do them if they hear *please*, e.g. If they hear *stand up please*, students stand up, but if they just hear *stand up*, students should not move. Demonstrate the game by calling out a range of instructions, some with please and some without, e.g. *Stand up please, sit down please, open your books please, close your books* (*pause*). When students understand the game, you could continue as a class (and offer some students the opportunity to give some instructions) or have students play the game in small groups, taking turns to give instructions for about a minute each before swapping.

---

extra: mixed-ability classes

After you have demonstrated the game, invite some volunteers to come to the board to write up the instructions you used. This gives some students the chance to demonstrate their skills, and provides prompts for students that need them when taking a turn at being the caller.

Presentation tool:	Unit 4, Grammar
Workbook / Online Practice:	p36
Photocopiable activity:	4A
Grammar reference:	SB p122
Audioscript:	SB p146
Extra Practice App	

VOCABULARY 2 SB p47

To start

Draw the following grid on the board.

T	A	X	I	P
I	R	C	L	A
B	O	A	T	V
E	N	R	I	A
E	K	I	B	N

Put students into pairs to find as many words for vehicles as they can in two minutes (horizontally, vertically, diagonally). Then brainstorm any other vehicles they know.

Answers: train, plane, taxi, boat, van, car, bike

vehicles

1 Ask students to match the words with the signs then compare their answers in pairs. Don't check the answers yet as this will be done in Ex 2.

2 🔊 4.6 Play the recording for students to check their answers. Play it again for students to listen and repeat. Find out if there are other significant modes of transport in students' daily lives, e.g. *underground, scooter, ferry*, and take the opportunity to teach the relevant words.

> 1 **A** car   **B** plane   **C** lorry
> 2 **A** train   **B** helicopter   **C** boat
> 3 **A** bus   **B** taxi   **C** bike
> 4 **A** van   **B** motorbike   **C** tram

3 Ask students to work in pairs to look at the picture and take turns to say a vehicle in the picture. Elicit the answers.

> bus, motorbike, car, lorry, taxi, plane, helicopter, train

alternative

Students take turns to describe a vehicle for a partner, who finds the vehicle in the picture.

e.g. A: a black taxi   B: Here it is.

4 Students ask and answer the questions in pairs. Then ask and answer their own questions. Point out that students can change words in the questions to make new questions, e.g. *How many ~~motorbikes~~ lorries are there?*

> 1 3   2 between the lorry and the blue car   3 black
> 4 in front of the bus

extra: digital

Search for some sounds of vehicles in this lesson on the internet using the search terms *free sounds vehicles*. Ask students to number 1–5 on a piece of paper, then play five sounds and students need to write down the vehicle they think it is. Play each sound again and elicit what it is.

5 Start by asking: *Where's the tractor?* to teach the word *tractor*. Demonstrate how students can change words in the questions in Ex 4 to make new questions, e.g. *How many ~~motorbikes~~ buses are there?* Students can also form other questions if they want to. Point out that students will need to check they use the correct singular or plural form. Put students into pairs to ask and answer questions.

> How many bikes are there? (two)
> Where's the helicopter? (in the sky)
> What colour is the plane? (orange)
> Is the purple car behind a bicycle? (No. The purple car is behind a green lorry.)
> Which vehicle is in front of the bus? (a blue car)

extra: mixed-ability classes

If some students find it too challenging to ask questions without preparation, put students in pairs to write at least four of their own questions, with both students in the pair writing down the questions.

Then re-organise students into new pairs to ask and answer their questions.

explore language

watch out for

Check students' pronunciation of *train* /treɪn/, *bus* /bʌs/ and *cycle* /ˈsaɪkəl/.

6 Direct students to the language box and elicit when students would need to use the verb forms with *-s / es* (third person singular, *he / she / it*.). Students complete the sentences then check as a class.

> 1 go by   2 cycle   3 goes by   4 walk   5 go by

extra: fast finishers

For sentences 1–4, challenge students to write a question that would elicit that answer.

Possible answers
1 How often do you go by train?
2 How do you and Adam go to school?
3 How does Mum go to work? / How often does Mum go by bus?
4 How can they go to the station?

73

VOCABULARY 2 (Continued)

Speak up

7 Remind students that adverbs of frequency could be useful in this exercise. To the left of the board write *never* and, to the right, write *always*, and elicit the other adverbs of frequency students learned in Unit 3 (*often, usually, sometimes*) and write these between in appropriate places. Put students in small groups to ask and answer the questions. Conduct whole class feedback.

Possible answers

I usually walk to school, but sometimes I go by car.
My friend Mary often cycles to school. Sometimes she goes by bus.

> **extra:** mixed-ability classes
>
> Designate a confident student as a leader for the group discussion. Tell them that being a leader means encouraging everyone to participate, helping people take turns, and they can also be called on to report back to the class. This gives the stronger student a chance to lead and provides some support for weaker students.

Fun footer

Read the fun footer with the class. If you can, find a short clip of a hover taxi in Dubai to show the class. Point out that another kind of taxi which isn't a car is a *water taxi*.

To finish

Put students into groups of 3–4. Secretly allocate each group one of the vehicles from the lesson (or ask them to choose one). and ask them to work out how to create a team statue of the vehicle using their bodies. It can have some moving parts. Set appropriate guidelines for your class, e.g. whether students should avoid touching each other in the activity. Explain that each group will come to the front of the class and present their statue. Other students must guess what vehicle the statue is.

Presentation tool:	Unit 4, Vocabulary 2
Workbook / Online Practice:	p37
Photocopiable activity:	4B
Grammar reference:	SB p122
Extra Practice App	

LISTENING SB p48

To start

Ask students to close their books and tell them they are going to have a treasure hunt. They work in pairs and find as many colours they can see in the classroom and write them down in a list, trying to spell the colours correctly. Elicit colours and write them on the board for students to check their spelling.

Power up

1 Go through the instructions and example with the class. Put students into pairs to complete the activity. Conduct whole class feedback.

There's a white building.
There are blue bins.
There is green grass.
There's an orange jacket.
There's a pink umbrella.
There's a purple T-shirt.

Listen up

2 🔊 4.7 Ask students to read the questions. If necessary, clarify that *rules* here means the instructions for the game. Play the recording twice. Elicit the answers. For students preparing for A1 Movers or A2 Flyers, point out that the game 'colour me' is similar to what they will do in Listening Part 4 – Starters, Part 5 – A1 Movers and A2 Flyers. Starters will follow instructions to colour objects. A1 Movers and A2 Flyers will follow instructions to colour objects and write one or two words.

A game called 'Colour me'. You have to write a word or colour an object.

---

3 🔊 4.8 Tell students that Eva's friend Ben is going to have a turn with the game. They need to listen to the instruction he gets and write the missing word in the picture. Play the recording twice then elicit the answer.

Centre

> **extra**
>
> Play *Colour me* with the class. Write a list of words on the board and give students a few minutes to draw a picture with the items in a black or grey pen or pencil without colouring them: *lorry, bus, bus stop, bike, car, school, plane.*
>
> Read out instructions for students to colour in the items, e.g.
>
> *The lorry is green. Colour it now.*
> *The bus is red. Colour it now.*
> *The car is blue. Colour it now.*
> *The bike is orange. Colour it now.*
> *The school is brown. Colour it now.*
> *The plane is pink! Colour it now.*
>
> Alternatively, students could work in pairs, and give their partner similar instructions.

exam task: A1 Movers Listening Part 5

In the A1 Movers Listening Part 5 exam task, there is one example and five items. Read the exam tip with the class. Play recording 4.9 and ask students to write down the prepositions they hear.

4 4.9 Get students to read the sentences first to focus their listening. Play the recording twice for students to complete the sentences. Elicit the answers.

1 grey **2** green **3** orange **4** brown

explore **grammar**   → SB p122

Go through the grammar box and read the examples from the recording with the class. Refer students to the notes on *can / can't* on page 122. Ask students to complete the exam-like task Ex 3 on page 123. This is practice for A1 Movers and A2 Flyers, Part 2.

In A1 Movers Part 2 [Short dialogue with 3 multiple choice responses], there are six questions. In A2 Flyers Part 2 [Continuous dialogue with multiple-choice responses], students will choose the correct response by the second speaker in a continuous dialogue from eight options (A–H).

For Ex 4 on page 123, ask students to write their own answers down. Circulate checking for accurate use of *can / can't*. Put students into pairs to ask and answer the questions.

watch out for ①

Emphasise that the form of *can* is the same for every subject. (There is no third person, there is no *-s* on can or the verb that follows.) Write on the board the following two sentences for comparison of third person *-s* in present but not with can: *Eva often plays Colour Me. Now Ben can play Colour Me too.*

5 Students complete the conversation then check as a class. Students practise the conversation in pairs, then adapt it to make it true.

1 can **2** can **3** Can **4** can **5** can't **6** can

6 Direct students to the first gap and elicit the answer. Set the exercise. Students compare in pairs before checking as a class. For sentence 5, if students have used *he / she* for bus, point out that objects in English are referred to as *it* (not *he/she*).

1 you **2** them **3** us **4** him **5** it **6** her

explore **grammar**   → SB p122

Refer students to the Grammar reference on page 122 and go through the notes. Set Ex 5 on page 123 in class or for homework.

watch out for ①

Emphasise that it is incorrect to use subject pronouns as object pronouns.

e.g. *Give the phone to ~~she~~ her.*

To finish

Give students some challenges of increasing difficulty using *can*. Demonstrate for students to understand unknown vocabulary. After each instruction encourage students to call out *I can* or *I can't*. For example:

1 Can you stand on one leg? Can you stand on one leg and count to ten? Can you stand on one leg and count to ten with your eyes closed?
2 Can you rub your tummy? Can you pat your head? Can you rub your tummy and pat your head at the same time?

Presentation tool:	Unit 4, Listening
Workbook / Online Practice:	p38
Grammar reference:	SB p122
Audioscript:	SB p146
Extra Practice App	

SPEAKING SB p49

To start

Ask for a show of hands: *Who likes going to the cinema?* Write *3D* on the board. Ask: *What is a 3D film?* Students could answer in L1 if need be. (It's a film where people and things look like they are coming out of the screen. You wear special glasses to watch it.) Write *4D* on the board. Ask: *What is a 4D film?* (It's a 3D film with special effects you can feel, e.g. the seats move or you feel heat.)

Power up

1 Direct students to the map of Adventureland Theme Park. Ask: *Do you like theme parks? Have you ever been to a theme park? What theme parks would you like to go to?*

Ask students to read the advert to decide which activties they want to do. Write on the board *I want to … .* Conduct whole class feedback.

Possible answers
I want to see a 4D film.
I want to go on the Big Wheel.
I want to take a ride on a bike.

2 Put students into pairs and tell them that they are visiting the theme park together but they can only do two activities. They need to decide which two activities to do. Conduct whole class feedback.

Possible answers
We want to get a boat on the lake and catch a train around the park.
First, we want to visit the cinema. Second, we want to do a treasure hunt.

Speak up

3 Teach *left* and *right*. Students complete the conversation with the words. Check students understand *souvenir shop* (a shop that sells objects that you can buy to remind you of a place you've visited. Souvenirs may include T-shirts, bags, keyrings, etc.).

4 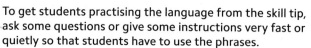 4.10 Play the recording for students to check their answers.

1 Where's
2 go left
3 Excuse me
4 opposite

extra
In pairs, students could practise the conversation.

skill tip

Read through the skill tip. Demonstrate the pronunciation of the phrases and give students time to practise saying them. Write or type out the useful phrases (or ask a fast finisher to do this) for display around the classroom.

---

extra: whole class

To get students practising the language from the skill tip, ask some questions or give some instructions very fast or quietly so that students have to use the phrases.

---

5 Ask two students to read the examples aloud. Then students take turns to follow the instructions.

Possible answer
A: Excuse me. Where is the cinema, please?
B: It's in Market Square. Go right.
A: Can you say that again, please?
B: Of course. Go right. The cinema is in Market Square.

Speaking extra

6 Students prepare a conversation similar to the ones in Ex 5, but for a place in their town. They could draw a map or show an online map. Ask each pair to present their conversation to the class.

A: Excuse me. Where is the supermarket, please?
B: Can you see the park? Go to the park then turn left.
A: OK. Thanks very much.

---

extra: project

Students design their own theme park individually or in pairs. They decide on a theme, draw a map of the theme park with at least five attractions, and make a list of things you can do there (in the style of the advert in Ex 2). This part could be done for homework if students are working individually.

Then students share their map with another student / pair. The listener chooses their favourite attraction and the presenter needs to give instructions on how to get there using the map.

Fun footer

Students read the fun footer. Bakken Theme Park was founded in 1583 and is the world's oldest theme park. You could show some pictures of Bakken Theme Park from the internet.

To finish

Share a tip for remembering *left / right*. Point out to the students that if they hold up their hands in front of them palms forward, thumbs separate from fingers, that the left hand makes an *L* (for left).

Repeat the game *please* from the *To finish* Grammar lesson on page 72 of the Teacher's Book. Add in the instructions with left and right, e.g. *Turn left please, turn right. Look left please, look right please. Wave your right hand please. Wave your left hand.*

Presentation tool:	Unit 4, Speaking
Workbook / Online Practice:	p39
Photocopiable activity:	4C
Grammar reference:	SB p122
Speaking file:	SB p137

WRITING SB pp50-51

To start

Write a message on the board to greet the class and give them the first instructions for the lesson. Indicate silently for students to read it as they come in, e.g.

Hi English class
Today's class is about writing messages. Can you understand this message?
Please find a partner. Open your book and turn to page 50.
Talk about the question in Ex 1 with your partner. Start now!
Mr Smith (your name)

Power up

1 Students discuss the question in pairs, using adverbs of frequency to say how often they write each one. During feedback, ask: *Which is not a message?* (a list). *Do you write lists?*

Possible answers

I often write text messages and lists. I sometimes write short notes, emails and posts on social media. I don't often write letters or postcards.

2 Ask students to read the messages and match them with a type of writing in Ex 1. Elicit the answers.

A text message **B** short note **C** list **D** email

3 If need be, give prompts for birthday/Christmas presents or other relevant present-buying occasion in students' country; list prompts could include food items or school supplies, etc. Lists could be made individually or in pairs. Ask students to read their list to the class.

Possible answer

pizza, apples, water, books

alternative

Put students into groups and get each group to choose one of the list types. On a piece of paper, they write a title for their list, and write as many items as they can in 30 seconds. Then they pass the list to a different group who has 30 seconds to add to the list.

4 Direct students to the bolded prepositions in the messages. Elicit the correct word for situations 1–3.

1 at **2** on/in **3** at

Fun footer

Read the fun footer with the class. See if students know any other message language (e.g. lol = laughing out loud). Get students to come and write a message to the teacher on the board or in a forum in the class online space using the language of messages and see if the teacher and class can work it out.

Plan on

skill tip

Go through the skill tip. Point out that useful information should include information on who, where and when.

watch out for

Point out that this language is informal so appropriate for messages to friends and family. Formal messages will be covered at A2 level.

5 Ask students to read the list and select the items to include. Elicit ideas.

day, time, place, maybe name (if it's a text message or social media message, name is not needed)

Write on

exam task: A2 Key for Schools Part 9

In the A2 Key for Schools Reading and Writing Part 9 exam task, students write a short message of 25–35 words. They will get instructions on who to write to and what to include.

6 **e** Go through the explore language box with the class. Encourage students to tick the task bullet points as they add them, to ensure that all the relevant information is included.

Possible answer

Hi Lee,
Come to town with me on Saturday.
I want to go to the cinema.
Meet me by the bus stop at two o'clock.
See you later,
Mary

Improve it

7 Students swap messages to check the points in Ex 6. Students could also check for full stops and capital letters for days of the week and names.

To finish

Tell students that you've got a text message, but you can't read it because there are no spaces, capitals or punctuation. Write the message and ask them to work in pairs to rewrite it correctly.

theresapartyforteachersat530onfridayatthesportscentreitsin mountainrdseeyouthere (There's a party for teachers at 5 p.m. on Friday at the sports centre. It's in Mountain Road. See you there!)

Presentation tool:	Unit 4, Writing
Workbook / Online Practice:	p40
Grammar reference:	SB p122
Writing file:	SB p137

SWITCH ON SB p51

School journeys

1 Put students into pairs to make a list of all the different types of transport from the unit (books closed). Give them three minutes to write as many as they can remember. You could make it a competition to see which pair can write the most. Elicit possibilities. Students could check Ex 1 on page 47 (or the wordlist on page 52) to see if there were any they missed, and add them. Students keep their list for use in Ex 2.

Possible answers

bike, boat, bus, car, helicopter, lorry, motorbike, plane, taxi, train, tram, van

2 ▶ Tell students that they are going to watch a video clip about different journeys to school. Ask students to watch the clip and tick the kinds of transport they see in the clip (on their list from Ex 1). Alternatively, for a bit of fun, get students to see who can call out the modes of transport as they appear in the video.

Possible answers

bus, car (in the background), walking, boat

3 ▶ Direct students to the table and elicit where each of the people live (Mexico, Lake Titicaca in Peru and Siberia). Elicit where Siberia is (Russia). Play the recording again, (you could start at 00:35) for students to complete the table. Make sure students know that more than one journey could match each sentence. Elicit the answers.

A Teresa, Ángela and Filomena
B Teresa, Ángela and Filomena, Vidal
C Teresa, Ángela and Filomena
D Vidal
E Teresa, Ángela and Filomena, Sayana

> **extra:** mixed-ability classes ⤮
>
> Reassure students that it's fine not to understand every word in the video, and encourage them that they can understand a lot from what they can see. To further push (stronger) students, tell them to write down any key words or pieces of information they hear about each journey. After going through the answers to Ex 3 for each journey, elicit anything extra students heard.

4 Get students to talk about the question in pairs and also decide which journey was the most difficult. Students may need to use both L1 and English. This is acceptable, but encourage them to use as much English as possible. Conduct whole class feedback.

Project

5 Write down the steps below on the board in a checklist for students to work through. Explain what is required at each stage and set a time limit, e.g. students need to complete steps (1) and (2) by the end of the class, and complete (3) (4) for homework by the following week.

For step (2), teach students a storyboard approach, i.e. drawing boxes of the different shots they are going take and plan what to say in each one. Point out that they can also add a voiceover afterwards.

(1) Ask and answer the following questions with a partner:

  a What transport do you use?

  b What time do you leave home?

  c How long is your journey to school?

  d What places do you see?

  e What animals or people do you see?

  f Who do you travel with?

(2) Plan your video diary on a storyboard.

(3) Record your video.

(4) Edit your video.

(5) Share your video.

For the presentation step (5), it may work well to allocate students different days and just show 2–3 videos per day, rather than everyone's on the same day. Encourage students who are watching to ask the person a question or give a positive comment about the video.

> **extra:** digital
>
> 1 If you have a private class online area, videos could be uploaded there instead. Group students to watch each other's videos and post a positive comment or question to the people in their group.
> 2 If it's not feasible for students to make videos, instead get students to make a comic strip about their journey to school. They could include the same information. Get students to share their comic strips in small groups, and then display them on the classroom wall.

Presentation tool: Unit 4, Switch on

Switch on videoscript: TB p139

UNIT CHECK SB p52

This Unit check covers vocabulary related to buildings and places in town, vehicles, instructions and *can*.

Practice

1 Put students into pairs and give them a time limit (e.g. two minutes) to look at the wordlist and write down as many words as they can for each category. During class feedback, elicit answers for each category, and find out which pair came up with the most words.

Possible answers

1 bus station, cafe, cinema, hospital, plane, playground, shopping centre, sports centre, square, supermarket, theme park

2 bus, car, taxi, van

3 bus station, shopping centre, sports centre, swimming pool, souvenir shop, text message

2 Give a few examples of true sentences about you and places or vehicles, e.g. *I usually go swimming on Saturday. I always take the bus to work.* Students write their sentences individually. Monitor and help as needed.

Possible answers

I usually cycle to school.

I sometimes go to the cinema with my family.

My family goes to the supermarket by car.

3 🔊 4.11 Play the recording and ask students to write down the sentences they hear. Play the recording again. Then elicit the sentences and write them on the board.

1 Give the bike to him please.

2 You mustn't run near the swimming pool.

3 Can you help me with my homework?

4 The café is opposite the museum.

4 🔊 4.12 Play the recording twice for students to complete the questions and answers. Then put students into pairs to ask and answer the questions. Conduct whole class feedback and elicit interesting answers from the pairs.

1 Can you travel on a tram in your town?

2 Which bus goes to the town centre from here?

3 What buildings are opposite, next to and near your school?

4 Who in your family can drive a .... ?

Possible answers

1 No, you can't. / Yes, you can.

2 Bus 45. / There is no bus to the centre / We are in the town centre.

3 There are houses opposite my school. There is a shopping centre next to my school. There is a hospital near my school.

4 My mother can drive a car./My father and my sister can drive a car./No one can drive a car.

GRAMMAR FILE SB p123

1 **1** Come **2** close **3** close/don't open **4** sit **5** don't play **6** read

2 **1** mustn't **2** must **3** mustn't **4** mustn't

3 **1** B **2** C **3** C **4** A **5** B

4 Student's own answers.

5 **1** them **2** you **3** me **4** us **5** it

6 Student's own answers.

Presentation tool:	Unit 4, Unit check
Workbook / Online Practice:	pp41–43
Grammar reference:	SB p122
Audioscript:	SB p146

Fun with food

5

VOCABULARY 1
food and drink

READING
topic: Mexican Day of the Dead
skill: thinking before you read
task: comprehension questions

GRAMMAR
present continuous (all forms)
countable and uncountable
nouns with a/some/any

VOCABULARY 2
the weather

LISTENING
topic: a kite festival
skill: finding people in a picture
task: matching

SPEAKING
topic: good and bad weather
skill: talking about pictures
task: find differences between two
pictures

WRITING
topic: planning a party
skill: making notes
task: write a description of a party

SWITCH ON
video: frozen museum
project: fun food museum

Lead-in SB p53

1 Read the quote with the class.
Direct students to the photo and
go through each colour ice cream
in turn, e.g. *What's the yellow
ice cream? Is it pineapple? Or is it
mango?*

With unknown words, see if
students can explain them to
each other. They could also do an
internet search for them, e.g. carrot,
or carrot ice cream. Ask: *Which ice
cream flavour is your favourite?*
Elicit some favourite flavours and
write these on the board. Then
ask students to vote by raising
their hands, and as quick review of
numbers, get students to count up
the number of votes (in English) for
you to record next to each flavour.

Possible answers
chocolate, orange, pineapple,
watermelon, mango, carrot, grape,
coconut and pear

2 Point out that these unusual ice
cream flavours all exist! You could
find some pictures of each one on
the internet, display them on your
projector and have students guess
which flavour each picture is.

Students discuss with their partner
these ideas for ice creams. *Do you
want to try an ice cream with these
unusual flavours? Do you think it
would be nice?* Conduct whole class
feedback. See who can come up
with the funniest and the nicest
ideas for a very unusual ice cream.

Possible answers
I choose bubble gum because it
sounds great!

VOCABULARY 1 SB p54

To start

Write on the board *I'm hungry* and *I'm thirsty*. Indicate the meaning of the words by touching your tummy as if you are hungry, and your throat as if you are thirsty. Point out that we use *be* + hungry and thirsty. Drill the phrases with increasing intensity, e.g. *I'm hungry, I'm hungry! I'm very hungry!*

Power up

1 Direct students to the captioned pictures of drinks and drill the words. Ask a few students which drink they would like. Then put students into pairs to ask each other. Elicit some other flavours of juice and milkshakes by asking *what flavour juices do you like?* (e.g. orange juice, pineapple juice, grape juice); *What flavour milkshakes do you like?* (e.g. chocolate, banana, mango.)

> **Possible answers**
>
> apple juice / a milkshake please / I would like lemonade.

food and drink

2 Ask *Do you eat food from other countries?* Elicit some foods that students like from other countries and write the word for the food or country on the board, e.g. *pizza, sushi, Mexican food, Italian food, Chinese food*. Direct students to the meals. Ask students to guess where each one is from (Brazil, Italy, Britain, Japan). Students decide which lunch they like and tell a partner, using a reason if possible.

> **Possible answers**
>
> I like lunch B because I love pasta. / My favourite lunch is lunch C. I like the sandwich!

3 🔊 5.1 Students work in pairs to find the words in the photos. Play the recording for students to check.

> **Photo A** – 1 meat 2 vegetables 3 beans 4 rice
> **Photo B** – 5 cheese 6 pasta
> **Photo C** – 7 apple 8 carrots 9 sandwich
> **Photo D** – 10 bread 11 salad 12 egg
> **A** – **1** meat **2** beans **3** rice
> **B** – **4** cheese **5** pasta
> **C** – **6** carrots **7** apple **8** sandwich
> **D** – **9** bread **10** vegetables **11** egg **12** salad

exam task: A1 Movers Reading and Writing Part 1

In the A1 Movers Reading and Writing Part 1 exam task, there is one example and five items. Also, there are eight pictures with the words underneath them to choose from. This exercise follows on here from the previous vocabulary work.

4 🅴 Students choose the correct word to fit each definition.

> **1** fruit **2** sandwich **3** cheese **4** vegetables **5** pasta

---

> **extra: fast finishers**
>
> Students write a definition for one of the food or drink words from pages 53 or 54. Invite students to read the definition to the class (or write it on the board) for other students to guess.

5 🔊 5.2 Tell students that they are going to hear four short conversations. They need to match the conversation to the lunches. Play the recording twice, then elicit the answers.

> **1** C (British lunch) **2** A (Brazilian lunch)
> **3** D (Japanese lunch) **4** B (Italian lunch)

> **extra**
>
> Ask students to turn to the audioscript on page 146 and practise reading the conversations in pairs.

> **game** on
>
> Put students into small groups. Nominate one student as the writer (or ask students to choose a writer.) Write headings on the board *good for you, not good for you*. Give students two minutes to list as many foods as they can in each category. Invite each group to share their list.

> **alternative**
>
> Students play the two-minute list game but making lists of food they like / don't like.

Fun footer

Point out that scream means to shout or make a loud high noise with your voice. Encourage students to try saying the fun footer aloud. Point out or elicit that *I scream* sounds very similar to *ice cream* but there is a slight difference in sound. See if students can hear the difference. (The difference is the juncture i.e. where the division occurs between syllables: icecream /aɪs+kriːm/ and "I scream" /aɪ+skriːm/).

Say it as a class echo, in different ways. You say: *I scream*, indicate the class to say *you scream*, then everyone says together *we all scream for ice cream*. Do this in different ways, (without stopping in between), e.g.whispering, with finger snapping, mouthing silently, loudly, slowly, fast.

To finish

Ask students to imagine what their *best lunch ever* would be using some of the ideas from the trays or their own ideas. If there is access to computers, students could cut and paste pictures of food on to a plate, and either present it on the projector, or print off for display.Students talk about the food in their nice lunch in pairs, e.g. *I've got some rice and beans, watermelon, cheese and an ice cream.*

Presentation tool:	Unit 5, Vocabulary 1
Workbook / Online Practice:	p44
Grammar reference:	SB p124
Audioscript:	SB p146
Extra Practice App	

READING SB p55

To start

Students keep their books closed. Write the words *fancy dress, happy, skeletons, skulls, fireworks, enchilada, Mexico* on the board. Ask students to discuss in pairs if they know what any of the words mean. See if any students can come up and draw a picture for one of the words to teach them to the class. Ask: *What's the connection between all of these things?* (Day of the Dead festival).

Power up

1 Direct students to the title and pictures. Put *Who / What / When / Where / How* on the board as prompts for possible questions. Brainstorm possible questions as a class. Write them on the board. Leave them there as it will be useful to refer back to them after they've read the text, in connection with the Skill for this lesson. (Forming such questions is a core skill enabling greater comprehension.)

Possible answers
What is the celebration?
Where is the celebration?
Does the girl like this food / the colour pink / this celebration?
What is the black / blue / purple food?
1 Mexico **2** Gabriela

2 Ask students to read the text and match questions 1–3 to the gaps in the text. Check as a class and elicit what the key words were in the text which helped them choose the correct answer.

1 C **2** A **3** B

3 Students answer the questions then check as a class.

1 Richard Collins
2 parties, dancing, singing, fireworks and food
3 because she doesn't want paint in her eyes
4 (lots of) beans, rice, a taco and some enchiladas

alternative

For a more communicative activity, organise students into groups of three. Student A reads text A, Student B text B and Student C text C. They then see which questions in Ex 3 they can answer. Then as a group students share the information about their text and as a group they complete all the questions in Ex 3.

extra: fast finishers

Refer back to the list of students' questions on the board. Ask students to see which questions they can answer from the text. If there are some questions which weren't answered in the text, encourage students to guess or do some research to answer them.

background: Day of the Dead

Share the following cultural notes or ask students to do further research into the festival.

In Mexico, 1 Nov is Day of the Innocents/Day of the Little Angels, and 2 Nov is officially Day of the Dead. Sugar skull: An important part of the tradition is also to write your name or the name of the person you are making it for on it in colour too. Skulls are not usually eaten, but placed on a small 'altar' that people make in their homes. The altar is usually decorated with flowers and food. It is customary for people to make the food of their loved ones and eat it to celebrate them. Specific food is eaten over this festival too, e.g. the enchiladas which are made from a special kind of corn that looks blue/purple.

Sum up

4 This is good practice for the A1 Movers Reading and Writing Part 5. Students complete the summary then compare in pairs before checking as a class.

1 November **2** Mexico **3** sugar **4** orange
5 costumes **6** faces **7** photo **8** food

Speak up

5 Divide students into small groups to discuss the questions. Sometimes asking students to write their ideas down can help keep them on track.

Fun footer

Ask students to read the fun footer, and check students pronunciation of sugar /ˈʃʊgə/. Look up how much sugar is in some popular food and drink your students like and then ask students to guess how much is in each.

To finish

Draw five small skulls (or apples if you prefer) on the board. Choose a word from the text, e.g. skeleton, and write up gaps on the board _ _ _ _ _ _ _ _ .

Students take turns to guess a letter. Fill in the correct letters. If a letter is not in the word, erase one apple off the tree. Students need to guess the word before the five skulls are erased. Elicit the meaning. Continue to play as a class or divide students into pairs or small groups to play.

Suggested words: *scared, happy, fireworks, flowers, fancy dress, special, beans, fruit, hot chocolate, hungry.*

Presentation tool: Unit 5, Reading
Workbook / Online Practice: p45
Grammar reference: SB p124
Extra Practice App

GRAMMAR SB p56

To start

Put class into pairs. Give each pair one of the words – *am | is | are*. (Big classes will end up with 3 or 4 pairs with the word *am | is | are*). In those pairs, students discuss these questions:

When do we use the word? (Elicit verb to be in present / with adjectives)
Who do we use it with? (Elicit pronouns)
Give 2 example sentences – one positive, one negative

Pair up with another pair that has the same verb. Compare answers.

Then regroup class into groups of three which has one student with each of the words *am | is | are*. They then take it in turns to present their verb, explanation and examples. Circulate to ensure the information is correct.

---

alternative

You may want to download the Grammar Presentation for this lesson from the Teacher Resources area of Pearson English Portal. This presentation has been created specifically for this lesson and is fully editable for teachers.

---

1 Ask students to read the grammar box which summarises the reference. Students write the -ing form for each verb. Write up the answers.

1 painting **2** doing **3** having **4** celebrating **5** sitting
6 playing

---

extra: fast finishers

Writing up a few more words for students to write the -ing form for, e.g. go, happen, get up, cycle, swim, jump.

Answers: *going, happening, getting up, cycling, swimming, jumping.*

---

explore grammar → SB p124

Refer students to the Grammar reference on page 124. Go through the notes and examples. Ask students to complete Ex 1 and 2 on page 125 then compare in pairs before you check as a class.

---

watch out for ⓘ

Point out that there are some verbs that we don't usually use in the continuous form, e.g. like

---

2 Encourage students to look at the picture before reading the text. Elicit what students know about *Halloween*.

1 is watching **2** is making **3** are having
4 aren't sitting **5** is wearing **6** isn't feeling

---

extra

Write on the board: *ghost, vampire, witch, skeleton*. Ask students to find these costumes in the picture.

---

3 Point out that students will need to choose *is* or *are* depending on whether the subject is singular or plural. Do this part as a class. Then put students into pairs to ask and answer the questions.

1 Are **2** Is **3** Are **4** Is

4 Students complete the sentences then check as a class.

1 is eating
2 is wearing
3 is drinking

5 🔊 5.4 Get students to read the questions then play the recording twice. Check as a class.

1 It's Halloween.
2 He is Lauren's brother.
3 She is drinking watermelon juice.
4 He's looking at the pumpkin soup.

Speak up

6 Students work in pairs to make sentences aloud rather than writing them down. Conduct whole class feedback.

Possible answer

This boy is wearing a vampire costume. He is smiling.
This girl is wearing a ghost costume. She isn't smiling.

To finish

Ask students to think of a festival they celebrate, perhaps one that they discussed in the previous lesson. Students draw three small pictures of something they do on that day. Students work in small groups and take turns to ask each other: *What are you doing in this picture?* Students reply using the present continuous. Alternatively, if students have photos of themselves on mobile phones, they could talk about those instead of drawing pictures.

Presentation tool:	Unit 5, Grammar
Workbook / Online Practice:	p46
Photocopiable activity:	5A
Grammar reference:	SB p124
Audioscript:	SB pp146–147
Extra Practice App	

VOCABULARY 2 SB p57

To start

Before class, make a slide show of a few pictures of some interesting extreme weather pictures. Use search terms like: *extreme rain, extreme wind, extreme snow, sunny paradise.* In class, show each picture in turn, and ask: *What's the weather like?* Try to elicit the words from Ex 1 and teach them if necessary.

Elicit the months of the year, (for a list of months, refer students to Student's Book page 8 Ex 7). For further review, replay track S.9 for students to listen and practise saying the months. Ask about the weather at other times of year, e.g. *What is the weather like in January? What about June?*

the weather

1 🔊 5.5 Ask students to match the pictures with the words. Then listen and check. Play the recording again for students to listen and repeat.

> **A** cold **B** sunny **C** windy **D** foggy **E** hot **F** warm
> **G** cloudy **H** rainy **I** snowy

2 Elicit some different cities or towns in your country for students to find / guess the weather for. If possible, make a live weather satellite map or an online forecast available, e.g. on your projector, student mobile phones, or bring in some newspapers. Otherwise, students can make good guesses.

> **Possible answer**
> What's the weather like today? In London, it's raining and cold. In Manchester, it's snowing! In Brighton, it's windy and cloudy, but it isn't raining.

explore **language**

Explain the two different forms: *It's* + adjective; *It's* + verb + *-ing* (present continuous).

> **watch out** for ⓘ
> We can't say *it's clouding, foggying,* etc. Point out that that *rain* and *snow* are verbs which is why we can use them in the present continuous.

3 Direct students to the title and the photos. Ask students to read the descriptions and match them to the pictures. Check the answers as a class.

> **1** B (Thai Pongal, Sri Lanka)
> **2** A (Pahiyas, The Philippines)
> **3** C (Maslenitsa, Russia)

4 🔊 5.6 Tell students they will hear three conversations. Play the recording twice and students choose the correct answer. Check as a class.

> **1** B **2** C **3** A

Speak up

5 Students discuss in pairs then conduct whole class feedback.

> **alternative**
> In pairs, students think of a place that has each type of weather, e.g. *Where is it hot? It's hot in Mexico. Where is it foggy? It's sometimes foggy in London.*

To finish

Explain that a word picture is a word and a picture, and draw one as an example e.g. the word *rain* inside a raindrop, or written in tiny raindrops. Ask students to design some word pictures for the weather words in Ex 1 to help them remember the words, then share in pairs.

Presentation tool:	Unit 5, Vocabulary 2
Workbook / Online Practice:	p47
Grammar reference:	SB p124
Audioscript:	SB p147
Extra Practice App	

LISTENING SB p58

To start

Tell students that you are going to read a shopping list for a picnic. (If necessary, teach the word *picnic.*) They need to listen and remember as many items as they can without writing anything down yet. Read the list twice. After you have read the list, students work in pairs and write down as many items as they can from the list. Elicit the answers and write them on the board.

Shopping list: some bread, some cheese, some butter, three tomatoes, six eggs, four pears, four bananas, some orange juice, some chocolate, and a big watermelon

Power up

1 Ask the questions to the class as a whole class brainstorm.

> **Possible answers**
> I eat lunch outside every day. / I sometimes have picnics on / at the weekend with my family. / I don't often eat outside. / I eat outside at festivals.
> I eat sandwiches and fruit. We sometimes eat eggs or cakes.

Listen up

2 Read the skill tip with the class, and quickly revise the verbs listed in the box by getting students to mime/ explain them. Direct students to the picture and demonstrate the pronunciation of *kite.* Elicit who / what is flying in the picture (the kites) and point out that we can say *The kites are flying* or *The people are flying kites.* Elicit answers to the questions.

background: kite festivals

Many places have kite-related festivals, from Pakistan to Afghanistan to Guatemala to Greece.

Possible answer

The weather is windy.

Some people are flying kites. Some people are watching kites. Here, the people are having a picnic.

Here, the people are sitting and talking.

exam task: A1 Movers Listening Part 1

In the A1 Movers Listening Part 1 exam task, there is one example and five items. Also, there are seven people to choose from. The task is completed by drawing lines from names to people in the picture, rather than matching letters.

3 e ▶ 5.7 Point out that as in the exam, you listen to people talking about what they can see in the picture. In the exam students draw lines from the names to the correct person in the picture. Play the recording twice for students to complete the activity. Check as a class.

A Kim (*Who's that in the blue jacket? … That's Kim.*)

B Ben (*… not the small boy. The boy next to him. Oh, yes. That's her brother, Ben. He's carrying a big rucksack!*)

C Mrs Sasaki (*Mrs Sasaki is putting some food out on plates.*)

D Jason (*Jason's drinking orange juice.*)

E Ella (*There's Ella. She's wearing a red cap.*)

explore grammar → SB p124

Refer students to the Grammar reference on page 124. Go through the notes and examples and set Ex 6 on page 125 in class or for homework.

4 Draw up the lists on the board. Ask students to work in pairs to divide the items then check as a class.

countable: an egg, olives, an orange, a sandwich, sweets, tomatoes
uncountable: bread, chocolate, cheese, pasta, rice
plural: olives, sweets, tomatoes

watch out for (!)

Point out that some countable nouns have a spelling change in their plural form, e.g. potato, tomato, mango, sandwich, add -es, *e.g. potatoes, tomatoes, mangoes, sandwiches.*

5 Encourage students to look back through the unit to find other words for food and decide which list they go in. Conduct whole class feedback.

Possible answers

countable: bananas, beans, carrots, enchiladas, pears
uncountable: butter, meat, salt, soup, spaghetti

extra: whole class

Teach students the following rhyme *one potato, two potatoes, three potatoes, four. Five potatoes, six potatoes, seven potatoes, more.* (The actions are putting fists on top of each other.) The rhyme repeats with increasing speed. Point out that this rhyme can only be done with countable nouns. Try some others, e.g. *one banana, two bananas, three bananas, four. Five bananas, six bananas, seven bananas, more.* Get students to make up appropriate actions to match different foods. For a challenge, get students to try saying the rhyme with the word *enchiladada!*

6 Review the explore grammar box point, that *any* is used for negatives and questions, and *some* is used before uncountable nouns. Students complete the text then compare their answers in pairs before checking as a class.

1 some **2** some **3** any **4** some/a **5** some **6** an
7 some **8** any **9** a

Speak up

7 Tell students what your favourite sandwich is as an example, e.g. say *I like chicken and salad sandwiches.* Put students into pairs to ask and answer.

Possible answer

A: What's in your favourite sandwich?

B: I like egg and tomato sandwiches. What's your favourite sandwich?

A: My favourite sandwich is cheese and chips!

To finish

Write on the board *I'm going on a picnic and I'm taking … .* Say this aloud and add a sandwich. Indicate a student repeat what you say and add an item, e.g. *I'm going on a picnic and I'm taking a sandwich and some sweets.* The next student repeats your items and adds another e.g. *I'm going on a picnic and I'm taking a sandwich, some sweets and an orange.* The game can continue to be played as a class or divide students into small groups to play. Monitor for accuracy of countable and uncountable nouns, and re-model as required.

Presentation tool:	Unit 5, Listening
Workbook / Online Practice:	p48
Photocopiable activity:	5B
Grammar reference:	SB p124
Audioscript:	SB p147
Extra Practice App	

SPEAKING SB p59

To start

Review words for things in the classroom using the questions in the useful language. Point to objects and ask: *How do you say … in English?* Suggested words: *bin, clock, cupboard, desk, laptop, noticeboard, pictures, shelf, window, door.*

Power up

1 Drill the phrases in the useful language box with the class. Put students into pairs to complete the exercise. Conduct whole class feedback.

> **Possible answer**
>
> **A:** Here's a dog. What's the word for *nube* in English?
> **B:** Cloud?
> **A:** Yes, a cloud. And I can't remember this word in English.
> **B:** Lemonade.

2 Drill the words in the box and elicit where each one is in the picture. Then ask students to work in pairs to ask *How many … ?* questions about each item. Elicit the answers.

> **Possible answer**
>
> How many bottles are there? 2
> How many bowls are there? 1
> How many cups are there? 1
> How many glasses are there? 5
> How many plates are there? 6

3 Go through the instructions with the class. Elicit a couple of differences then put students into pairs to find as many as they can. The check list covers the types of differences that might occur in the exam. After the task, check what differences students have found.

> **Possible answer**
>
> Here the boy's shirt is orange but here it's red.
> In the second picture, the salad is behind the bottles. But in the first picture, it isn't!
> Look, in this picture the dog is eating the sandwiches but in this picture he's just looking at the sandwiches.
> In this picture there's a sun. But in this picture, there isn't.

Speak up

> **exam** task: **A1 Movers Speaking Part 1**
>
> **4 e** Go through the examples and the exam tip. Elicit a few examples of differences using the example structures. Students work with their partner to practise talking about the differences they identified in Ex 3. Remind students that in the A1 Movers Speaking Part 1, the examiner can help with an unknown word.
>
> > **Possible answer**
> >
> > In picture A the dog is looking at the sandwiches, but in picture B he's eating them.
> > In the first picture there's a sun. But in the second picture, there isn't.

Speaking extra

5 With supervision, students could find two pictures on the internet using the search terms: *spot the difference, kids.* Students use the example structures in Ex 4 to prepare at least three differences to share with the class.

> **Possible answer**
>
> **A:** In picture 1, the child is drinking orange juice but in picture 2, the child is drinking milk.
> **B:** Yes, and in the first picture, there are four cakes, but in the second picture there are three cakes.
> **A:** And in the first picture, the mum is standing up, but in the second picture, she is sitting.
> **B:** Yes, and look, here the mum's t-shirt is blue, but here, it's purple.

> **alternative**
>
> Before class, find two similar but different pictures and either bring in copies or upload them to your class online area for students to access via their mobile device.
>
> Put students into pairs. Student A only looks at picture A, and student B only looks at picture B. Students take it in turns to describe what they see without revealing their picture. If the picture is different from what they heard they can say: *But in my picture …*
>
> e.g. A: In my picture, a boy is eating an ice cream.
> B: But in my picture, the boy is eating a sandwich.
>
> To finish, students reveal their pictures and make three sentences about the differences.

6 Students work in pairs to do another spot the difference task. Give students a couple of minutes to talk about the differences then conduct whole class feedback.

Fun footer

Ask students to read the fun footer. Point out that barbie is an informal shortened version of barbecue. Give another example of a shortened word: *choccy bickie* and see if students can work out what it is (a chocolate biscuit.) Point out that in the USA, biscuits are cookies.

To finish

Ask students to reflect on the lesson and think of:

… something you liked.
… something you already knew.
… something you learned for the first time today.

Put students in pairs to talk about their answers then conduct whole class feedback.

Presentation tool:	Unit 5, Speaking
Workbook / Online Practice:	p49
Photocopiable activity:	5C
Grammar reference:	SB p124
Speaking file:	SB p138
Pairwork file:	SB p143

WRITING SB pp60-61

To start

Consider playing some happy party music in English as students enter the classroom to set the scene for the topic of party planning. Gradually reduce the volume to indicate you're going to start. Brainstorm some reasons for a party on the board, e.g. *birthday, New Year, Halloween, summer, a new house, a new baby etc.*

Power up

1 Give students a moment to think about which celebration they would choose. Put students in pairs to share their ideas.

> **Possible answer**
> I am planning a birthday party.

2 Direct students to the photos and elicit the types of meal in each one *barbecue, picnic, pizza*. In the same pairs, students decide which food they would choose.

> **Possible answer**
> We would choose pizza.

3 Go through the sample menu with the class. Ask students to write their own menu. Tell them to include both food and drink.

> **Possible answer**
> Menu for a pizza party
> food: pizza, salad, chips, birthday cake, ice cream
> drinks: orange juice, lemonade

4 Tell students that the Outdoor Activity Centre is a place where people can have parties. Ask students to read the form and answer the questions. Elicit the answers.

> **1** His name is Adam Fraser.
> **2** His email address is afraser12@engmail.com.
> **3** He is twelve/12.
> **4** He wants to have a barbecue for twenty/20 people.
> **5** His friends from school are coming. His phone number is 07997 474395. The party is for his thirteenth birthday. His friends from school are coming. Their favourite food is burgers and pizza. They want fruit juice and water.

Fun footer

Read the fun footer with the class. Ask: *Are birthday cards popular in this country?*

Find a suitable website in English for students to make an e-card for a classmate's birthday. You can often specify a future date for delivery. Alternatively, students could write a message for a friend in a card. Suggest ways to start and finish the message, e.g. *To / Dear … From / Love from …*

> **background:** text messages ⓘ
> Point out that in English, people don't usually end messages to family and friends with the word *kisses* but people often write x or xxx for kisses instead.

Plan on

5 Get students to work in pairs to plan their own party and make notes using the questions given.

> **Possible answer**
> **1** date: 3 April
> **2** time: 5.30 p.m.
> **3** 10
> **4** a picnic

Write on

6 Go through the skill tip. Point out the instruction near top of the form in Ex 3 *Please write your name in BLOCK CAPITALS* and elicit what this means = every letter of the word is a capital (uppercase) letter. Get students to write answers to the application form in Ex 3.

> Last name: TAN First name: LILY
> Home phone or mobile: 45660 542 980
> email: lilytan89@blue.com
> Age (years): ten/10
> Meal: B picnic
> Number of guests: thirty/30
> About the party: It is a birthday party for my sister. Our family and friends are coming. We like pizza and ice cream. Our favourite drink is lemonade.

7 Students swap their descriptions with a partner and create an application form. They must ask and answer questions to get all the information. Circulate, helping as required. Remind students to use the application form on page 60 to help them.

Improve it

8 Tell students to check their partner's form for capitals for names, months, days of the week, spelling and that the student has included all the information required. Invite students to share their partner's party with the class.

> **Possible answer**
> Roman is having a picnic party for his mum's birthday on 15 March. There are twelve guests. They are having cheeseburgers, chocolate cake and apple juice.

To finish

Consider finishing this lesson with a class party at the end of this class, e.g. you could play music (in English) and play some party games. If appropriate at your school, students and teacher could bring in some party food to share.

Presentation tool:	Unit 5, Writing
Workbook / Online Practice:	p50
Grammar reference:	SB p124
Writing file:	SB p138

SWITCH ON SB p61

Frozen Museum

1 Tell students that they're going to watch a video clip about an ice cream museum. Tell students that it's a real place, in San Francisco, USA. Direct students to the title of the video, and elicit what *frozen* means. (Many students will likely be familiar with the Disney's animated film *Frozen* which may help them guess the meaning of this above-level word.) Put students into pairs to write down as many facts (or ideas) about ice cream as they can. Elicit ideas.

Possible answer

Ice cream is frozen / cold.

I like ice cream.

Ice cream has got cream in it.

There is chocolate ice cream, banana ice cream and mango ice cream.

> **extra:** whole class
>
> Pre-teach the following words by writing them on the board and getting students to talk in pairs about whether they know what each one is, then draw or show some images. Leave the words displayed during the lesson for students to use in Ex 2 and 3: *sweets*, *whipped cream can*, *mochi* (a Japanese rice cake sweet), *sprinkles*, *peach*, *swing*.

2 ▶ Get students to read the list of possible things. Encourage students to note down any other things they can do at the museum if they can. Elicit the activities students ticked or noted, and list these on the board. Don't give any extras yet, as you can elicit any more students noticed after you play the recording again in Ex 4.

---
2 eat ice cream   **3** play games   **4** take photos.
(Other activities include: play in a sprinkle pool, eat mochi, go on a swing.)

---

3 ▶ Get students to read the question. Tell them to consider the question as you play the recording again, and also to see if there are any other activities you can do at the museum that haven't been noted yet. Play the recording. Elicit any other activities to add to the list from Ex 2, then put students in pairs to discuss the question.

Possible answer

It isn't a museum because you can't learn about ice cream.

---

4 ▶ Get students to discuss the question in small groups and say what they would like or wouldn't like about going to a museum like this. Get each group to briefly report back to the class.

Possible answer

We would like to go to the ice cream museum because we love ice cream.

Yes, because we want to play in the sprinkle pool.

We want to go because we want to play games and have fun.

Project

5 Get students to reflect on what kind of food would make a good food museum, e.g. *Is it a delicious food? Is it a special food from your city or country?* Divide students into groups of four, and assign each group a leader whose job it is to help keep everyone on task and encourage every member to participate. Tell students to brainstorm ideas for each question, make decisions, and then decide how to present their museum, e.g. a radio advertisement, an oral presentation with slides, a brochure, acting out a visit to the museum for the class. Give a clear time limit, and monitor, providing assistance as required.

> **alternative**
>
> 1 For a longer project, get students to plan and present their museum in more detail. Students could begin by researching some other real museums for ideas – many museums have virtual tours or 360 degree videos.
> 2 Make ice cream. There are lots of simple internet recipes for making plastic bag ice cream from just a few ingredients: milk (or soy / rice milk), sugar, salt, ice, plastic bags. Students could work in groups to plan different flavours, and take photos of the different stages and label the pictures.

Presentation tool: Unit 5, Switch on
Switch on videoscript: TB p140

UNIT CHECK SB p62

This Unit check covers food and drink, weather, countable and uncountable nouns, and present continuous.

Practice

1 Quickly review examples of countable and uncountable nouns with *a/any/some* with the class. Ask students to find and write down as many words as they can for each category, then compare their answers with a partner.

Possible answers

1 apple, grape, mango, orange, pear, coconut, pineapple, watermelon.

2 hot chocolate, lemonade, milk, milkshake, orange juice

3 three countable nouns: sandwich, bottle, kite
   three uncountable nouns: fruit, pasta, rice

4 pizza, rice, salad

2 Students work individually to write their sentences about food. Go over the example sentence with the class. If necessary write another example on the board, e.g. *I love Japanese food because it's interesting and delicious.* Encourage students to give reasons why they like/don't like the food in their answers. Elicit answers from around the class during feedback.

Possible answers

I love pasta, but I don't like cheese.
I think Mexican food is delicious.
I like fruit. Watermelon is my favourite.

3 🔊 5.8 Play the recording twice for students to write the sentences they hear. Then invite students to write the sentences on the board for the whole class to check.

1 I'm eating some chicken salad.
2 She's sitting next to her friend.
3 We're making a cake for you.
4 They aren't flying kites today.

4 🔊 5.9 Play the recording and ask students to write down their answers to the questions. Put students into pairs to compare their answers.

Possible answers

1 (Is it snowing now?) No, it isn't.
2 (What's the weather like today?) It's cloudy. It's cold.
3 (Who are you sitting next to?) Tom / I'm sitting next to Tom.
4 (What are you looking at?) My book / I'm looking at my book.

GRAMMAR FILE SB p125

1 **1** Peter is painting a picture.
   2 Rachel and Joy are listening to music.
   3 Max and Paddy aren't playing football now.
   4 I'm not eating lunch at the moment.
   5 Is Elana drinking lemonade?
   6 Are you watching this programme?

2 **1** am/'m having **2** is eating **3** is sitting **4** are having
   5 am/'m learning **6** am/'m having

3 Student's own answers.

4 **1** 'm **2** isn't **3** 's **4** Are **5** aren't **6** 're

5 **1** A **2** C **3** A

6 **1** any **2** any **3** an **4** a lot of **5** any **6** some

Presentation tool:	Unit 5, Unit check
Workbook / Online Practice:	p51
Grammar reference:	SB p124
Audioscript:	SB p147

Back in time

6

VOCABULARY 1
adjectives to describe things

READING
topic: a TV show about the past
skill: finding the right type of word
task: gapped text with picture cues

GRAMMAR
past simple: *be*
past simple: regular verbs

VOCABULARY 2
things we do (verbs)

LISTENING
topic: a night in a castle
skill: identifying information you need
task: multiple choice (pictures)

SPEAKING
topic: life in the past
skill: supporting a partner
task: talk about a picture

WRITING
topic: a pirate museum
skill: choosing the right word
task: write a blog post

SWITCH ON
video: Frontier House
project: life in the past

Lead-in SB p63

1 Direct students to the photo and ask them to read the questions. Allow one minute for them to discuss their answers in pairs before eliciting the correct answers. Then go over the background notes and find out if any students have seen this phone (or similar) before and where, e.g. in an old film.

Possible answer
It's a mobile phone. It's old.

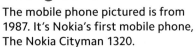

background: Nokia
The mobile phone pictured is from 1987. It's Nokia's first mobile phone, The Nokia Cityman 1320.

2 Direct students to the box and elicit the opposite adjective pairs, e.g. Ask: *What's the opposite of beautiful?* (beautiful – ugly, big – small, dirty – clean, old – new). Put students into pairs to discuss the question then conduct whole class feedback.

Possible answer
It's big. It's old. It's ugly.

3 Tell the class about something old that you've got, e.g. say: *This watch is very old. It was my grandfather's. It's special. It's about fifty years old.* Students discuss the question in pairs then conduct whole class feedback.

Possible answer
I've got an old radio. It's about thirty years old.

extra

Conduct a challenge. Put students into small groups and give them two minutes to think of and write down as many other objects as they can that are old and not used anymore. Then get students to swap their list with another group and discuss the other ideas. Elicit answers from around the class.

VOCABULARY 1 SB p64

To start

Say: *My friend wants a new mobile phone. What is a good mobile like?* Elicit qualities, especially adjectives, e.g. small, quick, easy, a good camera, a lot of apps.

Power up

1 Ask students to match the words to the poster then check as a class. Use the poster to teach *gadget* (a small machine or tool) and *exhibition* (a show of paintings, photographs, or other objects that people can go to see). Drill the pronunciation of the words in the box.

A radio   **B** TV   **C** computer game   **D** mobile phone
E computer   **F** record player

alternative

Ask students to keep their books closed. On your projector, zoom in really close to one object on The Gadget Show poster, e.g) the computer, so that only part of it is visible. Get the class to guess what it is as you gradually zoom out so that they get a clearer picture (without showing the date). Then get students to guess the decade the gadget is from. Repeat with some or all of the other objects.

2 ◀)) 6.1 Play the recording for students to hear the dates. Play it again for students to repeat.

nineteen fifty
nineteen sixty
nineteen seventy-nine
nineteen eighty-five
nineteen ninety
two thousand
two thousand ten

3 Students discuss in pairs whether or not they use the gagets. Elicit answers from around the class. Take a class vote to find out which of the gadgets students find most interesting/unusual.

Possible answer
I use a computer and mobile phone.
I don't use a radio.
The record player looks interesting.

adjectives to describe things

4 ◀)) 6.2 Go through the adjectives in the box one by one, eliciting the meaning for each. Direct students to the first example, and ask a student to read it aloud. Elicit the word to complete the sentence (slow) and point out that the bolded word *quick* is the opposite of slow. Students complete the sentences then play the recording for them to check their answers.

1 slow   **2** old   **3** small   **4** interesting   **5** easy

5 ◀)) 6.3 Explain that students are going to hear a series of sounds and need to write down an adjective from the box in Ex 4 which matches the sound. Tell students to number 1–5 on a piece of paper. Play the recording twice for students to write an adjective next to each number. Play the recording again, pausing after each sound to elicit the answer.

Possible answers
1 slow   **2** quiet   **3** loud   **4** quick   **5** boring

6 Elicit the order of the first sentence with the class. Elicit what is needed at the beginning of the sentence (a capital letter.) Ask students to rewrite the sentences in the correct order. Students compare in pairs then check as a class. Ask: *Have you started all your sentences with a capital letter?*

1 Dad's car is dirty.   **2** We're watching a sad film.
3 My teacher isn't old.

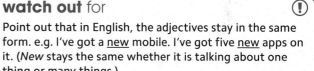

explore language

Read through the language box. Give another example of possible adjective placement before a noun and after the verb to be, e.g. *I often play difficult computer games.* (Before noun *computer games*.) *Today's computer games are difficult.* (After *to be*).

watch out for

Point out that in English, the adjectives stay in the same form. e.g. I've got a new mobile. I've got five new apps on it. (*New* stays the same whether it is talking about one thing or many things.)

extra: fast finishers

Write up two more jumbled sentences for students to order.

4 loud / are / motobikes / the /
5 the homework / easy / is
Answers:
4 The motorbikes are loud.   5 My homework is easy.

alternative

In pairs, students take turns to call out an adjective from Ex 4, and their partner must call out its opposite as quickly as possible, e.g.

A: Loud.   **B:** Quiet.

Speak up

7 Explain that students need to work in pairs to think of an easy subject, a difficult subject, a loud song and a quiet song. Encourage students to give a reason if they can.

Possible answers
English is an easy subject. I think history is difficult.
Big Party is a loud song. Sleep Baby Sleep is a quiet song.

game on

Students will need to coordinate in pairs to write down all the adjectives in the box in Ex 4 plus *large* and *new* between them. Students cut the words into cards. Explain that a *pair* means two words that are opposites, e.g. dirty and clean.

VOCABULARY 1 (Continued)

To finish

Get students to stand in a circle. Choose one of the adjectives from Ex 4, e.g. *small*. Give students a moment to think something small, e.g. mouse, baby, grape, mobile (or get students to write their word down without showing anyone). Get everyone to say *small* in unison. Then immediately go around the circle with everyone saying their word in quick succession – it doesn't matter if some words are the same – it is interesting to see who thought of the same or different things. Finish with everyone again saying *small* in unison. It works well to record the poem, e.g. on your mobile, and play it back to the class. Repeat the activity with a different adjective.

Presentation tool:	Unit 6, Vocabulary 1
Workbook / Online Practice:	p52
Grammar reference:	SB p126
Extra Practice App	

READING SB p65

To start

Find a few pictures of interesting cars to display on your projector for students to describe in pairs. Try to get a range for which students could use the adjectives *old, new, slow, dirty, clean, beautiful*.

Alternatively, bring or choose some objects in the classroom for students to describe.

Power up

1 Check students understand *modern*. Ask students to work in pairs to describe the room. Write some prompts on the board, e.g. *The room is … because …, It's got … I think it's …*

Possible answers

The room isn't modern. I think it's from the 1970s. There are orange cupboards. There are three flowers on the wall. I like the room!

2 Emphasise that students only need to read the first paragraph at this point. Elicit the boy's name and surname.

The boy's name is Fred Robshaw.
First name = Fred. Surname = Robshaw

---

exam task: A1 Movers Reading and Writing Part 3

In the A1 Movers Reading and Writing Part 3 task there is an example, and there are three options to choose from for the title, not six.

3 Remind students to read the whole sentence around the gap, and that each gap should only have one word. Go through the skill tip. When students have completed the task, ask them to compare their answers in pairs then check as a class.

1 parents (reason = noun needed here. Links to word 'sister' in next part of the sentence.)
2 house (reason = noun needed here. Links to word 'furniture and paint' in previous sentence.)
3 kitchen (reason = noun needed here. Links to word 'bathroom' in same sentence.)
4 difficult (reason = adjective needed here. Links to words 'clothes and food weren't very nice' in the next sentence.)
5 boring (reason = adjective needed here. Links to words 'quiet' in previous sentence and 'weren't any mobiles etc in next sentence.)

---

extra: fast finishers

Write up the following words for students to find in the text. Students decide what they think they mean and write an example sentence. Invite students to share the meaning and sentences with the class.

Words: a time machine / paint / nightmare / bright / clothes

Sum up

4 There are more options here than there would be for an exam task to get students thinking. In the exam, there will be a choice of three. Point out that students are looking for an idea which represents the whole story not just part of it.

Possible answer

Fred Robshaw's adventure / My house was a time machine / Time travellers.

---

extra

Put students into pairs. Say: *Imagine the TV company asks you to try life in the past like Fred did. Do you say yes or no? Why or why not?* Each pair should decide and then share with the class what they decided.

Speak up

5 Ask students to make two lists of the adjectives in the article. One of the words in bold and one for other adjectives.

adjectives in bold: modern, different, surprised, old-fashioned, quiet, fun, exciting, good.
other adjectives: happy, sure, orange, terrible, green, bright yellow, nice, easy.

Possible sentences:

I am happy today.
Our classroom is modern.
I don't like old-fashioned clothes.
I have got a bright yellow bag but my friend has got a different colour.

To finish

Put students into groups. Allocate each pair an adjective from pages 65. Get them to match the adjective to its opposite and write the opposite in brackets. Give them 30 seconds to make a list of as many things as they can that could be described with that adjective, then pass the list to the next group to add to. The lists could be passed a few times around the groups. Conduct whole class feedback.

Presentation tool:	Unit 6, Reading
Workbook / Online Practice:	p53
Grammar reference:	SB p126
Extra Practice App	

GRAMMAR SB p66

To start

Prepare a tray of about ten items and a blanket or cover. Put the tray in the middle of the class. Give students thirty seconds to look at the tray. Get students to close their eyes or turn away. Cover the tray and remove one of the items from the tray without saying what it was. Students open their eyes and look at the tray. Elicit guesses of what is missing, using the following form, *there <u>was</u> a pen here, there <u>were</u> some sweets*, etc.

---

alternative

You may want to download the Grammar Presentation for this lesson from the Teacher Resources area of Pearson English Portal. This presentation has been created specifically for this lesson and is fully editable for teachers.

1 Ask students to match the sentence halve then check as a class.

1 C (There was a record player.)
2 A (There weren't any computer games.)
3 D (Was there a TV?)
4 B (Yes, there was.)

---

explore **grammar** → SB p126

Refer students to the Grammar reference on page 126 and go through the notes with the class. Set Ex 1 and 2 on page 127 for homework or to do in class.

---

watch out for

Pay attention to the pronunciation of *was / were*. Point out that in English, the pronunciation doesn't always match spelling, e.g. *was* doesn't rhyme with *has*. *Were* doesn't rhyme with *here*.

2 6.5 Ask students to read the statements then play the recording twice. Elicit the answers.

1 T **2** F **3** T **4** F

---

extra: mixed-ability classes

To stretch stronger students, get them explain why the false statements are false.

2 The trip wasn't to a science museum, it was to a ….
4 There weren't hot drinks in the café, there was …

---

3 6.6 Play the recording for students to notice the pronunciation. Point out the weak forms for the first two sentences. Play the recording again for students to listen and repeat.

Fred was hungry.
The clothes were old-fashioned.
The weather wasn't good.
The cars weren't new.

GRAMMAR (Continued)

4 Direct students to the example. Get students to write sentences individually. Monitor students carefully.

Possible answers
1 Yesterday wasn't Sunday. It was Monday.
2 Yesterday wasn't 3 April. It was 9 April.
3 Yesterday, it wasn't raining. It was sunny.
4 Yesterday, I wasn't at home. I was at school.
5 Yesterday, my friends weren't at the park. They were at school.

5 Point out that these are five separate parts of a conversation (it isn't one complete conversation). Look at part 1 with the class. Elicit the words for the gap. Point out that each question needs two words and that all the questions refer to the past. Check as a class.

1 Were they   2 were you   3 were you   4 Was it
5 Were there

6 6.7 This is good practice for the A1 Movers Reading and Writing Part 2. Students match the responses to the questions then play the recording to check.

A 4   B 1   C 3   D 5   E 2

Speak up

7 Give students a few minutes to re-read the article on page 65. Students take turns to ask and answer questions. This could also be done as a whole class.

Possible answers
A: Was the living room blue?
B: No, it wasn't. It was orange. Were there any mobiles in the house?
A: No, there weren't. Was there a TV in the house?
B: Yes, there was.

alternative

Before class, find some old photos of the local area / your country / school. Print one photo for each group. Students should work in groups of 3–4. Place the photos around the classroom. Each group spends a minute looking at one photo and making as many sentences as possible about the pictures using *there are, there was, there wasn't, there weren't* … Then, get students to move to the next picture.

To finish

Write the following prompts on the board. Students reflect on their learning and complete the sentences individually before sharing in pairs. Conduct whole class feedback.

.............., ... and .... *were useful words from the last lesson. Something useful from today was* … .

Presentation tool:	Unit 6, Grammar
Workbook / Online Practice:	p54
Photocopiable activity:	6B
Grammar reference:	SB p126
Audioscript:	SB p147
Extra Practice App	

VOCABULARY 2 SB p67

To start

Introduce dictionaries, either paper-based or online, e.g. Longman Dictionary of Contemporary English. *www.ldoceonline.com.* Write three words for students to race to find definitions for: *farmhouse, together, woods, boot.*

Conduct whole class feedback. Elicit what information can be found in a dictionary definition, e,g, what kind of word it is (verb, noun, adjective etc), examples of use, pronunciation, word stress.

things we do (verbs)

1 This exercise is a reminder of the present simple form before going on and start learning the Past Simple -*ed* endings. Use this task to give students practice in two skills: guessing meaning from context and using a dictionary. Students read the story individually then talk about their guesses in pairs. Conduct whole class feedback.

Possible answer
visit – to go and spend time in a place or with someone
stay – to remain in a place rather than leave / to live in a place for a short time as a visitor or guest
travel – to go from one place to another
arrive – to get to the place you are going to
text – to send someone a written message on a mobile phone
help – to make it possible or easier for someone to do something by doing part of their work or by giving them something they need
tidy – to make a place look tidy, i.e. neatly arranged with everything in the right place
walk – to move forward by putting one foot in front of the other
talk – to say things to someone as part of a conversation
wash – to clean something or your body using water and a type of soap
clean – to remove dirt from something by rubbing or washing
change – to become different, or to make something become different

2 6.8 Play the recording for students to listen and repeat. Play the recording again, pausing after each verb. Elicit an example of how to use each verb, a simple definition (which can include gestures or pictures) or a translation of each verb.

visit	tidy
stay	walk
travel	talk
arrive	wash
text	clean
help	change

3 Students complete the activity then compare in pairs before checking as a class.

1 B (wash)   2 A (travel)   3 E (clean)   4 D (change)
5 C (talk)

explore language

Go through the language box. Give or elicit some examples from Ex 1.

Hanna visits Gran. (i.e. Hanna goes to Gran's house. Hanna is the subject. Visits is the verb. Gran is the object). Point out that Gran visits Hanna has a different meaning i.e. Gran goes to Hanna's house.

> **watch out** for ⓘ
>
> If students speak a language with more flexible word order, e.g. Russian or Turkish, emphasise that in English, you can't reverse the word order without changing the meaning.

4 Take the opportunity to revisit positions of adverbs of frequency with to be and other verbs, see language box on page 34 and Grammar reference on page 120. Then direct students to sentence 1, and elicit the word order *I often text* and write it on the board. Point out the who in brackets and ask: *Who do you often text?* Complete the sentence on the board with a student's idea, e.g. I often text my cousin. Students complete the remaining sentences then invite students to compare in pairs before conducting whole class feedback.

Possible answer
1 I often text my best friend.
2 I sometimes wash my clothes.
3 I sometimes help my teacher.
4 My family and I often stay at home on Sunday afternoon.
5 I sometimes tidy my room.

> **game** on
>
> If students haven't already compared their answers in pairs, ask them to do so. Then go through the game instructions with the class.

To finish

Write up these gapped instructions in speech bubbles on the board. Students work in pairs to work them out. To extend the activity, students could write one that their parent / guardian always tells them to do for another pair.

T_ _ _ your room!

S_ _ _ here!

C_ _ _ _ your desk!

T_ _ _ me when you a_ _ _ _ _!

(Tidy, Stay, Clean, Text, arrive)

Presentation tool:	Unit 6, Vocabulary 2
Workbook / Online Practice:	p55
Photocopiable activity:	6A
Grammar reference:	SB p126
Audioscript:	SB p147
Extra Practice App	

LISTENING SB p68

To start

Write the sets below on the board and ask students to work in pairs to decide which is the odd one out in each set and give a reason. Elicit the answers, remember that any answer with a sensible reason is acceptable. Circle the word from the suggested answer. Tell students that the circled words all appear in today's lesson. Clarify the meaning of any of the circled words if necessary.

1 January, May, September, summer
2 journey, museum, bank, shop
3 yellow, large, grey, orange
4 mobile phone, laptop, record player, app
5 sheep, ghost, dog, cow.

Suggested answers:
1 Summer is the odd one out because it is a season. The other words are months.
2 Journey is different because it is a trip. The other words are places.
3 Large is the odd one out because the other words are colours. Large means big.
4 A record-player is different because it's old-fashioned. The other gadgets are modern.
5 Ghost is the odd one out. All the other words are animals.

Power up

1 Teach *castle* using the picture. Elicit responses to the question in the class.

Possible answer
A famous castle in Spain is the Alcázar of Segovia. It's on a hill. It's old. It's very beautiful. There is a museum inside.

2 If possible, show an image of Warwick castle to the class then share the background notes. Give students time to read the report then elicit the answers.

Possible answer
They were at Warwick Castle for one night. They were there with their history teachers.

> **background:** Warwick Castle
>
> Warwick castle is in England. It is a large castle made out of stone. Some parts of it are more than 1000 years old. Now it is open for people to visit and stay the night.

Listen up

3 Read through the exam tip with the class. Direct students to Ex 4 questions. Elicit the kind of information required for each question.

Possible answers
1 a time
2 a number
3 a game (a noun)
4 an adjective describing the beds
5 a thing that made a noise (a noun)

LISTENING (Continued)

To finish

Dictate the following riddle for students to write down. Read it slowly through multiple times without stopping. Put students into pairs or small groups to reconstruct the full riddle. Then, see if students can solve it.

There is a castle near my house. I arrived at the castle on Monday. I stayed one night. Then I arrived home on Monday. I didn't stop on the way home. How can this be?

Answer: I arrived on a horse. The horse's name was Monday!

Presentation tool:	Unit 6, Listening
Workbook / Online Practice:	p56
Photocopiable activity:	6C
Grammar reference:	SB p126
Audioscript:	SB p147
Extra Practice App	

---

exam task: A1 Movers Listening Part 3

In the A1 Movers Listening Part 3 exam task the items are not inter-related, but in the A2 Flyers Listening Part 4 exam task they are, as in this task. In both exams, all the distracting options should be mentioned in the script. In both exams, there is an example followed by five items.

4 6.9 Play the recording twice. Check the answers as a class.

> **0** B (*we arrived at about* **half past two** *in the afternoon*)
> **1** C (*There were about* **fifty** *students in the castle*)
> **2** A (*We played* **card games**.)
> **3** C (*the beds were* **old**!)
> **4** B (*The 'ghost' was a* **sheep**!)

---

explore **grammar**   ➥ SB p126 ☑

Point out that the story about the castle was in the past and the past simple was used. Refer students to the Grammar reference on page 126. Go through the notes and set Ex 3 and 4 on page 127 for homework or in class.

---

watch out for   ⓘ

Point out that not all verbs in English follow the pattern of adding -*ed* for the past simple. Common irregular verbs will be covered in Unit 7.

---

5 6.10 Play the recording for students to hear the different endings. Then give students a chance to practise saying them. Play the recording again for students to listen and repeat.

6 Point out that this exercise has two stages. First, students need to select the correct verb for each sentence. Then they need to write it in the past simple. Remind them that at least one verb will need a spelling change (tidy).

> **1** My uncle **visited** us yesterday.
> **2** I **cleaned** the bathroom last week.
> **3** My dad **cooked** the dinner yesterday evening.
> **4** We **arrived** home at 3.30 yesterday.
> **5** Jo **listened** to music all weekend.
> **6** We **tidied** our room yesterday.

---

extra   💬⁺

Ask students to write two true sentences and a lie about things they did yesterday using some of the verbs from Ex 5. Students share in pairs, ensuring that they use the correct pronunciation.

SPEAKING SB p69

To start

Write three years on the board that are important for you, e.g. 1999, 2000, 2016.

Get students to check in pairs that they can pronounce the years. Then get a student to ask you about each year, e.g. S: *Why was nineteen ninety-nine special?* T: My son was born. *Why was two thousand speciall?* I travelled to the USA. *Why was 2016 special?* I started working at this school. (Use regular verbs with -*ed* or *was* if you can.)

Get students to choose three years that are special for them and write them down. In pairs, students ask and answer about the years they chose.

Power up

1 Give a few example sentences. Point out that students can use other words that aren't in the box as well. Organise students into pairs to make up sentences. Conduct whole class feedback

Possible answers (boxed words underlined)

I <u>texted a friend</u> <u>yesterday</u>.
I <u>travelled by train</u> last year.
I <u>washed my hair</u> on Sunday.
I <u>watched a film</u> at the weekend.
I played basketball <u>last week.</u>
I started English lessons <u>in 2017</u>.
I tidied my room <u>on Friday</u>.

2 Ask students to write down one of the sentences they made in Ex 1. Then students walk around the class finding someone else who has the same answer (although they may have a different sentence written down).

Sample answer

A: I travelled by train last year.
B: I didn't travel by train last year.
A: I travelled by train last year.
C: Me too.

Speak up

3 Read the useful language box with the class and drill the phrases. Go through the quiz as a class, teaching vocabulary as required, and have students mark each question true or false. Then students compare their answers in pairs.

4 🔊 6.11 Play the recording for students to check their answers.

1 T   **2** F (it was in Italy)   **3** F (it was around 1900)
4 F (it was in 1972)

5 Direct students to the picture and the instructions. Organise students into pairs to take turns to say things that are wrong, and to encourage their partner using the phrases in the useful language box.

> **extra:** fast finishers
>
> Students make a poster of the useful language for supporting a partner to display in the classroom.
>
> **Possible answer**
> **10** things are wrong

Speaking extra

6 Conduct whole class feedback of Ex 5. Listen for and remodel any incorrect use of past simple.

Possible answers

There is a car but people didn't use cars in 1820.
The man is wearing a watch but there weren't any wrist watches in 1820.
There is a radio on the pizza stand but there weren't any radios in 1820.
The boy is drinking cola but people didn't drink cola then.
This woman is wearing trainers but people didn't wear trainers then.
There's a cinema but there weren't any cinemas then.
This man has a mobile phone but there weren't any mobile phones in 1820.
There's a boy listening to music on his headphones, but there weren't any headphones in 1820.
There's a boy wearing jeans but jeans weren't made in 1820.
There is a boy holding a laptop, but laptops didn't exist then.

Fun footer

Ask students to read the footer. Elicit the pronunciation of 1800s (eighteen hundreds). If you have internet, you could show some pictures of early bicycles.

To finish

Ask students to turn to the wordlist on page 72. In pairs, students take turns to give each other a word from the sections: gadget, an adjective or things we do. The writer needs to write the word with their eyes closed. If necessary, the speaker can spell it out. The speaker should encourage the writer using the phrases *Well done. Very good. Great. Yes, that's right.*

Presentation tool:	Unit 6, Speaking
Workbook / Online Practice:	p57
Grammar reference:	SB p126
Speaking file:	SB p139
Audioscript:	SB p148

WRITING SB pp70–71

To start

Ask: *What museums do you know or have you visited?* Elicit the names of museums in your area or that students have been to. Write the following list of museums on the board.

Museums: dinosaur film art technology pirate

If necessary, teach dinosaur and pirate. Students order the museums from the one they are most to least interested in, then compare their list in pairs. Conduct whole class feedback

Power up

1 Elicit what the class knows about pirates from films or stories. If necessary, ask: *Do you know any famous pirates?* (E.g. Blackbeard, Captain Jack Sparrow, Captain Hook.)

2 Put students into pairs to discuss what they know about pirate ships and pirate flags. Conduct whole class feedback.

Possible answers

Pirates travelled by pirate ship. Pirate flags were on the ships. They were black.

3 Ask students to quickly read Daniela's post to find which flag is correct without completing the gaps yet. Elicit the answer. If you have the internet, you could show where the Bahamas are on a map or show some images from the Pirate Museum in Nassau.

Possible answers

Pirate flags weren't all the same.
The pirates slept in hammocks.
Blackbeard was a famous pirate.

4 Point out how *family* is crossed out because it is used and encourage students to cross out the words as they use them to keep track. Students complete the post then compare in pairs before checking as a class.

1 visitors **2** beds **3** women **4** like **5** interesting

5 Ask students to find an example of each thing then conduct whole class feedback. Point out that the names of specific places are capitalised.

Possible answers

1 large, black, same, different, loud
2 visited, opened, looked, learned, listened, loved, was, were
3 My brother and I liked the pirate flags, but Mum didn't like them … !/It was a very interesting day./I loved it!
4 Bahamas, the Pirate Museum, Nassau.

explore **language**

Go through the language box with the class. Get students to find and underline the time words in Daniela's post.

6 Direct students to the language box and give another example of time words for past and present, e.g. *I have maths at 9 a.m. I had maths class on Tuesday at 9 a.m.* Put students into pairs and ask them to use time words to talk about a museum they visited. Ask them to describe what they liked/didn't like about the museum.

Possible answers

In April I visited the Food Museum. I loved looking at the different meals people ate around the world in the 1900s.

Fun footer

Read the fun footer with the class. If students want to, see who can say the phrases in the most pirate-y voice. If students like jokes, tell the following one: *Why are pirates called pirates? Because they arrrrgh! (are)*

7 Go through the instructions then ask students to talk in pairs about which place they will choose to write about. Circulate while students write notes under each heading.

Possible answer

1 Amazing Dinosaur Exhibition
2 In my town in a park.
3 My class.
4 9 a.m.
5 9.30 a.m.
6 Dinosaur models. Large and small. Some dinosaurs moved.
7 Some dinosaurs lived near here.
8 It was fun.

Write on

8 Circulate while students write their paragraph. Remind students to use past simple. Students can use sentences from Daniela's post as a model but it doesn't need to be as long.

Possible answer

My class went to the Amazing Dinosaur Exhibition last year. It was in a park in my town. We travelled by bus and arrived at 9.30 a.m. There were a lot of dinosaurs in the park. A large dinosaur moved its head. I screamed because it looked very real. I learned that in the past some dinosaurs lived near here. The trip was fun! I loved it!

---

extra: fast finishers

Fast finishers could act as editors for other students' work – giving them feedback and helping them check their word order as per the skill tip.

Improve it

9 Get students to check that they have the items listed and add them in if necessary. Students could work with a partner to peer check items 1–4.

> **extra:** whole class
>
> Ask students to share their paragraphs in small groups.

To finish

Write up the following sentences about a trip and ask students to work in pairs to discuss how they could make it more interesting by changing the adjective *good*. Conduct whole class feedback.

I went on a good trip to a good art museum. The paintings were good. We had some good food. It was good!

Presentation tool:	Unit 6, Writing
Workbook / Online Practice:	p58
Grammar reference:	SB p126
Writing file:	SB p139

SWITCH ON
Frontier House

1 Put students into pairs. Ask students to think of three animals on a farm. Get students to check the spelling of their words (e.g. on the wordlist for animals on page 40), and then scramble the letters on a piece of paper for each word. Pairs swap with another pair and see how quickly they can unscramble the letters.

Possible answer

cow, pig, sheep

---

2 Tell students that they're going to watch a video clip about some people that took part in a TV show where they had to live like the old days, a similar idea to the TV show that they read about on page 65. Ask students to read the sentences in Ex 2 and elicit the pronunciation of 1883 (eighteen eighty-three). Play the video for students to answer the question. Students check in pairs. Elicit the answer.

Some teachers were very old isn't true. The narrator says *Some teachers were very young.*

---

3 Ask students to read the jobs 1–4. Check students understand *looks* after, *field* and *carries*. Tell students they must listen for which person does which job and tick the best table heading. Play the clip. Ask students to check in pairs before eliciting the answers.

---

1 Erinn   **2** Logan   **3** Aine and Tracy   **4** Logan

> **extra:** whole class
>
> Ask students to discuss the following questions in small groups: *What was good about life in 1883? What is good about life today?* Get each group to briefly report back to the class.

Project

4 Give some examples of times from the past that students could choose, e.g. 1970s, 1920s, 1800s, medieval times, ancient times. Ask students to work in pairs and discuss what time they are going to choose. Then students should discuss anything they already know about the questions. Then students could divide the questions so that they each research two (in class or for homework).

5 Ask students to create a poster advertising their time in history they have researched. This could be a paper poster or a digital poster. Tell them they can draw (or find pictures of) the clothes, the hobbies and activities, as well as any other appropriate ideas. Give each pair the opportunity to present their work to the class.

> **alternative**
>
> 1 Students could create booklets about their chosen time, with one page per question, and more information on each section.
> 2 If your students enjoy drama, they could plan a presentation about a time period in the first person, e.g. *We live in 1300. We live on a farm.*

Presentation tool:	Unit 6, Switch on
Switch on videoscript:	TB p140

UNIT CHECK SB p72

This Unit check covers past simple forms, and vocabulary for gadgets, adjectives and verbs for things we do.

Practice

1 Put students into pairs and set a challenge. Ask each pair to find and write down three words from the wordlist for each category, and then raise their hand. The pair who completes the task first, and has the correct answers, wins.

Possible answers

1 things you do in the classroom: help, stay, talk, tidy, walk

2 adjectives to describe the classroom or things: boring, clean, difficult, easy, interesting, large, loud, new, old, quick, quiet, slow, small.

3 adjectives to describe you or your family: interesting, beautiful, fun, good, modern, old-fashioned, small, surprised, loud, quiet.

2 Students write down sentences about things they did this morning. They can refer to the verbs on page 67 if needed. Put students into pairs to compare their answers. Ask students to report interesting answers from their partner during class feedback.

Possible answer
I walked to school.
I arrived at school at 8 a.m.
I talked to my friends.

3 🔊 6.12 Play the recording twice for students to write the sentences they hear. Ask one student to write the sentences on the board and ask the class to check if they are correct. If necessary, play the recording again.

1 It was my birthday at the weekend,
2 There weren't any TVs in 1900.
3 I played a computer game yesterday.
4 She used her mobile to call a friend.

4 🔊 6.13 Ask students to complete the questions first. Then play the recording for them to check their answers. Put students into small groups to ask and answer the questions.

1 Was
2 Were
3 Was
4 did

Possible answers

1 Yes, it was. It was sunny and hot. / No, it wasn't. It was cold and windy.
2 Yes, there were. I watched a programme about pirates. / No, there weren't.
3 Yes, it was. / No, it wasn't.
4 The teacher gave us Ex 6 and 7 for homework. / The teacher didn't give us any homework.

REVIEW 2: UNITS 4-6 SB p73

Vocabulary

1 **Possible answers**
1 loud **2** sunny **3** beans **4** travel **5** café
6 Monday **7** stay **8** boat

2 **Possible answer**
1 Loud is the odd one out because the other words are verbs.
2 Sunny is the odd one out. Sunny is the only word about weather.

3 **1** cinema **2** boring **3** travel **4** sandwich **5** difficult
6 museum **7** motorbike **8** sunny **9** wash **10** tidy

4 🔊 R2.1
1 G = sports centre   Z = swimming pool
2 G = pasta   Z = tomato sauce
3 G = bus   Z = bike
4 G = warm weather   Z = rain

5 **e** This is similar in format to the Movers Reading and Writing Part 4 task, but the Movers task tests grammar, not lexis.
1 C (*snowing* is correct because only snow is *white*)
2 B (*hot* is correct because they talk about a temperature – thirty degrees – which is *hot*)
3 B (*clean* is correct because kitchens *must* be clean)
4 A (*talks* is correct because it comes before the word *about food*. We can't say *eats about food* or *does about food*.)
5 C (*chicken* is correct because you don't usually cook *salad* or *cheese* for dinner)

Grammar

1 **1** G **2** A **3** E **4** H **5** D

2 **Possible answer**
B You can't take photos here.
F You mustn't use your mobile.

3 **1** 'm **2** 're **3** isn't **4** 're **5** is **6** are

4 **1** wasn't **2** was **3** Was **4** was **5** Were **6** weren't
7 was **8** were

5 🔊 R2.2 **1** A **2** C **3** B **4** A

6 **Possible answer**
Hi Luis, what are you doing at the moment? I'm doing English homework, but it's difficult. Can you help? Thanks.

GRAMMAR FILE SB p127

1 **1** were **2** wasn't **3** was **4** were **5** weren't **6** was

2 **1** B **2** F **3** E **4** D **5** A **6** C

3 **1** studied **2** danced **3** played **4** used **5** listened
6 travelled

4 **1** B **2** C **3** F **4** A **5** D **6** E

Presentation tool:	Unit 6, Unit check
Workbook / Online Practice:	pp59–61
Grammar reference:	SB p126
Audioscript:	SB p148

Bright sparks

7

VOCABULARY 1
jobs

READING
topic: amazing teenagers

skill: identifying words that go together

task: sentence completion

GRAMMAR
Past simple: irregular verbs and questions

Past simple: question words

VOCABULARY 2
irregular verbs

LISTENING
topic: making a robot for a competition

skill: spelling words carefully

task: gap fill

SPEAKING
topic: the model plane (picture story)

skill: using linking words

task: tell a story from pictures

WRITING
topic: a personal story

skill: making your writing clear

task: write about a famous person

SWITCH ON
video: skateboard star

project: improvement action plan

Lead-in SB p75

Read the quote *I'm good at making things.* with the class. Give them an energising challenge to make something, e.g. some origami, or put students into teams, give each team a newspaper and a roll of tape (or marshmallows and sticks), and see who can make the tallest tower in five minutes.

1 Get students to look at the photo. Ask: *What are the students making?* (vehicles / cars). Put students into pairs to ask and answer the question.

Possible answers

I'm usually good at making things.
I like making things.

extra

To extend the activity, if students' answers are yes, encourage them to talk to their partner for two minutes about what they are good at making and why. Elicit some interesting answers from around the class.

2 Check students understand and can pronounce the school subjects with correct syllabic stress. However, emphasise that they can also talk about other things they are good at, e.g. *I'm good at helping my gran. I'm good at playing baseball. I'm good at listening to my friends.* If students are reluctant to say what they are good at, encourage their partner to make suggestions.

Possible answer

I'm good at music and maths. I'm good at cooking. I'm good at playing games.

3 Give students some time to talk in pairs about other subjects they enjoy, e.g. history, geography.

Possible answer

history, geography, drama

extra

Ask students to chose their favourite school subject and write it down on a piece of paper. Then do a class mingle and ask students to find as many people as possible with the same favourite subject as them, forming a group. After three minutes, tell students to stop and find out which group is the largest and what the subject is.

VOCABULARY 1 SB p76

To start

Ask each student to write down two jobs of people in their family or people they know on a post-it note. It is acceptable for these to be L1 at this stage.

Collect in the post-it notes. Divide the notes among 2 or 3 of the stronger students and asks them to write up the jobs in English on the board. Any jobs that are unknown in English can be written up in L1. Whole class checks spelling of the jobs as they are being written up. Students can ask the 'assistant teachers' (ie stronger students standing in front of board) for definition or pronunciation of any new jobs. Any jobs left written in L1 on the board the teacher deals with at the end with the whole class. Keep these on the board for use in Ex 2. With unusual jobs or those which have specialist terms, you could provide a more general term, e.g. if given words like financial analyst, entrepreneur, advertising executive, small business owner, you could use the general word *business person*.

Power up

1 Take the opportunity to share with students why you like being their teacher, e.g. say: *I like being a teacher because I like helping you learn new things.* Put students into pairs to ask and answer the questions. Ask students to suggest things that are easy/difficult about being a teacher. Conduct whole class feedback.

Possible answers

Yes (I would), because I like school!

No (I wouldn't), because it is difficult.

It's easy because students are nice.

It's easy because there are long summer holidays.

It's difficult because teachers read a lot of homework.

It's difficult because sometimes students don't listen.

extra

Say: *you're a teacher for one day: what subject do you choose? Why?* Students answer in pairs then conduct whole class feedback, e.g. *art, English, geography, history, maths, music, science, sport.*

2 🔊 7.1 If you used the *to start* activity, ask students to see if any of the jobs listed are on the board. Then students match the jobs with the pictures then compare in pairs. Play the recording for students to check their answer.

A game developer **B** artist **C** basketball player **D** dentist
E doctor **F** farmer **G** nurse **H** photographer **I** scientist
J singer **K** taxi driver **L** journalist

extra

Play the recording again for students to listen and repeat the jobs. Watch out for the pronunciation of *photographer* – check the stress is on the second syllable.

jobs

3 🔊 7.2 Tell students that they are going to hear four short conversations or sounds of people doing a job and they need to choose the correct job. Play the recording twice. Check as a class.

1 C (singer) **2** A (dentist) **3** A (basketball player)
4 B (game developer)

4 Use questions to check students understanding of *enjoy* and *be good at something*. On the board write: *I love singing but everyone covers their ears when I sing!* Ask the following questions: *Do I enjoy singing?* (Yes.) *Do people like my singing?* (No.) *How do you know?* (People cover their ears.) *Am I good at singing?* (No!) Direct students to the questionnaire. Ask students to underline things they enjoy and circle things they are good at – some things may be both.

5 Students practise asking and answering questions in pairs. Demonstrate by asking a student questions about items in the questionnaire then suggesting a job, e.g. *Do you enjoy computers? (Yes?) You can be a game developer.*

alternative

Get students to look at their answers in Ex 4 and choose a job they would like to do from the jobs in the lesson. Students move around and ask each other questions to guess each other's job.

example:

A: Do you enjoy helping people?
B: Yes, I do.
A: Do you enjoy science?
B: Yes, I do.
A: Would you like to be a doctor?
B: Yes!

To finish

Ask students to close their books and work in pairs. Give them a minute to see how many jobs from the lesson they can write down. To help, you could write the first letters of the jobs from Ex 2 on the board.

Presentation tool:	Unit 7, Vocabulary 1
Workbook / Online Practice:	p62
Photocopiable activity:	7A
Grammar reference:	SB p128
Extra Practice App	

READING SB p77

To start

Write on the board:

- play sport in a world championship
- win a science competition
- make an app

Ask: *Would you like to do any of these things in the future?* Tell students they are going to read about young people who are famous for doing these three things.

Power up

1 Ask students to quickly read the article to find out what each person's job is (and match them to the list on the board if you used the *To start* activity). Elicit the answers.

A (Mo'Ne Davis) baseball
B (Ben Pasternak) app designer
C (Kiara Nigrin) scientist

---

exam task: A2 Flyers Reading and Writing Part 5

In the A2 Flyers Reading and Writing Part 5 exam task there are five items and two examples. The text is just one story: a narrative.

2 **e** Go through the example and skill tip with the class. Students complete the remaining gaps then check as a class.

1 a big match (*Mo'ne helped her team to win a big match.*)
2 children (*… Mo'Ne wrote a book for children about …*)
3 was (very) happy (*Over one million people bought the app and played the game. Ben was very happy!*)
4 another idea (*He had another idea. This time he made an app for young people.*)
5 South Africa (*Kiara Nighrin is a young scientist from South Africa …*), fifteen (*When she was fifteen, Kiara wrote an essay about her idea and …*)

---

extra: fast finishers

Write up two extra sentences for fast finishers to complete:

6 Ben made his second app for young people in
.... (the USA).
7 Mo'Ne became famous after lots of people watched
.... (her on TV).

---

3 Go through the questions with the class.

Possible answers

1 It isn't interesting.
2 It tells us that there are three stories but it doesn't tell us what the stories are about.
3 Three famous young people / Young people changing the world

Sum up

4 After students close their books, elicit the first names of the three people and write them on the board. Ask students to talk in pairs about what they remember about each one then conduct whole class feedback

Possible answers

Mo'Ne: She's from the USA. She loves sports. She played in the Baseball World Series. She's famous. She wrote a children's book about playing baseball.

Ben: He's from Australia. He is an app designer. He made a colour matching game and an app for selling things.

Kiara: She's from South Africa. She had an idea for farmers. She wrote an essay. She won $50 000. She wants to be a scientist or science writer.

Speak up

5 Put students into small groups to discuss the questions.

Possible answers

I am similar to Mo'Ne because I'm good at sports. / I'm different from Mo'Ne because she loves basebal, but I don't play baseball.

I am similar to Ben because I like apps. / I'm different from Ben because I don't make apps.

I am similar to Kiara because I love science. / I'm not similar to Kiara because I'm not from South Africa.

Fun footer

Ask students to read the fun footer. Check students understand the double meaning of the words cool (great, cold) and fan (someone who likes a sport or famous person, a machine / object you can use to cool the air).

To finish

Invite students to try the online version of the game Ben designed called *Impossible Rush*, either on the projector or on their mobile phones. Give students two minutes to try the game. Ask: *Did you like the game? Do you think it is easy or difficult?*

To extend the activity, put students into pairs and see if they could write instructions for the game for someone who is new to games, e.g. a grandparent.

Presentation tool:	Unit 7, Reading
Workbook / Online Practice:	p63
Grammar reference:	SB p128
Extra Practice App	

GRAMMAR SB p78

To start

Start by reviewing the past simple of regular verbs. Write on the board *walk*, and elicit the past simple form, and add *-ed*. List following verbs on the board: *arrive, change, stay, tidy, like, open, stop, travel, be.*

Ask students to decide which have a spelling change in the past tense and write down the past simple form of each. Check as a class and recap the pronunciation of the endings /id/, /t/, /d/.

Answers: (spelling changes underlined) arri<u>v</u>ed, chang<u>ed</u>, stay<u>ed</u>, tid<u>i</u>ed, lik<u>ed</u>, open<u>ed</u>, sto<u>pp</u>ed, trave<u>ll</u>ed, *was / were*.

alternative

You may want to download the Grammar Presentation for this lesson from the Teacher Resources area of Pearson English Portal. This presentation has been created specifically for this lesson and is fully editable for teachers.

1 Students match the verb forms. Encourage students to re-write the past form next to the present form. Check as a class. Drill the pronunciation, of present and past forms, paying special attention to *bought* with the silent *gh*.

1 C 2 D 3 I 4 E 5 J 6 G 7 F 8 A 9 H 10 B

explore grammar → SB p128

Point out that some verbs in English are irregular (i.e. that they don't use *-ed* for past simple). Students have already met the irregular form of *be* (*was / were*).Read through the box with the class and then refer them to the notes on page 128. After going through the notes, set Ex 1, 2 and 4 on page 129.

watch out for ⓘ

In the negative sentences, make sure that students use the verb stem (not the irregular form) after *didn't*, e.g. *I didn't <u>buy</u> anything* NOT *I didn't bought anything.*

2 ▶ ◀)) 7.4 Tell students that they are going to watch/ hear three speakers talking about what they did last weekend. Get students to read the sentences before listening. Tell them that each sentence (A–C) is said by a different speaker (1–3). Play the video/recording for students to match speakers and the sentences.

A We went to the park and I played baseball. (Speaker 3)
B After school I had pancakes with my family. (Speaker 1)
C I bought a new skirt and a new T-shirt. (Speaker 2)

3 ▶ ◀)) 7.5 Ask students to read the questions. Play the video/recording for students to answer the questions. Elicit the answers.

1 No, he didn't. (extra info: He went to his mum's party.)
2 Yes, she did. (extra info: She also bought a new skirt.)
3 No, she didn't. (extra info: She woke up at 11 o'clock.)

4 Direct students to the photo and tell students that a young interviewer, Emma, is asking Pedro and Paulo about their YouTube channel. Ask them to complete the sentences. Check as a class.

1 make 2 sing 3 write 4 know 5 go

5 Students work individually to decide on a response (A–E) to each of the questions in Ex 4. They compare their answers in pairs.

1 A 2 E 3 B 4 D 5 C

extra

Ask students to find and highlight the following words in Ex 3 and 4: *online, fans, social media, followers, interview*. While they are doing that, write the following definitions on the board:

1 Facebook, Instagram, etc.
2 People who like / admire someone
3 People who choose to see your posts
4 on the internet
5 someone asks you questions

Put class into groups and give each group a different board marker. Then one person from each group runs up to the board and writes up the word that means the same as the definition on the board. If it's wrong, wipe off their answer. If it's right, leave it up. Carry on until all definitions have matching words. The winner is the team/ colour with most correct answers.

Answers: 1 social media 2 fans 3 followers
4 online 5 interview

Speak up

6 Go through the example question then circulate providing assistance while students write three questions starting with *Did*. (Question words will be covered on page 80.) Put students into pairs to ask and answer.

Possible answers
1 Did you go to the swimming pool at the weekend?
2 Did you make your bed at the weekend?
3 Did you buy anything at the weekend?

alternative

Write up these scrambled questions for students to rewrite the questions in order. Then ask students to move around the classroom asking and answering the questions with different partners.

Did / go / you / at / weekend / the / anywhere? (Did you go anywhere at the weekend?)

you / Did / buy / at / the / weekend / anything? (Did you buy anything at the weekend?)

the / weekend / in / anywhere/ did / you / go? (Did you go anywhere in the weekend?)

Fun footer

Ask students to read the fun footer. Check students can say the date correctly (twenty third April, two thousand and five). Ask students to guess what the first video was about: *Was it (a) an interview with a famous sportsperson (b) a music video (c) a person at a zoo talking about elephants.*

Answer: C
You could search on YouTube to show the first video, it's called *Me at the zoo.*

Ask students to guess how many hours of video are uploaded to YouTube every minute (300 hours).

To finish

Ask students to draw a three by three grid and write in it nine of the past forms from Ex 1, one in each cell, in any order. Call out the present tense forms out of order, and have students cover the past form with a counter or small piece of paper. When a person gets three in a row, they call out *bingo*. They can call out bingo every time they get a new three-in-a-row.

Presentation tool:	Unit 7, Grammar
Workbook / Online Practice:	p64
Photocopiable activity:	7B
Grammar reference:	SB p128
Audioscript:	SB p148
Extra Practice App	

VOCABULARY 2 SB p79

To start

Carefully draw the notation above on the board, or alternatively show some braille notation on the projector from a braille generator. See if students know what it is. (It's braille notation. These symbols indicate the word *went*. Note that it isn't actual braille which is when it is printed with raised dots so that blind people can read by touching the paper with their fingers.) With books closed, ask: *Who invented this?* Braille (Louis Braille). *Where was he from? How old was he when he invented Braille?*

Fun footer

After students guess answers to the questions above, get students to open their books and read the fun footer to find out the answers. Ask: *Were there any surprises?*

irregular verbs

1 Direct students to the picture and ask students to quickly read the article to find out what Subham's idea was about braille. (He made a braille printer out of Lego. It was much cheaper than other braille printers.) Then ask students to replace the verbs in brackets with the past simple forms.

---
1 left   **2** thought   **3** said   **4** found   **5** could   **6** gave
7 learnt/learned   **8** built   **9** took   **10** saw
---

2 ◀)) 7.6 Play the recording for students to listen and repeat the verbs. Note that students will learn to recognise *could* as the past tense of *can* here, but will not practise it yet as the form is so different from other verbs here.

> **watch out** for
>
> Pay special attention to the pronunciation of *could* (silent *l*) and thought (silent *gh*). Also, encourage students to pay special attention to the various sounds of the vowel cluster *ou* in *could, found, thought* – there are three different sounds.

3 This is an opportunity to revise how to form questions in the past with auxiliary *did*. Elicit how to complete the first question on the board as an example. Students complete the questions then compare in pairs before checking as a class.

---
1 **Did** Shubham's family **leave** Belgium? **Yes, they did. They moved to the USA.**
2 What **did** his parents **say** when he asked them a question? **They said 'Google it'.**
3 **Did** Shubham **think** about blind people's problems? **Yes, he did. He thought about their problems.**
4 **Did** the big printer **give** Shubham an idea? **Yes, it did.**
5 What kind of printer **did** Shubham **build**? **(He made) a Lego braille printer.**
6 **Did** some news reporters **take** photos? **Yes, they did.**

VOCABULARY 2 (Continued)

> **game** on
>
> Put students into teams of three to four and organise the teams to play each other. Students need to say the past form as quickly as possible.

> **alternative**
>
> Teams take turns to call out present forms for the other team for one minute and see how many the other team can get in that minute. Which team can get the most?

4 Go through the example with the class then have students rewrite the other sentences following the example. Ask various students to come and write part of the answer on the board then hand the pen to another student to continue. Alternatively, if you have collaborative software, e.g. Google docs, allocate a certain student to type in each answer to a shared document (from their device), then review as a class.

1 She/Lily didn't take a laptop to school yesterday. She took a mobile phone.

2 She/Lily didn't see her friend George at school. She saw her friend Georgia.

3 Her/Lily's teacher didn't say 'Hello' when the pupils arrived. He/She said 'Good morning'.

4 Her/Lily's English class didn't learn about irregular verbs. They learnt about regular verbs.

5 Her/Lily's friend didn't find some sweets in her bag. She found some chocolate.

Speak up

5 Give students a moment to reflect on the question. Then invite each student to share.

> **Possible answers**
> I learnt about past simple forms and words for jobs.
> I learnt the words journalist and dentist.

To finish

Ask students to work in pairs to imagine they work together doing one of the jobs from the unit, e.g. look at the wordlist on page 84. Together, they write three sentences about things they did today using regular or irregular verbs. Pairs take turns to read their sentences for the class, and the other students guess their jobs.

e.g. *We sang at a concert. We learnt a new song. We visited children at a hospital. (We are famous singers.)*

Presentation tool:	Unit 7, Vocabulary 2
Workbook / Online Practice:	p65
Grammar reference:	SB p128
Audioscript:	SB p148
Extra Practice App	

LISTENING SB p80

To start

Write the following verbs on the board in one colour at random places: *say, visit, make, see, have, find, go, think, sing, learn, took, arrive*. Get students to work in pairs to think of the past simple form for each (some are irregular and some are regular). Invite a few students to come to the board and replace the present with the past form, using a different coloured pen. Other students can provide assistance. When all the present are changed to past, ask students to use the past forms to tell each other about some things that happened between the last class and this one.

Power up

1 Elicit what students can see in the photo.

> **Possible answer**
> a robot

2 Ask students to think of famous robots from a film they have seen, or from history. Elicit a few ideas from the class, then put students into small groups to discuss.

> **Possible answer**
> R2 -D2 is a famous robot from the film *Star Wars*.

Listen up

> **exam** task: **A2 Key for Schools Listening Part 4**
>
> **3** 7.7 Go through the skill tip with students. Direct students to the rubric and title, and elicit the meaning of engineer (someone who designs and builds things) and robotics (the science of making robots). Give students a moment to read the notes. Play the recording twice. Elicit the answers, and get students to carefully check the spelling of *First* which was spelt out in the recording.
>
> **1** twelve/12 (Clare and her friend are both **twelve**.)
> **2** Matt (Well, my friend **Matt** and I …)
> **3** FIRST (It's called **FIRST** Robotics Competition. F-I-R-S-T.)
> **4** blue (And why did you paint it **blue**?)
> **5** six/6 weeks (Yes, we did. About **six** weeks.)
> **6** Yes (they did). (We're very happy. We **enjoyed** it a lot.)

> **explore grammar** ⟶ SB p128
>
> Go through the explore grammar box and point out that students have already used these question words for asking and answering questions in the present tense (see the Unit 3 Grammar reference on page 120). They work the same way in the past simple with a change in the form of *is* / *do* to the past. Refer students to the Grammar reference on page 128 and go through the notes with the class. Set Ex 3 on page 129 as homework or an activity in class.

> **watch out** for ⓘ
>
> Although most past simple verbs have only one form, *was* / *were* is the exception. Students need to select the correct form for questions, i.e. *was* for I/she/he/it/singular thing, *were* for you/we/they/plural thing.
>
> *Where <u>was</u> the competition? What colour <u>were</u> the robots?*

4 🔊 7.8 Students complete the questions then see if they can remember the answers. Play the recording again then check as a class.

1 When 2 Why 3 What 4 Where

5 🔊 7.9 Play the questions for students to notice the intonation. Play again for students to listen and repeat.

The voice goes up towards the end of the question.

6 Ask students to think about when they were younger. Direct students to the example. Then get students to write two questions each for their partner about when they were younger.

Where did you live?
What did you like?

Fun footer

Ask students to read the fun footer. Check they have got the pronunciation of the year (fourteen ninety-five). Ask students if they know what jobs Leonardo da Vinci did. He did many things, for example he was a painter, inventor, scientist, writer, engineer. You could find and show a clip of some of Da Vinci's inventions, e.g. search for the flying scene from the film *Mr Peabody and Sherman* for a fun animated clip.

To finish

Write an answer on the board and ask students to work in pairs to come up with a possible question using a question word and past simple. Elicit the questions.

e.g. Answer: Spaghetti.

Possible questions: What did you eat for dinner last night? What was your favourite food when you were a child? What did you buy at the supermarket?

Answer: Monday.

Possible questions: What day was yesterday? When did you play football? When was our last class?

Presentation tool:	Unit 7, Listening
Workbook / Online Practice:	p66
Photocopiable activity:	7C
Grammar reference:	SB p128
Audioscript:	SB p148
Extra Practice App	

SPEAKING SB p81

To start

Choose two short YouTube clips to start the lesson. Choose something light-hearted and appropriate for your class level. Then ask students to discuss in pairs:

What were the videos about?
What happened in the videos?
Which video did you enjoy more?

Conduct whole class feedback.

Power up

1 Ask students to discuss the question in pairs then conduct whole class feedback. Monitor closely to check that all examples are appropriate.

Possible answer

I like watching films on YouTube. For example, I like watching videos about funny animals and music videos.

I sometimes make films for YouTube, for example, I talk about films.

I don't often go on YouTube but I like to make videos for my friends, for example when I go places.

2 Direct students to the picture and the title *The model plane*. Ask: *Have you ever flown a model plane?* Students answer the questions then check as a class.

1 A
2 B
3 A

3 Make the first question with the class as an example. Ask students to work individually to make the questions with the words given while you circulate. Check as a class.

1 Where **did** Paul go with this plane?
2 What **was** the weather like?
3 What **did** his friend Sandy do?
4 Why **did** they make a film?
5 Where **was** the plane?

4 Encourage students to use fuller sentences if they can. If students are preparing for an exam, point out that speaking examiners can award more marks when students use fuller sentences, even if they're not completely correct. Single words and short phrases on their own can only score medium marks on the scale of 0–6 (Vocabulary), even if they are totally correct.

Possible answers
1 Where did Paul go with this plane?
   He went to the park.
2 What was the weather like?
   It was warm and sunny. It was windy.
3 What did his friend Sandy do?
   Sandy filmed the plane on her mobile phone.
4 Why did they make a film?
   She made a film to put on YouTube.
5 Where was the plane?
   It was in a bush.

SPEAKING (Continued)

Speak up

exam task: A1 Movers Speaking Part 2

5 Read the rubric, skill tip, and explore language box with the class. In the A1 Movers Speaking exam, students can tell the story in the <u>present tense</u> too. Most students will probably opt for the present tense in the exam. However, they should choose before they start, and stick to one or the other. Here, we're using the past tense for practice.

Possible answer

1 Paul and Sandy went to the park and Paul took his plane.

2 When they were at the park, Paul said 'Make a video, Sandy!'.

3 Sandy made a video, but it was very windy. 'Oh no!' said Sandy.

4 Paul and Sandy lost the plane. They looked for the plane, but they didn't find it. Then a dog found the plane.

alternative

Ask students to speak about the pictures in the present tense first, then change to past tense. Or get one student to tell the story in the present tense then their partner retells the story in the past tense. The student who is listening corrects the speaker if any mistake is made in the tense.

Speaking extra

6 Encourage students to think of a video and answer the questions. Students could share with the class, or in groups.

Possible answer

1 I watched a video about water bottles. Kids showed different tricks with the bottles of water.

2 I watched it last week.

3 I watched it at home.

4 First, four kids flipped water bottles and they landed on the table.

5 Then different kids showed different tricks. One kid's bottle landed on top of another bottle.

6 I liked it, but I don't know if the tricks were real. Maybe it was a camera trick! I want to try the tricks!

extra: digital

Choose a short video to show the class which is appropriate in content and interest for your class. Have the students watch it and answer the questions.

Or, make it a jigsaw video watching exercise if logistics allow. Choose two videos. Half the class watches one (e.g. in another room or on their device) and half the class watches the other. Group students into pairs of A and B to ask each other the questions.

7 Advise students to prepare for upcoming pairwork on page 143: they need to think of/search for a the funniest video they've seen (e.g. on YouTube) that they like and be ready to answer some simple questions about it, like the ones in Ex 6. As above, monitor carefully that the choices are appropriate.

alternative

Ask students to prepare answers to the questions about their video for homework then bring them to class to discuss the next day.

To finish

Ask students to work in pairs to think of their own plan for a funny video about losing something like Paul did. They should draw a storyboard of three pictures. Combine pairs for students to tell each other about the story in their video. If time allows, students could film their videos on mobile phones to share with the class (or act out their story).

Presentation tool:	Unit 7, Speaking
Workbook / Online Practice:	p67
Grammar reference:	SB p128
Speaking file:	SB p140
Pairwork file:	SB p143

WRITING SB pp82–83

To start

Choose a famous person students will know of, and say five things about their life. Try to include the phrases in the useful language box: *He / She is from … He / She grew up in … He / She was born in …* Students guess who you are talking about. For a bit of fun, tell students they need to guess another famous person and share five things about your own life, and see if they can guess it's you. Ask students to repeat the activity with their own famous people.

Power up

1 Ask students to discuss the question in pairs. Conduct whole class feedback.

Possible answer

My favourite famous person is Simone Biles. She's a gymnast from the USA and won gold medals at the Olympics.

2 Direct students to the picture of Adriana and the caption.

Possible answer

Her famous person is Tatiana Calderón. She's a racing driver from Colombia.

3 Say: *Later on we're going to work on a writing project. Your writing project will be similar to this one in exercise 3.* Give students a few minutes to read the text and find five things. Conduct whole class feedback.

Possible answers

She's from Colombia.
She was born in March, 1993.
She was five when she went on a go-kart track.
She won the EasyKart National Championship in 2005.
She became a driver for Sauberon in 2017.

4 Go through the explore language box and ask students to find the phrases in the text and highlight them.

She's from Colombia.   She was born in March, 1993.
She grew up in Bogotá.

5 Students should use the phrases in the language box. Point out that *in* is used for year and place. Put students into pairs or small groups to share their sentences.

Possible answers

I'm from the Czech Republic.   I was born in April, 2011.
I grew up in Prague.

Fun footer

Ask students to read the fun footer aloud with a partner and see if they can say the year (nineteen fifty-eight). If possible, show a picture of Maria Teresa de Filippis racing. Tell students that Maria Teresa de Filippis started racing cars because her brothers said she couldn't drive fast. They were wrong!

Plan on

6 Tell students to use the text information to answer the questions. They will need to speculate about the last question. Check as a class.

Where is she from? She's from Colombia.
When was she born? She was born in March, 1993.
Where did she grow up? She grew up in Bogotá.
What is her job? She is a racing driver.
Why does Adriana like her? Because she is from her country.

7 Students choose their own famous person to write about. It could be the person they chose in Ex 1 or someone else.

Possible answer

What is her name? JoJo Siwa
Where is she from? The USA
Where did she grow up? Nebraska, USA
When was she born? 19 May 2003
What is her job? Singer, dancer, actor, YouTuber
Why do you like her? She is good at singing and dancing.
I like her YouTube videos. Her JoJo bows are fun.

Write on

8 Give students some head-down quiet writing time for ten minutes. Circulate providing assistance as required. Then students compare their answers in pairs. Ask: *Have you included all the information from the table? Have you used the phrases from the useful language box? Have you included any linking words (see page 81)?*

Possible answer

JoJo Siwa is a famous singer and dancer from the USA. She was born in Nebraska in 2003. She makes YouTube videos. I like JoJo because she is good at singing and dancing. Her big JoJo bows are famous and popular.

Improve it

9 Point out that a caption is text that explains a picture. It usually goes below the picture. Students could find and print pictures off the internet, or if they are unable to do that, they could draw a picture or relevant. Then write a caption. Display the projects in your classroom or invite students to post them to your private class online area.

> **extra:** fast finishers
>
> After you check their work for accuracy, get students to create a gapped version of their text by removing the verbs in the past simple (and write them in a box). Collect and photocopy the texts for other students to try.

To finish

Get students to work in new pairs and ask them to speak for a minute about the person they wrote about (without looking at their text). In a mixed-ability class, give students the choice how long they want to speak for: 30 seconds, 45 seconds or a minute.

To make it easier, tell students they can write down six words before their time starts. Get students to swap partners again and see if they can talk for longer. To extend the activity, you could give other topics for students to speak about, e.g. your school, what you did yesterday.

Presentation tool:	Unit 7, Writing
Workbook / Online Practice:	p68
Grammar reference:	SB p128
Writing file:	SB p140

SWITCH ON SB p83

Skateboard star

1 Draw a star on the board, elicit the word *star* and write it on the board. Then ask: *what does it mean if person is a star?* (They are really good at something, special or famous.) Tell students that they are going to watch a video about a boy called Zion who is a skateboard star and is really good at skateboarding. Put students into pairs to think of three things they want to be good at. These could include school lessons, free time activities, personal qualities like being a good friend.

Possible answer

I want to be good at science. I want to be good at art. I really want to be good at helping people.

2 ▶ Play the recording and pause at 00:4. Ask *where is Zion skateboarding?* (On the road). Then play the rest of the recording. Pause the recording at 1:33 and elicit some places Zion skates. Then play the rest of the recording. Elicit some more places.

Possible answers

on the road, at a park, on steps, on a skateboard ramp, at a skatepark, near the sea, at home, at a carpark, on a bench.

3 ▶ Get students to discuss each sentence in pairs and see if they can remember. Then play the recording for students to check, and pause after each question is answered, and elicit the answer. If students have found this difficult, after eliciting the answer, skip back about 10 seconds so students can hear the section again before the clip proceeds. See if students can correct the false statements.

1 F (*Zion is eight years old. He has already been skateboarding for five years. When he was three …*)
2 F (*Zion has five brothers and sisters.*)
3 T
4 T

Project

4 Organise students into pairs. Go through the full rubric for Ex 4 and Ex 5 so that students understand that the activity they choose will be used for an action plan. Students may like to choose something that they're already interested in or good at, and want to get even better at. For the discussion part, students could work through the questions listed in Ex 5. Make sure they understand: *experts, professionals, change.*

5 Go through the example sentences with the class. Students write five things they can do to improve. Monitor and provide assistance as required. Combine pairs to form small groups to share their action plans.

alternative

For a longer activity, students could research some ways to improve in their chosen activity (in class or for homework), and then decide which are the most practical suggestions to use to incorporate in a plan. They could present their ideas in two columns: *Dream world* and *My world*, (e.g. *Dream world: I can get lessons from a pop star. My world: I can watch singing lessons from a pop star on YouTube*). It could also be presented as a lift-the-flap poster, where the dream is on a flap / post-it note, and the reality suggestion is written underneath.

Presentation tool: Unit 7, Switch on

Switch on videoscript: TB p140

UNIT CHECK SB p84

This Unit check covers vocabulary for jobs and things we do, and irregular past simple forms.

Practice

1 Set a time limit of one minute. Ask students to find and write down words from the wordlist for the two categories. Elicit the real people and their jobs.

Possible answers
1 racing driver (Tatania Calderón), farmer (my aunt), nurse (my cousin).
2 learn, think, write

2 Ask students to write three sentences about things they didn't do yesterday, then compare their sentences in pairs. During feedback, ask students from some pairs to share one thing their partner didn't do, e.g. *Alicia didn't fly a model plane yesterday.*

Possible answer
I didn't see an elephant.
I didn't find any money.
I didn't build a robot.

3 ◄)) 7.10 Tell students they are going to listen to things people did yesterday. Play the recording for students to write down the sentences. During feedback, write the sentences on the board and find out if any students did similar things yesterday.

1 I saw the doctor yesterday.
2 My team won the football match.
3 She took some photos of the basketball player.
4 We sang *Happy Birthday* to our teacher.

4 ◄)) 7.11 If necessary, review the past simple question words on page 80 of the Student's Book. Play the recording for students to complete the questions and write their answers. Then put students into pairs to ask and answer. Conduct whole class feedback.

1 What **2** Where **3** When **4** Where

Possible answers
1 I learnt about jobs.
2 I went to the cinema.
3 I got up at 6.30.
4 I was here at school!

GRAMMAR FILE SB p129

1 **1** built **2** found **3** bought **4** left **5** could **6** gave

2 **1** Did you see your friends yesterday?
2 Did your parents have breakfast with you?
3 Did you all sing in the music lesson this morning?
4 Did you find some money in the street on the way to school?
5 Did you go to the cinema at the weekend?

3 **1** When did Carol go home?
2 What animal did Olivia and Lina see?
3 Why did Harry sing a song?
4 How did you travel to London?
5 Where did they find a music player?

4 **1** good **2** competition **3** saw **4** won **5** wrote

Presentation tool:	Unit 7, Unit check
Workbook / Online Practice:	p69
Grammar reference:	SB p128
Audioscript:	SB p148

Top to toe

8

VOCABULARY 1
parts of the body

READING
topic: friends and twins –
physical appearance
skill: reading quickly
task: multiple-choice cloze

GRAMMAR
comparative adjectives
superlative adjectives

VOCABULARY 2
clothes

LISTENING
topic: people with world
records
skill: guessing an answer
task: gap fill

SPEAKING
topic: unusual world records
skill: making a guess
task: make guesses about pictures

WRITING
topic: a visit to a pet shop
skill: writing a story based on pictures
task: write a short story

SWITCH ON
video: meet my family
project: record breakers

Lead-in SB p85

Draw a face on the board, adding only one feature at a time, and eliciting the words as you go. Start by drawing an eye on the board and elicit the word *eye*, then draw another eye, a nose, mouth, one tooth, teeth, an oval for *face*, ear, hair, beard and moustache. If no students know the words, say them.

1 Ask students to open their books to page 85 and direct them to Ex 1. Put students into pairs to take turns to find the things that they can in the picture. Elicit what they can see and what they can't.

Possible answer
In the picture: ear, eye, face, hair, mouth, nose, teeth; Not in the picture: beard, moustache.

2 Describe one of the faces for students to guess which one it is, e.g. *She has got brown eyes. She is smiling. We can see her teeth.* Get students to guess which face it is. Tell students to work in pairs to take turns to describe a face and guess which one it is.

Possible answer
This person has got brown eyes. We can see his teeth. He has dark hair. He isn't smiling.

---

alternative

Instead of Ex 2, tell students about an imaginary alien and get them to listen and draw, e.g. *My alien has got four eyes and five ears. My alien has a big mouth with one tooth. My alien has blue hair.* If students have different coloured pens, include colours in the description.

Get students to compare pictures and see whether they included all the features you said, and whose is the funniest. Then get students to draw their own alien face and describe it to a partner to draw.

Students compare their original alien and what their partner drew. Was it similar?

VOCABULARY 1 SB p86

To start

Teach / revise the following vocab by touching or indicating it on your body. Give a slight pause before saying each word so that students can call out the word if they know it.

head, neck, feet, back, shoulders, arms, hands, fingers, legs, knees, toes.

Then call out different body parts for students to touch, e.g. *Head. Knee. Fingers.* (Demonstrate yourself as well.) When students get confident, occasionally call out a word while touching another part of your body, e.g. *head* (touch your head), *back* (touch your back), *arms* (touch your toes), *fingers* (but touch your toes). Pause for students to adjust if they touched their toes! As an extension, students could play the game in pairs or small groups.

Power up

1 Direct students to the photo and magnify it on the Presentation tool, if using. Ask the question as an open question first and elicit possible answers. Then go through the options A, B, and C, clarifying *world record* and *taking part in a tradition* if required. Ask students to tick A, B, or C then quickly read the first text in Ex 2 to check their answer. Elicit the answer, and anything students know about Castells, then share the background information.

***

C taking part in a tradition (*It's a very old tradition.*)

***

> **background:** Castells
>
> This tradition is hundreds of years old and is most popular in Catalonia. Castells are made as part of a competition or display at a festival. There are lots of different styles of castell – the one in the picture is just one of many. They can be six or seven people tall, sometimes more. It's important that each person gets down from the castell carefully!

parts of the body

2 Point out the people A, B and C in the photos. Ask students to read descriptions 1–3 and match them to the people A–C.

***

1 C **2** B **3** A

***

> **useful language**
>
> Go through the language box with the class. Ask students to find and underline *at the bottom, in the middle,* and *to the top.* Ask students to work in pairs to describe the castell starting with the following prompts, *At the bottom, there are … In the middle, there are … At the top, there is … .* Elicit possible answers.

3 Ask students to look at the words in bold with a partner, and check they know what all of them are by pointing to the parts of their own bodies. Play the recording for students and ask students to point to relevant parts of the picture when each part of the body is mentioned. Chorally drill the words. Point out that *feet* is an irregular plural of *foot.*

> **watch out** for
>
> Check students know that we have two different words for *fingers* and *toes* in English.

> **alternative**
>
> Play audio 8.1 and ask students to follow the text in the book. There is one extra sentence for each part 1–3 which is not written. Ask students to listen for the extra sentences and write them down. (Look at person C. Look at person B. Look at person A.)

4 Do a few similar examples as a class, e.g. Say: *It is below your leg. What is it?* (foot). *It's above your neck, what is it?* (head) Ask students to work in pairs and take turns to read the questions aloud and answer them.

***

1 hand **2** neck **3** toes

***

> **extra:** fast finishers
>
> Students could write their own clues for a body part from Ex 2 or from the parts of the face on page 85. Give students the opportunity to read their clue(s) to the class for the others to guess.

5 🔊 8.1 Elicit the first answer as an example then get students to work in pairs and choose the correct word. Go through the answers as a class.

***

1 straight **2** long **3** wavy **4** fair **5** red **6** dark **7** short **8** brown **9** blonde **10** curly

***

> **extra:** whole class
>
> Draw on the board three columns and label them:
> 1 What colour is your hair? 2 How long is your hair?
> 3 How straight is your hair? Ask students to divide the adjectives from Ex 5 into the relevant columns and see if they can add any more words to each column.
>
> Answers: 1 long, short, (shoulder-length)
> 2 blonde, brown, red, fair, dark (black, grey, white, purple!)
> 3 straight, wavy, curly, (spiky)

VOCABULARY 1 (Continued)

> **game** on
>
> Demonstrate the game and write some prompts on the board demonstrating the two alternative ways to use adjectives talk about hair, i.e. before a noun, or after the verb *to be*, e.g. *She has curly hair. Her hair is brown. It's long.*
>
> If your students wear ponytails or pigtails, consider teaching these nouns, checking that students understand the animals and *tail*, e.g. *She has pigtails. He has a ponytail.*

To finish

Tell students that you are thinking about a new hairstyle. Ask students to work in pairs to draw you a new hairstyle. Each pair should share with the class what they chose using adjectives from the lesson. e.g. *Your new hair is long, curly and red!* Alternatively, they could choose a new hairstyle for themselves.

Presentation tool:	Unit 8, Vocabulary 1
Workbook / Online Practice:	p70
Grammar reference:	SB p130
Audioscript:	SB p148
Extra Practice App	

READING SB p87

To start

Review parts of the body calling out two parts of the body and getting students to see if they can touch the two parts together, e.g. *Can you touch your fingers and back* (students have to touch their fingers to their knees), *toes and knees, shoulder and leg, tongue and nose?*

Power up

1 Teach the word *twin*. Ask students to answer the questions individually then compare their answers in pairs. Conduct whole class feedback.

Possible answers
1 Twins are usually born on the same day but sometimes they are born on different days.
2 Yes.
3 They sometimes look similar (see footer).

Fun footer

Ask students to read the footer. Clarify that *identical* means *exactly the same.* Chorally drill identical. Ask students to look around the classroom for any identical or similar objects, e.g. *Look! Ivan and Pablo have got identical bags. Everyone has identical books! Our pencil cases are similar, but not identical.*

Read on

2 Direct students to the photos and ask them to guess and tick which pair are twins. Then ask students to read the article to find out without worrying about the gaps yet. Elicit the answer.

> **extra**
>
> Find or ask students to find an internet picture of Lucy and Maria Aylmer when they were younger. Ask: *Did they look more similar when they were young or now?*
>
> ### Possible answers
> Guessing: I think the boys / the girls are twins.
> After reading the article: The girls are twins.

> **exam** task: A1 Movers Reading and Writing Part 4
>
> In the A1 Movers Reading and Writing Part 4 exam task, there is one example and five items. No keys would be given away elsewhere in the text.
>
> **3** **e** Direct students to the first gap and model reading the words before and after the gap (pausing briefly for the gap). Try to get students to think about what the word might be before looking at the options A, B and C. Then direct students to the options and ask them to circle the correct option. Students complete the activity then compare in pairs before checking as a class.

1 C (*your* links to you in the question, addressing reader)
2 A (*got* to form have got for possession, belonging)
3 C (*in* preposition of place, in correct for classroom; at/ on not possible)
4 B (*an* we use *an* before a singular word beginning with a vowel)
5 B (*were* to form were born, plural of was born)
6 A (*their* plural possessive adjective for more than one person – *there* refers to a place and *there're* the short form of *they are*)]

> **extra:** fast finishers
>
> Ask students to find and highlight six words in the text for parts of the body or face, and circle six adverbs of frequency.
>
> Answers: face(s), eyes, teeth, feet, hair, skin; often x 2, sometimes x 2, always x 2, never x 3

Sum up

4 Students close their books. Students work in pairs and say two things about the twins and two things about the friends. Conduct whole class feedback.

Possible answers

twins: They aren't identical. Their skin is different. Maria's hair is black but Lucy's hair is red.

friends: They look the similar. They sometimes change names and seats. Their names are Aaron and Miguel. Miguel is taller than Aaron.

Speak up

5 Students take turn to describe someone in their family, e.g. their hair, whether they are tall or short, their age, or their interests. Their partner needs to guess who it is. Some students may choose to use or attempt to use comparative adjectives from the text but this will be covered in more detail in the next lesson.

Possible answer

A: He's tall. He's thirty-eight. He's got dark hair.
B: Your dad?
A: No. But he looks like my dad.
A: Your uncle?
B: Yes.

To finish

Find and show (or ask students to find) some pictures of famous twins or famous people who have a twin. Students discuss how they are the same and how they are different.

Presentation tool:	Unit 8, Reading
Workbook / Online Practice:	p71
Grammar reference:	SB p130
Extra Practice App	

GRAMMAR SB p88

To start

Write the adjectives listed on the board and ask students to work in pairs. Can they think of the opposite adjective for each one? If students find it challenging, give them the first letter of each opposite.

new (old)	easy (hard)	quiet (loud)
sad (happy)	hot (cold)	soft (hard)
curly (straight)	young (old)	clean (dirty)

> **alternative**
>
> You may want to download the Grammar Presentation for this lesson from the Teacher Resources area of Pearson English Portal. This presentation has been created specifically for this lesson and is fully editable for teachers.

1 Get students to use the spelling patterns in the box to write the comparative form. Get different students to come up to the board and write the correct form.

1 sadder **2** straighter **3** hotter **4** happier **5** longer
6 easier

explore grammar

Go through the grammar box with the class. Emphasise the irregular forms for good and bad are better (not gooder) and worse (not badder). You could ask students to find and underline the examples of *better* and *worse* in the first text on page 87. *I'm <u>worse</u> at maths than Miguel, but <u>better</u> at sport.*

Refer students to the notes on page 130 then get students to complete Ex 1. Set Ex 2 and 3 for homework and check in the next lesson and get students to compare their answers to Ex 3 in pairs.

> **watch out** for ①
>
> Point out that these patterns only work for short adjectives. Comparative adjectives for longer adjectives (i.e. three syllables + or two syllables that don't end in -y, like *beautiful* or *modern*) with *more / less* will be covered in A2.

2 8.3 Read through the rubric with the class and elicit the meaning of *triplets*. Get students to complete the sentences with the word in brackets then play the video/recording for students to check their answers. Elicit the answers.

1 shorter **2** younger, taller **3** heavier **4** older

3 🔊 8.4 Play the video/recording for students to listen first. Ask them to focus on weak forms of the -*er* ending and of *than*. Then play it again for students to listen and repeat.

1 I'm older than my brother.
2 Today's homework is easier than yesterday's.
3 My eyes are bigger than my sister's.

4 After checking the answers to the exercise, ask: *when comparing two adjectives which is the word that will always be before the second noun?* (than). *How about if there is no second noun – as in item 4?* (We don't use *than*).

1 better **2** prettier **3** fairer **4** happier **5** worse

GRAMMAR (Continued)

5 Go through the rubric and elicit which picture the example relates to (the middle picture). Students write sentences about the pictures.

Possible answers
Nikki's hair is longer than Beth's hair.
Nikki's hair is darker than Beth's.
Dad is shorter than Robert.
Robert is younger than Dad.
Mum's hair is curlier than Grandma's.
Grandma is older than Mum.

---

extra: mixed-ability classes

With a mixed-ability class, you could adjust the expected output, for example, some students could write eight sentences while others write four.

Speak up

6 Ask students to work in pairs. Circulate providing assistance as required.

Possible answer
My brother Adam is taller than my sister Jess.
Jess is older than Adam.
Jess has longer hair than Adam.

---

alternative

Get students to choose a favourite famous person. It could be the person they used for the writing project on page 82. Ask students to work in pairs to compare the people they chose using comparative adjectives.

Fun footer

Get students to read the joke in the footer. Check they understand *worm*. Ask *why is it worse to have half a worm?* (You ate the other half!)

To finish

Write up this tongue twister using *better* for students to read. *Betty Botter bought a bit of butter. But the butter was bitter so Betty bought some better butter.*

Say it with some expression to convey the general meaning of bitter. Elicit what verb bought is the past simple of (buy). Underline better butter. Ask: *How many bits of butter did Betty buy? Which was the better butter – the first one or the second one?* second.Then ask students to try the tongue twister and see how fast they can say it.

Presentation tool:	Unit 8, Grammar
Workbook / Online Practice:	p72
Photocopiable activity:	8A
Grammar reference:	SB p130
Audioscript:	SB p148
Extra Practice App	

VOCABULARY 2 SB p89

To start

Tell students an anecdote about someone you saw on the way to school that was wearing something unusual, for example, dressed in very unseasonal clothing, or a costume. Use expression and mime a bit to indicate the clothes, e.g. say *On my way to school, I saw something strange. I saw a man at the bus stop. He was wearing shorts, a T-shirt and sunglasses. No jacket! No boots! No coat!*

clothes

1 8.5 Ask students to match as many of the clothes as they can. Play the recording for students to check their answers.

A cap B hoodie C jeans D socks E sunglasses F dress
G sandals H shirt I shorts J trainers K T-shirt L skirt
M tights N boots

---

extra: whole class

Play the recording again for students to listen and repeat the words. As an extension, students could stand up and sit down, whenever an item they are wearing right now is called out.

---

exam task: **A2 Flyers Reading and Writing Part 1**

In the A2 Flyers Reading and Writing Part 1 exam task, there is one example and fifteen options. More lexical sets are tested, but this exercise relates to the theme of the unit.

2 Students complete the activity then compare in pairs before checking as a class.

1 trainers 2 sunglasses 3 jeans 4 cap 5 sandals
6 hoodie 7 tights 8 boots 9 shorts 10 skirt

---

3 8.6 Tell students that they will hear four short dialogues and to decide which person in the picture is being spoken about in each. Play the recording twice then elicit the answers.

1 Sam 2 Jack 3 Jack 5 Sarah

---

explore **language**

Go through the explore language box. Point out that you can say *I've got a shoe*, but you can't say *I've got a jean / short*.

---

extra: whole class

Ask students to turn to the audioscript on page 149 and find and underline the adjectives and comparative adjectives.

Answers: (adjectives) great, nice, good, long, cool, right; (comparative adjectives) smaller, cooler

---

watch out for ⓘ

Make sure students understand that *jeans, shorts, tights, glasses* are plural in English. Even though they are only one piece of clothing, each pair has two legs or two eyes!

---

4 Students can use the sentences in the audioscript as further examples. Ask students to make a sentence about each person and share it with the class.

> **Possible answers**
> Sarah's dress is longer than Emma's skirt.
> I think Sam's trainers are cooler than Jack's.
> Jack's sunglasses are smaller than Sarah's.
> Emma's pink tights are brighter than her black boots.

> ### game on
> Go through the instructions for the game and example. Ask a volunteer to describe one of the people for the class to guess. Then students play in pairs.

Speak up

5 Students choose two items each, and then tell their partner about them. Conduct whole class feedback.

> **Possible answer**
> I've got a yellow T-shirt. My T-shirt is brighter than yours. I've got black trainers. I think my trainers are bigger than yours.

> ### extra: mixed-ability classes
> Encourage stronger students to use other comparative adjectives in their description if they want to. The four in the rubric are a prompt not a limit.

Fun footer

Ask students to read the footer. Ask students why they think the jeans were stronger than normal trousers. (They are made of special cloth called denim.) Ask: *Who wore jeans? What jobs did they do?* The jeans were strong because they were for working on farms and in mines.

To finish

Ask students to answer the following questions in pairs: *What do you like wearing? What don't you like wearing? Why?*

> ### extra
> Bring in a small suitcase or bag with some different items of clothing from the lesson. These could include some funny items like a silly hat. Get students to take turns to open up the bag and pull something out, hold it up and get students to say what it is and even make some comparisons between items. Pack everything back into the suitcase. Put students in pairs to make a list of everything they remember from the suitcase.
>
> Alternatively, you could get some internet pictures of clothing items and flip through them on a slideshow one by one. See what students can remember.

Presentation tool:	Unit 8, Vocabulary 2
Workbook / Online Practice:	p73
Photocopiable activity:	8B
Grammar reference:	SB p130
Audioscript:	SB p149
Extra Practice App	

LISTENING SB p90

To start

Put students in pairs. One is the runner and one is the writer. Write Text 1 on a piece of paper and put in on a table at the front of the room (if you have a large class, you may have to put the text in more than one place). The runners take turns to come and read the text, and then run back and tell it to their partner who writes it down. Ask: *Which team was the fastest?* Students swap roles and play again.

Text 1: The longest ice cream in the world was more than one kilometre long! It was in the USA.

Text 2: The record for most selfies with different people is 134 in three minutes. It was at a school in the UK.

Power up

1 Direct students to the photo of Usain Bolt. Read the rubric with the class and elicit some other things people can get a world record for.

> **Possible answers**
> being the strongest, being the first person to do something or go somewhere, doing something big, being a singer / writer who sells a lot of work.

> ### extra
> Elicit anything else students know about Usain Bolt, then share the following information: Usain Bolt is from Jamaica. Usain Bolt set world records in 100 metres, 200 metres and 4 x 100 metre relay. He won eight gold medals at the Olympics. When he was twelve, he was already the fastest runner in his school.

2 Direct students to the pictures and elicit guesses of what the records might be.

> **Possible answers**
> I think this record is for texting the fastest.
> Maybe this record is for travelling to the North Pole.

Listen up

3 🔊 8.7 Direct students to read the names 1–5 and the records A–E before they listen. Play the recording. Elicit the answers.

1 B   2 D   3 E   4 A   5 C

> ### background: texting record ℹ
> The twenty-five word message Marcel had to type was: *The razor-toothed piranhas of the genera Serrasalmus and Pygocentrus are the most ferocious freshwater fish in the world. In reality they seldom attack a human.*

> ### exam task: A2 Flyers Listening Part 2
> In the A2 Flyers Listening Part 2 exam task, there is one example and five items.
>
> **4** 🅴 🔊 8.8 Get students to read the notes and guess the answers or see if they can remember any. Then play the recording again for students to complete the gaps.

LISTENING (Continued)

---

1 Brazil (*And the person who holds the record is. Marcel Fernandes Fihlo from* **Brazil***.*)

2 16/sixteen (*She was* **sixteen** *when she pulled her father's van!*)

3 jump (*the world record for the highest* **jump***.*)

4 6/six (*her hair was nearly* **six** *metres long!*)

5 pizzas (*They made one hundred* **pizzas***.*)

---

explore **grammar** → SB p130

Read through the box with the class. (Note that long adjectives with 'the most' are not covered at this level.) Draw a tall stick figure on the board and say *tall*, draw a taller one and say *taller*, then draw an even taller one and say *the tallest*. Refer students page 130. Ask students to complete Ex 4 and 5 in class. Set Ex 6 for fast finishers in other exercises or for homework.

---

watch out for ⓘ

Some students may forget to use irregular forms *the best* and *the worst*. Check students' pronunciation of *worst*, it rhymes with *first*.

---

5 Fill in the first two gaps as an example with the class, then have students fill in the remaining gaps. Students ask and answer the questions in pairs. Students may want to take some notes so that they can share something about their partner in Ex 6.

---

1 best   **2** the youngest   **3** the easiest   **4** the worst
5 the longest

---

6 Ask each person to share something they learned about their partner in Ex 5.

Possible answer

The easiest subject for Dasha is maths. / Dasha's easiest subject is maths.

Fun footer

Read the fun footer with the class. Some of Ashrita's world records are underwater cycling the longest distance, fastest time to run a mile with a milk bottle on the head and making the world's largest pencil.

To finish

Ask students to work in small groups to think of the best and the worst in each of these categories. Conduct whole class feedback.

thing to put on a pizza
place to visit in your area
thing about having 6 m long hair!

Presentation tool:	Unit 8, Listening
Workbook / Online Practice:	p74
Grammar reference:	SB p130
Audioscript:	SB p149
Extra Practice App	

SPEAKING SB p90

To start

Ask students to discuss in pairs: *What is the best animal in the world? The fastest? The biggest? The nicest? Why?* Conduct whole class feedback.

Power up

1 Focus students on the photos and generate discussion about each one, e.g. ask: *What animals are in the photos? What are they doing?* Then get students to guess which animal holds each record but don't check the answers yet.

A the biggest (Geronimo the rabbit has **the biggest** ears.)
B the fastest (Bertie the tortoise is **the fastest** tortoise.)
C the best (Purin the dog is **the best** goalkeeper.)

Speak up

---

exam task: **A1 Movers Reading and Writing Part 2**

In the A1 Movers Reading and Writing Part 2 exam task, there is one example and five items.

2 🄴 Ask students to read the questions, and choose an appropriate response to each from the options A, B, C. Don't check the answers yet.

---

3 🔊 8.9 Play the recording for students to check their answers to Ex 1 and 2. Focus students on the useful language box and play the recording again for students to tick the phrases used.

Ex 1
A the biggest (Geronimo the rabbit has **the biggest** ears.)
B the fastest (Bertie the tortoise is **the fastest** tortoise.)
C the best (Purin the dog is **the best** goalkeeper.)

Ex 2
1 B   **2** A   **3** C

---

4 Go through the rubric and example and point out the clues. Then put students into pairs to guess the world records.

Possible answer

A: What's the record in photo D?
B: Is it the smallest horse?
A: Maybe it's the cutest!
B: Look at photo E, what's the world record here?
A: Perhaps it's the biggest cow?
B: Yeah, or maybe it's the tallest?
A: Now, what's the record in F?
B: I guess it's the biggest shoe.
A: Good idea.

---

5 🔊 8.10 Go through the exam tip with the class. Play the recording twice.

Photo D: the smallest horse
Photo E: the tallest cow.
Photo F: the biggest feet and shoes

Speaking extra

exam task: A1 Movers Speaking Part 3

6 Direct students' attention to the photos A–F and
ask them to identify which one is different. They
compare in pairs and give their reason. Elicit answers
from the class, encouraging students to explain why.

Photo F is different. (There is no animal in the photo.)

7 Students decide which of the records from Ex 4 they
would like to break and why. Then have a class mingle
for students to compare their answers and find someone
who agrees with them.

Possible answers

I would like to break the record for world's fastest teenager
because I love to run.
I would like to break the record for world's highest jumper
because it would be cool.

extra: digital

Ask students to look up *world records kids can try* and
choose the easiest and hardest record they find. There are
even some online games where you can break a record.
Tell the class about it.

To finish

Students could try to break a record, e.g. see who can clap
the fastest. The world record is 1080 claps in one minute!

Presentation tool:	Unit 8, Speaking
Workbook / Online Practice:	p75
Photocopiable activity:	8C
Grammar reference:	SB p130
Speaking file:	SB p141
Audioscript:	SB p149

WRITING

To start

Write the following pairs on the board. Put students in pairs
to discuss which is better. Encourage them to give a reason.

reading | watching TV
paper book | ebook
scary story | funny story

Power up

1 Ask the questions as a class discussion and elicit ideas.

Possible answer

I think J K Rowling is the best writer. I love the *Harry Potter*
books!

2 Direct students to the title *The pet shop* and the pictures.
Then get students to read the story and answer the
questions. Elicit the answers.

1 Nina Carmen.
2 a girl called Rose
3 in a pet shop
4 The story is about a girl who goes to a pet shop to get a
pet. First she sees a mouse. Then a cat. Finally she sees a
dog and decides she wants that.

3 Point out that *look* can be used in a range of ways.
Students complete the phrases then check as a class.

1 looks **2** looks **3** looks

4 Elicit which meaning matches each sentence.

A 2 **B** 1 **C** 3

explore **language**

Go through the explore language box. Point out that speech
marks can be single or double. Ask students to find the
speech marks in the story and notice how they are around the
speech.

5 Get students to add the speech marks then check as a
class.

1 'I like cats,' says Daniel.
2 Mum says, 'Do you want a pet?'
3 'That's a great idea!' says Dad.
4 'Sam's the tallest boy in the class', says the teacher.
5 The man says, 'The parrots cost twenty pounds.'
6 'You're our favourite cousin', say the boys.

watch out for

Check that students have both an opening and closing
speech mark.

Fun footer

Ask students to read the fun footer. Zoella (Zoe Sugg)
is an English vlogger. She makes YouTube videos about
clothes, hair and makeup. She sold 78,109 copies of her
book *Girl online* in the first week.

WRITING (Continued)

Plan on

6 Students work in pairs to look at the pictures and discuss the questions. Point out that it's fine for them to make up an answer.

Possible answer

1 There are two women and a man. There are three dogs. The young woman's dog is Lulu. They are at a dog training class.

2 The other dogs are good but Lulu is barking and jumping. Lulu is the worst dog.

3 It is windy. Betty's hat is in the water. Lulu is swimming. Lulu has got the woman's hat. It is a happy ending.

Write on

> **exam** task: A2 Flyers Reading and Writing Part 7
>
> In the A2 Flyers Reading and Writing Part 7 exam task, there would be no words in any of the pictures, and the story line would be clearer.
>
> **7** **e** Read the exam tip with the class. Ask students to write their story using some of the ideas they discussed in Ex 6. Students can use present or past tense but should generally stay consistent within their story.
>
> ### Higher level answer
>
> Lulu is at a dog training class with other dogs. She is the worst dog. The other dogs are good but Lulu is barking and jumping. It's windy and this woman's hat goes in the water. Then Lulu swims in the water. She has got the hat. Now everybody says 'Lulu is the best dog!'
>
> ### Lower level answer
>
> Lulu is at dog training class. She is bad. The hat is in the water. Lulu has got the hat. Thank you Lulu!

Improve it

8 Get students to check their ownwork first. Then change students' partners to a different partner from Ex 5 to share their stories and check the things listed.

To finish

Write or type up this story on the board (or photocopy).

rose and lulu are at the dog training class go says rose but lulu doesnt go it is windy and a womans hat goes into the water help she says lulu swims to the hat now lulu is the best dog (Rose and Lulu are at the dog training class. 'Go', says Rose but Lulu doesn't go. It is windy and a woman's hat goes into the water. "Help", she says. Lulu swims to the hat. Now Lulu is the best dog!)

Divide students into small groups. Get them to discuss what changes need to be made, then give them different coloured pens, and get them to take turns to come and add a capital letter or punctuation mark.

Presentation tool:	Unit 8, Writing
Workbook / Online Practice:	p76
Grammar reference:	SB p130
Writing file:	SB p141

SWITCH ON SB p93

Meet my family

1 Put students into pairs to do the activity.

Possible answer

A: He has got brown hair. He is seven. He is shorter than me.

B: Is it your brother?

A: Yes, your turn …

2 ▶ Play the video clip and pause at 1:11. Elicit what is special about the Van Ness family. Ask students to predict what might be special about their home. Then play the rest of the clip to see if they were right.

The people in the Van Ness family are very tall.
Their house is bigger than a normal house. Every room is higher, the benches are higher.

3 ▶ Get students to read the questions to check they understand them, and discuss in pairs any answers they can remember. Play the clip again for students to check, pause and elicit the answers as you go. For item 4, at 1:46, pause the clip with the groceries showing, and get students to talk in pairs about what food they can see. Elicit ideas.

1 Yes, they are the tallest family in Britain.

2 There are four children: Vincent, Lucas, Franklin, and Naomi.

3 Frank is 6 foot, 10 inches (208 cm – 2 m 08)

4 **Possible answers:** cereal, bananas, apples, pears, juice, cereal bars, flour, whipped cream, meat

Project

4 Students could do this research in class, or for homework. The Guinesss World Records website is an excellent resource for this. Students bring their answers to the questions to the next lesson.

5 Students make posters about each record. These could be digital posters made as individual slides on a slide presentation, which will make them easier for the other students to see when they are presented. Alternatively, the poster sets could be pinned around the classroom for students to walk around and note down which is the fake record from each group. Finally, conduct whole class feedback to see if students guessed the correct record.

> **alternative**
>
> Put students into pairs or small teams to plan a challenge for another pair, e.g. Which pair can make a paper plane fly the furthest? It may be helpful to bring in props, e.g. newspaper, tape, sports equipment. Get the students to plan under the following headings:
>
> *Challenge name:*   *Instructions for students:*
> *What we need:*   *How to decide the winner:*
>
> The challenges could be presented in one lesson. At the end, ask students to reflect on the challenges using superlatives, e.g. *Which challenge was the easiest/hardest/ funniest/best?*

| Presentation tool: . | Unit 8, Switch on |
| Switch on videoscript: | TB p140 |

UNIT CHECK SB p94

This Unit check covers comparative and superlative adjectives, vocabulary for parts of the body, face, hair and clothes.

Practice

1 Set this as a challenge. Divide the class into small groups and allocate one writer for each group. Set a time limit of one minute for students to come up with words from the wordlist for each category. Find out which group has the most correct answers at the end of the task.

Possible answers

1 finger, toes, ear, eye, moustache, nose, tooth
2 back, head, shoulder, leg
3 swimsuit, sunglasses, hat

2 Students write three sentences about their hair and clothes. Circulate and help as needed.

---

alternative

Fast finishers can work in pairs and write sentences about their partner's hair and clothes, e.g. *Natasha is wearing red trainers and a white T-shirt. Her hair is brown.* Encourage students to compare aspects of their partner's appearance with their own using comparative adjectives, e.g. *Liam's hair is darker and curlier than mine.*

Possible answers

I've got wavy hair.
I'm wearing a red sweatshirt and blue jeans.
My trainers are black.

3 🔊 8.11 Play the recording for students to listen and complete the sentences with the comparative and superlative adjectives they hear.

1 taller **2** bigger **3** nicest **4** best

4 🔊 8.12 Tell students they need to listen and complete the questions. Play the recording. Then ask students to write down their answers to the questions, comparing their answers in pairs. Elicit answers to question 4 and find out how many students chose the same answer.

Possible answers

1 (oldest) My grandfather. / My grandfather is the oldest person in my family.
2 (hardest) Music. / I think music is the hardest lesson.
3 (longest) Lara/ / Lara has got the longest hair in our class.
4 (best) The Voice. / The Voice is the best programme on TV at the moment.

GRAMMAR FILE SB p131

1 **1** A **2** C **3** C **4** C **5** A **6** C

2 **1** Adam is bigger than me.
2 Are Sam and Jack older than Ella?
3 Your trainers aren't newer than my trainers. / My trainers aren't newer than your trainers.
4 His hair is curlier than your hair. / Your hair is curlier than his hair.
5 I am happier today than yesterday.
6 Is the weather hotter now?

3 Student's own answers.

4 **1** C **2** B **3** B **4** C **5** C **6** A

5 **1** I'm the biggest of my brothers and sisters.
2 My dad isn't the oldest in our family. / The oldest in our family isn't my dad.
3 My jeans are my newest clothes. / My newest clothes are my jeans.
4 Maria's hair is the curliest of all my friends. / Of all my friends Maria's hair is the curliest.
5 Angelo and Rita are the happiest people I know. / The happiest people I know are Angelo and Rita.
6 Is today the hottest day of the summer? / Is the hottest day of summer today?

6 Student's own answers.

Presentation tool:	Unit 8, Unit check
Workbook / Online Practice:	pp77–79
Grammar reference:	SB p130

School's out

9

VOCABULARY 1
sport and activities

READING
topic: different sports to try
skill: transferring information
task: matching

GRAMMAR
be going to
like/love + -ing, want to + infinitive

VOCABULARY 2
health problems

LISTENING
topic: future dreams
skill: checking answers
task: multiple choice (short texts)

SPEAKING
topic: talking about plans
skill: interacting with a partner
task: plan an activity weekend

WRITING
topic: holiday activities
skill: setting out a clear message
task: write a postcard

SWITCH ON
video: survival fun
project: survival school

Lead-in SB p95

Introduce the unit title *school's out* and explain that this means *school's finished for the holidays* and that the unit is related to activities that are done outside school time like interests and holidays.

Direct students to the photo and read the quote *Let's go to the beach!* Ask: *Do you like to go to the beach? What do you like to do there?* If your students don't live near an ocean, you could adapt this to a local river / lake / park, or ask: *Would you like to go to the beach one day? What do people do at the beach?*

1 Put students into pairs to discuss the question. Elicit the answer from the class. Find out if any students have played or play football on the beach.

He is playing football.

2 Ask students to join up with another pair to discuss the questions. Give each group one minute to discuss. During feedback, ask students to share the activities of their team members with the class, e.g. *Ellie does kung fu. She does it twice a week, on Wednesdays and Fridays. She doesn't play football.*

I play football and do dancing.
I sometimes play basketball at school.
I don't play volleyball. I don't do kung fu.

3 Ask students to discuss the question in their groups. During feedback, elicit answers from around the class and encourage students to share favourite sports that aren't listed in Ex 2.

My favourite sports are swimming and tennis.

---

extra

To extend the activity, ask students to think of reasons for their answer in Ex 3. Give an example if necessary, e.g. *My favourite sport is basketball because I love running, jumping and playing in a team.*

Ask students to work in small groups and take it in turns to share their reasons with the group.

VOCABULARY 1 SB p96

To start

In small groups, get students to make a list of sports they do in lessons at school. Elicit ideas (e.g. swimming, running, volleyball) and write them on the board, but leave a little space before each one to add verbs before each activity later in the lesson. Then ask: *What different sports can you think of (sports you don't usually do at school)?* Write up any ideas, e.g. rock climbing, sailing. Leave the sports listed on the board for use later in the lesson.

Power up

1 Ask students to read the sentences and tick the ones that are true for them. Put students into pairs to compare their answers.

Possible answer

A: Is sentence 1 true for you?

B: Yes, I like watching sport.

A: Me too. Is sentence 2 true for you?

B: No, it isn't true. I like team sports. I play volleyball. Is sentence 2 true for you?

A: Yes, it is. I don't really like team sports. I like swimming and rollerblading.

B: Sentence 3 is true for me. I love competitions.

A: I don't like competitions.

B: I like trying different sports. Is sentence 4 true for you?

A: Yes, I like trying different sports. I tried rock climbing last year. It was fun.

sport and activities

2 🔊 9.1 Direct students to the photos and ask students to work in pairs to talk about what the people are doing in each photo, naming the sport or activity if they can.

1 swimming **2** mountain biking **3** skateboarding
4 basketball

exam task: A1 Movers Speaking Part 3

In the A1 Movers Speaking Part 3 exam task, the layout is different: there are four sets of four pictures, covering different lexical areas.

3 e Direct students back to 1–4 in Ex 2. Remind students of some of the phrases they can use in 'odd one out' and write these on the board as a prompt, e.g. *I think … is different because … .*

… is the odd one out because … . Elicit a possible odd one out for the first group with the class. Then put students into pairs to discuss the remaining.

Possible answers

1 I think beach volleyball is different because it isn't in water.
2 I think dancing is the odd one out. Rock climbing and mountain biking are in the mountains but dancing is usually inside.
3 Yoga is different because the other activities are on wheels.
4 The odd one out is rollerblading because the other sports use a ball.

explore **language**

Go through the notes in the useful language box. Refer back to the list of sports that you made in the *to start* activity and ask students to work in pairs to decide whether we use *play*, *go* or *do* with each one.

watch out for ①

Demonstrate the pronunciation of skiing /ˈskiːɪŋ/.

4 Ask students to complete the text individually with the correct verb forms. Remind students of the third person -s, and elicit the spelling change in *goes* / *does*. Students can compare their answers in pairs but don't check the answers as a class yet because this will be done in Ex 5.

1 goes **2** play **3** does **4** plays **5** goes **6** go

5 🔊 9.2 Play the recording for students to check their answers to Ex 4. Ask some students to write up the answers on the board to check spelling, especially the -es in *goes* and *does*.

1 goes **2** play **3** does **4** plays **5** goes **6** go

6 Direct students' attention to the photos. Ask students to work with a partner and discuss what activities they do at the weekend. Circulate, checking the correct use of the verbs play, do and go, and helping as needed. During feedback, ask students to share something their partner does on the weekend.

Fun footer

Ask students to read the fun footer. Consider showing a short clip of Ashima Shirashi climbing. She is one of the world's best rock climbers. Note: there is another exercise related to Ashima Shirashi on page 106 with a photo. You may like to assign it at this point to do in class or for homework

To finish

Write on the board the following categories: sport/activity, food, animal, part of the body, country

Students work in pairs. Call out a letter, and students need to write down something for each category that starts with the letter called out. They have one minute. Elicit ideas. Pairs get a point for each item. As a variation, students can write down more than one item in each category starting with a given letter, and get a point for each.

Suggested letters and sample answers:
C (cycling, cake, cat, cheek, China)
M (mountain biking, melon, monkey, moustache, Mexico)
S (swimming, sandwich, spider, shoulder, Spain)
T (tennis, tomato, tiger, toe, Turkey)

Presentation tool:	Unit 9, Vocabulary 1
Workbook / Online Practice:	p80
Photocopiable activity:	9A
Grammar reference:	SB p132
Extra Practice App	

READING SB p97

To start

Find a short video clip of young people from Finland riding hobby horses to show the class. (Alternatively, show the picture of the hobby horses on Student's Book page 95.) Ask: *Would you like to try this sport? Why | Why not?*

Power up

1 Read through the options and check students understand *relatives*. Add the option *other* to encourage students to consider other activities as well. Ask students to ask and answer the question in pairs, encouraging them to expand their answers if they can. Elicit some responses.

Possible answer

I usually go to a beach with my family. We go swimming and eat ice cream.

I always stay with my aunt and uncle. They live on a farm.

I often play sports in the park with my friends.

> **extra**
>
> Direct students to the picture and introduce the idea of hobby-horsing.

2 Ask students to look at the title, opening lines and profile shots and picture without reading in detail yet. Elicit where the text is from.

Possible answer

an advert

> **exam** task: **A2 Key for Schools Reading and Writing Part 4**
>
> This is similar in format to one of the task options for the current A2 Key for Schools Reading and Writing Part 4 exam task, and for the 2020 onwards Key for Schools Reading and Writing Part 2 exam task, apart from the fact that there is an example in addition to the seven items.

3 Read the exam tip. Ask students to read the text then attempt the questions. If you need to, clarify *hobby horse* and *fence* using the picture, and *theme park* by reminding them of the one on page 49. Check as a class.

---

1 C Max (only one that mentions theme park)
2 A Milla (only one that mentions buying something – hobby horse)
3 B Charlie (We like unusual sports)
4 A Milla (not very good at ball sports like football and basketball)
5 B Charlie (We're going to go surfing)
6 C Max (grandparents)
7 B Charlie (summer camp)

> **extra: fast finishers**
>
> After they have rechecked their answers, ask fast finishers to write their own response post like Milla, Charlie and Mac did, which says what they think about hobby horsing and what they are going to do this summer. Ask them to read it for the class or share in pairs.

Sum up

4 Students should talk about what each of the three people are going to do. Elicit the answers.

Possible answers

Milla's going to try hobby-horsing

Charlie's going to go to a summer camp.

Max is going to visit his grandparents.

Speak up

5 Students work in pairs and discuss the plans. Conduct whole class feedback.

To finish

Tell students about some other unusual sports events in Finland. Ask: Which of these would you try?

Swamp soccer: You play football but in a swamp. It is very dirty!

Air guitar: People wear a costume and pretend to play a guitar to music.

Berry picking: Who can pick the most berries in an hour?

Mobile phone throwing: Who can throw a mobile the furthest?

As an extension, put students into small groups. Give each one an item from around the classroom. Give them five minutes to invent some sort of new sport competition using the item. They could come up with rules. Have each group present their idea to the class (this could be done as a poster / digital slides or online) and have students vote on which is the most fun or most unusual idea.

Presentation tool:	Unit 9, Reading
Workbook / Online Practice:	p81
Grammar reference:	SB p132
Extra Practice App	

GRAMMAR SB p98

To start

Ask students to look back at the text *Try something different* on page 97. Give students one minute to count the instances of the phrase *be going to* / *be not going to* in the text including the introduction, subheading and paragraph. Elicit how many there are (thirteen).

alternative

You may want to download the Grammar Presentation for this lesson from the Teacher Resources area of Pearson English Portal. This presentation has been created specifically for this lesson and is fully editable for teachers.

1 Get students to complete the sentences then check as a class.

1 to   **2** Are   **3** not   **4** going

explore grammar → SB p132

Get students to read the grammar box. For more detail, refer students to the Grammar reference *be going to* on page 132. Go through the notes with the class then set Ex 1–3 on page 133 for homework or in class.

watch out for ⓘ

Check that students are including the relative form of *be* in their sentences, e.g. *I'm going to try hobby horsing.*

2 Put students into pairs to read the conversation aloud first, taking turns to do each part (sentences 1,3,4 are said by one student, sentence 2 by the other). Then, give an example of how it can be changed (see below). Students make up their own similar conversation by changing a few words.

Possible answer
A: I'm going to go to the beach this summer.
B: Are you going by car to the beach?
A: No, I'm not. I'm going to go by bus.

3 9.4 Elicit how to complete the first gap as an example. Play the video/recording. Students complete the remaining gaps then compare their answers in pairs before checking as a class.

1 going to go   **2** going to bring   **3** going to do
4 going to visit

4 9.5 Go through the items in the box first. Tell students that they are going to watch/hear three people speaking about their summer plans. Play the video/recording again. Students should tick the things in the box they hear.

America
beach
water skiing

extra: whole class

Play the recording again, and ask students to make notes on where each speaker is going to go and what they are going to do. Students compare in pairs then conduct whole class feedback.

Answers:
A: Marbella, Spain. Chill by the pool or go to the beach with friends.
B: Greece. Go to the beach, go water skiing.
C: America. In New York, go to the Statue of Liberty. In Florida, go to Universal Studios theme park.

5 Ask: *Do you go on a summer camp? What do people usually do at summer camps?* Elicit ideas. Direct students to the chart. Ask: *How many activities is Tara going to do?* (four) *How many activities is her brother Fraser going to do?* (four) Ask students to complete the paragraph then compare in pairs before checking as a class.

Possible answers
1 going to go rock climbing   **2** going to go rock climbing
3 play baseball   **4** going to go surfing   **5** swimming
6 going to do dancing   **7** go cycling

6 Direct students to the example question. Demonstrate substituting another activity with *play baseball* to form a new question, e.g. *Is Fraser going to go swimming?* Remind students that they will need to select the correct verb *play* or *go* before each activity.

Possible answer
A: Is Tara going to go rock climbing?
B: Yes, she is.
A: Is Fraser going to go dancing?
B: Yes, he is.
A: Is Tara going to go surfing?
B: No, she isn't.

extra: fast finishers

Ask students to imagine that they are attending the same summer camp as Tara and Fraser. Without showing their partner, they need to choose four activities they are going to do from the list in Ex 3 and place a tick next to them (and a cross next to the two they aren't going to do). Students work in pairs to ask and answer questions about what they are going to do. e.g, A: *Are you going to go surfing?* B: *Yes, I am.*

7 Point out the example which is a question using the prompts in item 1. Ask students to write questions from the remaining prompts then ask their partner and take notes.

1 Are you going to visit your grandparents?
2 Are you going to play a lot of sport?
3 Are you going to go swimming?
4 Are you going to read some books?
5 Are you going to sleep a lot?
6 Are you going to meet your friends?
7 Are you going to watch a lot of TV?
8 Are you going to have fun?

GRAMMAR (Continued)

8 Ask each student to share something about their partner. The smaller your class, the more each student could share about their partner.

Possible answer

Jay is going to sleep a lot and he's going to read some books.

Speak up

9 Tell students something about your plans for summer as an example, e.g. say, *I'm going to visit my friend Mary in London.*

Possible answer

I'm going to go camping with my family. We're going to go swimming every day.

> **alternative**
>
> If another holiday is coming up soon, e.g. spring break, New Year, winter holidays, ask students to talk about their plans for that instead.

To finish

Ask students to complete at least three of the following sentences about future intentions. Put students into small groups to share their ideas.

Tomorrow, I'm going to …
Next week, I'm going to …
Next year, I'm going to …
When I'm fifteen, I'm going to …
When I'm twenty-one, I'm going to …

Presentation tool:	Unit 9, Grammar
Workbook / Online Practice:	p82
Grammar reference:	SB p132
Audioscript:	SB p149
Extra Practice App	

VOCABULARY 2 SB p99

To start

Play *Simon says* to review the parts of the body, include the new words *stomach* and *throat*.

health problems

1 Direct students to the pictures and ask them to match the words. Check the answers as a class. Drill the phrases.

1 D **2** H **3** E **4** F **5** C **6** G **7** A **8** B

explore **language**

Go through the language box with the class. Write up: *He's got a sore throat.* Demonstrate that you can change in other words for *throat*, e.g. *He's got a sore leg / toe / arm / finger / shoulder.*

> **watch out** for
>
> Check that students are comfortable pronouncing the words ending in *-ache* and *cough*.

2 9.6 Tell students that they are going to hear what is wrong with each person and they should write it down. Play the recording twice. Check answers by asking a question in the following form: *What's the matter with Nadia?*

1 has got a headache   **2** has got a sore throat
3 has got a temperature   **4** has got a cold
5 has got a cough

3 Students complete the nurse's notes. Check as a class.

1 sunburn   **2** a stomachache   **3** toothache

4 Get students to start by reading aloud the example conversation in pairs. Then get students to take turns to pretend that they have a health problem and use the questions in the example to ask and answer. Point out that if students travel to an English-speaking country in future, it's very useful to be able to say if they have a health problem.

Possible answer

A: Are you okay?
B: No, I'm not.
A: What's the matter?
B: I've got a sore throat and a headache.

> **extra:** mixed-ability classes
>
> To extend the activity for stronger students, suggest that they offer their partner some advice for the problem, e.g. *go and lie down. / Go and see the school nurse. / I'm going to make you a lemon drink.*

game on

Tell students to choose four of the bolded health problems from Ex 1 and write them down. Call out the health problems out of order (use the full phrase from Ex 1 for students to cross out).

alternative

Instead of saying the word, give a description so that students need to think quickly about which word to cross out, e.g. *I've been in the sun all day and now my face is red!* (sunburn). *I'm going to go to the dentist* (toothache).

Fun footer

Read through the footer with the class. Get students to think about what their own families do when they have some of these health problems. Ask: *What do you do in your family when you have a sore throat? What helps a cold? What about a headache?*

To finish

Tell the class that you are going to give them some words / phrases that rhyme with one of the health problems in the lesson. Write the following words / phrases on the board one at a time and get students to work out what health problem it rhymes with. When they guess correctly, write up the word next to its rhyme. Encourage students to practise saying the words.

off (cough)
gold (cold)
poor boat (sore throat)
red snake (headache)
truth cake (toothache)

Presentation tool:	Unit 9, Vocabulary 2
Workbook / Online Practice:	p83
Grammar reference:	SB p132
Audioscript:	SB p149
Extra Practice App	

LISTENING SB p100

To start

If possible, make a collage of pictures for your IWB/projector of famous sports people that your students are likely to know. Ask students to talk in pairs. Which people do they know? What sports do they play / do?

For a non-tech option, ask students to work in pairs to think of the three most famous sportspeople from their country in any sport (present or past). Conduct whole class feedback.

Power up

1 Ask students to ask and answer the questions in pairs. Conduct whole class feedback.

Possible answer
My favourite sportsperson is Serena Williams from the USA. She plays tennis.

Listen up

2 9.7 Get students to write down 1–4. Play the recording for students to write down two sports for each person.

Matt: swimming, running
Kate: dance, football
Beth: swimming, surfing
Dean: surfing, sailing

extra

Ask students to discuss the following question in pairs. *Do you watch or play the sports in Ex 2?*

exam task: A2 Key for Schools Listening Part 4

In the A2 Key for Schools Listening exam (Part 4, 2020 onwards), there are five items and the focus is on gist or the main idea. The extracts are not on the same topic, though here, these are all related to the topic of the unit.

3 **e** ◀)) 9.8 Read the exam tip aloud. Suggest that students put a mark next to the answer they think is the first time they listen, then choose their final answer the second time they listen. Encourage them to give their best guess if they aren't sure. Get students to read the questions first and highlight / underline key words. Then play the recording twice. Elicit the answers.

1 A (My dream is to open a gym.)
2 C (I think I'd like to be an ambulance driver.)
3 B (My dream is to go to the Olympics.)
4 A (My dream is to cycle round the country.)

explore grammar   → SB p132

Refer students to the Grammar reference on page 132. Go through the notes with the class and then set Ex 4–6 on page 133 to complete for homework or in class.

LISTENING (Continued)

---

watch out for

You may need to remind students of the spelling changes in -ing forms. Verbs that end with -e lose the e. Some, but not all, verbs which end in consonants take a double letter.

---

4 🔊 9.9 Get students to complete the conversation then play the recording for students to check their answers.

1 to do   **2** to be   **3** playing   **4** to play   **5** to work
6 to be   **7** talking   **8** playing   **9** watching

---

extra: whole class 👥

Divide the class in half to be Seb and Olivia. Play track 9.9 and get the students to try to read along aloud.

---

5 Students ask and answer the questions in pairs.

Possible answers

(What job do you want to do?) I want to be a dentist.
(Do you want to be a sportsperson?) I don't want to be a sportsperson.
(Do you like playing sports, too?) Yes, I do. I like playing tennis and going rock climbing.

6 Tell students that the dreams they write about could include what they want to do for a job, what activities they want to try in the future or where they want to travel to. Circulate while students write sentences about their dreams starting with *I want to ...* . Then put students into pairs to share their answers. Invite each student to briefly share what their partner said. If you have a very large class, put students into groups to share instead.

Possible answer

Sophie wants to be a wildlife photographer because she loves animals. She wants to travel to Africa. She wants to take photos of elephants and lions.

To finish

Students write three sentences about things they like/don't like/love, two should be true and one is not true. Students share in small groups and the other students have to guess which sentence is the lie.

Presentation tool:	Unit 9, Listening
Workbook / Online Practice:	p84
Photocopiable activity:	9B
Grammar reference:	SB p132
Audioscript:	SB pp149–150
Extra Practice App	

SPEAKING SB p101

To start

Say: *Imagine you won a holiday for your family somewhere in your own country. Where would you go? What would you do?* Put students in pairs to compare their ideas.

Power up

1 Get students to read both adverts and decide which activity they like best. Students compare their answers in pairs then conduct whole class feedback.

Possible answer

I like sailing best. / My favourite activity would be having dinner around a campfire.

Speak up

2 🔊 9.10 Play the recording then elicit the answer to the question.

No, they decide to go camping by the sea because the boy loves being near water.

3 Students plan their weekend of activities individually without showing anyone else. They can use ideas from their favourite advert or their own ideas.

Possible answer

Weekend plan
Saturday morning – go kayaking
Saturday afternoon – go sailing
Sunday morning – go water skiing
Sunday afternoon – go swimming and diving

Speaking extra

4 Read through the skill tip and the useful language box. Students talk about what they planned and negotiate a new plan for both of them.

Possible answer

A: What are we going to do on Saturday morning?
B: How about water skiing?
A: I'm not sure. I can't waterski. How about rock climbing?
B: Okay, let's go rock climbing on Saturday morning. What about sailing in the afternoon?
A: Yes, let's go sailing. Now, what are we going to do on Sunday?
B: I want to go kayaking. Do you want to go kayaking in the morning?
A: Okay, but I want to have a campfire. How about a campfire in the afternoon?
B: Great!

extra

Students design an advert for their own holiday experience similar to the ones in Ex 2.

To finish

Get students to work in small groups and take turns to choose a word from the unit so far to draw for the other students to guess. The student who guesses first draws the next picture.

Presentation tool:	Unit 9, Speaking
Workbook / Online Practice:	p85
Photocopiable activity:	9C
Grammar reference:	SB p132
Speaking file:	SB p142
Audioscript:	SB p150

WRITING SB pp102–103

To start

Write up the following words: *desert, rainforest, lake, volcano.* Ask students to discuss in pairs: *Which of these things do we have in this country? Where in the world could you see each thing?* Conduct whole class feedback.

Power up

1 Get students to decide where they would like to go then compare in pairs. Conduct whole class feedback.

Possible answer

I would like to go to a beach in Australia. I love the sea! I would like to try surfing.

2 Ask: *Do you often write postcards?* If students don't write postcards, or aren't familiar with them, you may need to bring some in or explain what they are and why they are written. Get students to read the postcard and answer the questions. Check as a class.

1 His grandparents 2 Colorado 3 Hi (hello) Love (goodbye)
4 Costa Rica

3 Get students to find the things on the postcard. This can be set along Ex 4 then check the answers to both.

1 2040 Mill Street, Denver, Colorado, USA
2 7 July
3 Jack (at the end)
4 Mr and Mrs Myers

4 Get students to find examples. Conduct whole class feedback.

1 We're having … We're seeing … (present continuous tense, general)
2 … we went / … we climbed (past tense)
3 Today we're walking through the rainforest. (present continuous tense, now)
4 … we're going to go swimming … I'm going to try white water rafting (*going to* for future plans)

Fun footer

Ask students to read the footer. Ask: *Do you collect anything? Postcards? Tickets? Bottles? Selfies? Something else?*

Plan on

5 Students can choose the place they suggested in Ex 1 or somewhere else. Students compare their answers in pairs.

Possible answer

I'm at Disneyland, Paris. I'm going on lots of rides.

6 Get students to plan their answer in the table.

Possible answers

where I am – Paris, France
what I did yesterday – arrived in Paris, went up the Eiffel Tower
what I'm doing today – rides at Disneyland, a parade
what I'm going to do – train to London

129

WRITING (Continued)

Write on

7 Go through the useful language box. Students could find a picture on the internet and print it if possible. Alternatively, students could type their postcard.

Possible answer

> Alaina Simons
> 76 View Drive
> Melbourne
> Australia

Hi Aunt Alaina,

I'm having a great time in Paris. Yesterday we went up the Eiffel Tower. Today we're at Disneyland Paris. The Space Mountain rollercoaster is the best ride! Tomorrow we're going to take the train to London.

See you soon,

Love,

Orla

Improve it

8 Read through the instructions with the class then get students to check they have used short forms.

To finish

Get students to place their postcards around the edge of the classroom. Students walk around to read the postcards. Ask students to read the postcards and find: 1 the person who travelled the furthest from home; 2 the person who had the most exciting holiday; 3 the person who had the most relaxing holiday. Conduct whole class feedback.

Presentation tool:	Unit 9, Writing
Workbook / Online Practice:	p86
Grammar reference:	SB p132
Writing file:	SB p142

SWITCH ON SB p103

Survival fun

1 Check students understand *team*. Elicit an example of a team activity, then put students into pairs to think of three more team activities, and discuss the question. Conduct whole class feedback.

Possible answer

Team activities: volleyball, football, English class games
I like playing sport in a team because I play with my friends.

---

extra: whole class

Tell students that they are going to watch a video about a survival school. Teach the word *survival*.

Write the following on the board:

days:
number of children:
children's ages:

Get students to copy these down and explain that they need to listen to answer these questions: *How many days is the school? How many children are there? How old are the children?* Tell students that each of the answers is a number. Play the first twenty seconds of the clip two to three times to see if students can get the answers (12, 10, 12–15).

---

2 ▶ Play the clip from 00:24 to 1:06. Elicit the bad news. Play the section again for students to note what is wrong with Callum, Abigail and Jasmine. Explain or elicit what a *twisted ankle* is.

The bad news is that some children are sick. (Callum has a stomachache. Abigail has a cold. Jasmine has twisted her ankle.)

3 ▶ Read through the questions with the class, and draw or show a picture of a *raft* to teach the word. Play the recording from 1:06 to the end for students to answer the questions. Get students to discuss their answers in pairs, then check as a class.

1 The challenges are to build a raft, get across a lake, and climb to safety. It's a race.
2 Three (There were five girls at school, but two girls are sick.)
3 The raft broke. (They didn't tie the knots well and their raft fell apart.)
4 The girls win the first challenge.

4 Students discuss the question in pairs. Conduct whole class feedback.

Possible answers

I would enjoy it because I like challenges.
I wouldn't enjoy it because it is cold and difficult.

Project

5 Get students to think about nature areas in their area or country which could be used for a survival school. Show some pictures of the areas to give students some inspiration, e.g. a beach, a forest, mountains. Go through the things to think about. Put students into pairs to plan their survival school challenges. Get students to show you their plan before moving on to Ex 6.

6 Students could present their ideas in a poster or video. If students make a video, encourage them to use space creatively, e.g. the trees by the school gate with clever framing could look like a forest, or filming with your hand over the camera so it's dark could be in a cave if you have voice over.

---

alternative

Survival list. Put students into groups of three. Tell them that they are going on an adventure experience in the mountains for three days and can only take what they are wearing now, and ten things. Brainstorm as a class two or three things they would take. Write these on the board. Get students to brainstorm more things in groups of three (they could use L1 if they don't have the language) – give them two minutes. After two minutes conduct open class feedback and write up their suggestions. For any words in L1, the teacher should ask students to try to describe the things, e.g. it's a small thing with a light. We use it to see in the dark = torch. Get students to decide together what they pack together. If they don't have the language, they can draw pictures or you can supply the vocabulary.

As an extension, say: *It's raining hard and half of your items are washed away. Which five items do you keep?* Students discuss in their groups for two minutes. Conduct whole class feedback.

Presentation tool:	Unit 9, Switch on
Switch on videoscript:	TB p141

UNIT CHECK SB p104

This Unit check covers health problems, sports and activities, likes / dislikes, and *be going to* for future plans.

Practice

1 Students can work individually or in pairs. Set a time limit and encourage students to come up with at least three words for each category. Elicit answers around the class and encourage students to share the different sports they play/do.

Possible answers

1 cold, cough, sore throat
2 baseball, cycling, tennis,
3 helmet, racket, skipping rope, surfboard

2 Student write sentences about the sports they like/ don't like.

---

alternative

Conduct a class mingle and ask students to walk around and find others with the same likes/dislikes as them. During feedback, elicit the most popular and least popular sports, and ask students to give reasons for their answers.

Possible answers

I like mountain biking. It's fun.
I don't like surfing. We don't live near the sea.
I like tennis. I play tennis on Fridays with my brother.

3 🔊 9.11 Play the recording twice for students to write the sentences. Then elicit the sentences and write them on the board.

1 I'm going to go camping this summer.
2 What's the matter? Have you got a headache?
3 I want to see the nurse.
4 We're going to play beach volleyball.

4 🔊 9.12 Play the recording for students complete the questions and answer them. Put students into pairs to ask and answer the questions.

1 going to teach
2 going to do
3 going to watch
4 going to go

Possible answers

1 Ms Grey is going to teach my next lesson.
2 I'm going to do it at four o'clock.
3 I'm not going to watch TV this evening.
4 I am going to go to my grandparent's home.

REVIEW: UNITS 7–9 SB p105

Vocabulary

1 **1** shoulders **2** shorts **3** take **4** baseball **5** wavy
6 cycling

2 **1** A **2** B **3** C **4** A **5** B **6** A

3 Things we do (verbs): give, build, see, learn, think, understand, walk, write.
Sports and activities: skiing, mountain biking, rock climbing, tennis, beach volleyball, skateboarding, photography, sailing

4 🔊 R3.1

1 left **2** went **3** found **4** saw **5** learnt **6** gave
7 said **8** made

5 **e** In the Movers Reading and Writing Part 1 task the keys are chosen from eight options with accompanying pictures. The options are all nouns.

1 artist **2** temperature **3** think **4** sunglasses
5 doctor / nurse

Grammar

1 **1** bigger **2** easiest **3** nice **4** better

2 🔊 R3.2
A Dora
B Anjit
C Oliver
F Holly

3 **Possible answers**
Chris painted a picture yesterday.
Laura went shopping yesterday.

4 **1** E **2** F **3** A **4** B **5** D **6** C

5 **e** In the Movers Reading and Writing Part 4 task, there is one example followed by 5 items.

In the current Cambridge English KEY for Schools Reading and Writing exam Part 5 task, there are no lexical items. There are eight items and one example. From 2020 onwards, the Cambridge English KEY for Schools Reading and Writing exam Part 3 task will have six items, as here, with a majority of lexical items.

1 B **2** C **3** A **4** C **5** A **6** B

6 **Possible answer**
Luis Scola, Marcos Delia and Patricio Garino are basketball players from Argentina. Marcos is older than Patricio, but Luis is the oldest. Marco is the tallest (2.10 m) and Patricio is the shortest (1.98 m). I think Luis Scola is the best.

GRAMMAR FILE SB p133

1 **1** You are going to go sailing.
2 I'm not going to go climbing.
3 They're going to play basketball.
4 Is he going to go swimming?
5 She isn't going to try hobby horsing
6 They are going to do yoga.

2 **1** Dan's going to play
2 We're going to talk
3 Are you going to go
4 You're going to go
5 We aren't going to go
6 Are your parents going to phone

3 Josh is going to play football.
Harry is going to play tennis.
Dave is going to play tennis.
Emma is going to do kung fu.
Pete is going to play baseball.
Cara is going to play basketball.
Jenny is going to go skiing.
Megan is going to go skiing.

4 **1** I love climbing.
2 My brother likes playing baseball.
3 My sister wants to be a dancer.
4 My mum and dad want to go to Mexico.
5 My cousin doesn't like rollerblading.
6 Our dog loves swimming in the sea.

5 **1** want to play **2** like playing **3** want to do **4** want to go
5 like doing **6** want to do

6 **A** 1, 2 or 4 **B** 1, 2 or 4 **C** 5 **D** 6

7 Student's own answers.

Presentation tool:	Unit 9, Unit check
Workbook / Online Practice:	pp87–89
Grammar reference:	SB p132
Audioscript:	SB p150
Extra Practice App	

Films and friends 10

READING
topic: film academy
task: multiple-choice cloze

LISTENING
topic: making a film
task: multiple-choice (dialogue)

SPEAKING
topic: different types of films
task: exchange opinions

WRITING
topic: favourite films
task: write a review

Lead-in

Introduce the unit title *Review: films and friends*. If you can, find and show some pictures of recent films for the students' age group. Ask students to discuss in pairs whether they have seen any of the films, and if they have seen any films recently. Conduct whole class feedback.

Direct students to the photo and use it to teach *animation* by asking: Do you think this is real? (No.) How can we include things in a photo that are not real?

Then direct their attention to the quote (*There are a lot of ideas in my head*) and get them to discuss it in pairs. Elicit some ideas about what they think it means.

1 Ask students to discuss the question in pairs. Elicit answers from around the class and find out how many students have the same favourite animation film, and what it is. Encourage students to give reasons for their answer.

Possible answer

My favourite animation films are the *How to train your dragon* series. The animations are fantastic!

2 Give students one minute to think of a good idea for a film, if they don't already have one in mind. Students share their idea in pairs, saying what type of film it is, e.g. animation, sci-fi, and what it is about.

My idea is to make a film about finding treasure in caves near our town.

READING SB p108

To start

Write on the board: *Do you want to be a … ?*

ctodor
ramfre
regsin
uilbred
flim-kamer

Ask students to work in pairs to unscramble the words for jobs. Then ask and answer the question in pairs.

Answers: doctor, farmer, singer, builder, film-maker. For further review of jobs, students could review Ex 2 on page 76.

Power up

1 Start by eliciting the kinds of films students like and why (funny films, animal films, animated films, etc).

> **Possible answer**
> I like science fiction films because I like seeing aliens.

2 Direct students to the advert on page 109. Ask students to work in pairs to describe what the people are doing.

> **Possible answer**
> In the animation film, the people are holding a clay figure near a video camera.
> In the action film, they are filming a mountain biker doing tricks.

alternative

Write the following prompts on the board and get students to work in pairs to make sentences about each picture on page 109.

The person is using a large / small camera.
The person is filming clay figures / a person on a bike.
The person is making an action / animation film.
It is outside / inside.

Read on

3 Students read the advert and answer the questions. Encourage students to try and find the information even if they don't understand every word of the text. To revise the present simple in more detail, refer to the Unit 2 Grammar reference on the present simple on page 118. If your students haven't already completed the Grammar reference exercises on page 119, you could set them in class or for homework.

> **1** animation or action movies **2** $100
> **3** there's a big party and you get a certificate
> **4** present simple because it happens every summer

extra: whole class

List the following words and phrases on the board and ask students to find and underline / highlight them in the text: 1 film-maker, 2 certificate, 3 stop frame animation, 4 tricks 5 opinion, 6 make up Write up the following definitions and ask students to match the words to the definitions. Check as a class.

A your ideas about something
B a person who makes films
C taking photos of objects and moving them a little bit before each photo then playing the photos in a series to make a film
D actors put this on their faces
E a paper which says a person completed a course
F special tips for doing something well

Answers:
A opinion   D make up
B film-maker   E certificate
C stop frame animation   F tricks

exam task: Multiple-choice Cloze

4 Students complete the cloze activity then compare their answers in pairs before checking as a class. Remind students that with multiple choice activities, it is best to answer every question even if they are not sure. They sometimes may be able to eliminate one answer, then choose a best guess from the other two options.

> **1** B **2** C **3** B **4** A **5** B **6** C **7** B **8** A

Sum up

5 In pairs, encourage students to think of at least three differences and three similarities.

> **Possible answer**
> Differences: The action film course is difficult but the animation course isn't.
> In the animation course, students make their film in two days, but in the action course, they have three days.
> In the action film course, students learn about acting, costumes and make up. In the animation course, students use Lego or clay figures. They don't learn about costumes or make up.
> Similarities: Both courses are one week long. Both courses cost $100. Students enjoy both courses.
> There is a party for both courses and students show their films.

extra: mixed-ability classes

To support weaker students, point out that similarities can be found in the introduction paragraph. Differences can be found in the sections on the courses.

6 Put students into pairs. Elicit the word from the grammar quiz that fits 1–4. Then get students to find four examples in the advert. Remind students that in the present simple the third person singular has an -s.

1 present simple
2 regular activities
3 often
4 do/does

Four more examples of this tense on this page: happens, do you pay, learn, join

Speak up

7 Ask each student to tell their partner which course they would prefer to do. Conduct whole class feedback and ask students to give reasons for their choices.

Possible answers

I want to do the animation course because it is easier.
I want to do the action film course because I think it is the best. I like acting and costumes.

To finish

Choose two short videos from the internet to show, e.g. two that use stop animation. Ask students to watch the videos and note down three similarities and three differences. Which did they like most? Why? Conduct whole class feedback.

Alternatively, ask students to select two films or TV programmes that they both know well or have seen recently. They should think of three similarities and three differences, then decide which is the better programme and why.

extra: project

As a project, ask students to plan and make a short film in pairs or groups. You could put some links to stop frame animation examples off the internet for students to watch at home, and come up with some ideas for their own film. Then in class, students work together to plan using a storyboard (a *set* of *drawings* like a comic that are done before a *film* is made in order to show what will *happen* in it) and a script. This could be done over a period of several days, and students could be encouraged to bring in costumes, etc. if they want to. If time allows, students could make their film then show them to the class.

Presentation tool:	Unit 10, Reading
Workbook / Online Practice:	pp90–91

LISTENING SB p110

To start

Write up the following prompts and ask students to finish the sentences with a partner about right now. Some students may want to turn to page 89 to review clothes vocabulary for the first prompt.

I'm wearing …
I'm thinking about …
I'm feeling …

Alternatively, make it a quiz. e.g. I'm thinking about (a) English (b) what I'm going to do after school (c) lunch (d) other. I'm feeling (a) fine (b) tired (c) hungry (d) other.

Power up

1 Put students into pairs to describe what people are doing and saying. Conduct whole class feedback.

Possible answer

In picture A, the people are watching a film. They are sitting outside. I don't think they are saying anything.
In picture B, there are five people. They are dancing. I think they are at a party. Maybe this woman is saying 'Let's dance!'

2 Ask students to match the words with sentences in the grammar quiz, then check as a class. For a more detailed review of present continuous, refer students to the Grammar reference on page 124, and ask students to complete any of the exercises on page 125 which they haven't done yet.

1 present continuous
2 things that are happening now
3 now
4 is/are

Possible answers
(Four more examples of this tense on the page):
Where <u>is</u> the kung fu group <u>filming</u>? How many people <u>are dancing</u> in the *Sunny Day* film? Who <u>is making</u> an animation? <u>Are</u> you <u>taking</u> photos?
1
Interviewer: Are you making a new film?
Henry: Yes, **I am**.
2
Interviewer: Is your sister acting in the film?
Henry: Yes, **she is**.
3
Interviewer: Are your parents helping you?
Henry: No, **they aren't**.
4
Interviewer: Are you enjoying it?
Henry: Yes, **I am**.

LISTENING 1 (Continued)

Listen up

3 🔊 10.2 Play the recording for students work out which conversations the photos relate to. Elicit the answers.

    Picture A: 5
    Picture B: 3

---

exam task: A2 Key for Schools Listening Part 3

This is similar in format to the A2 Key for Schools Listening Part 3 task from 2020 onwards, but in the exam, feelings and opinions will also be tested. In the current A2 Key for Schools Listening Part 3 exam task, there is an example.

4 🅴 🔊 10.3 Get students to read the questions. Then play the recording. Finally go through the answers as a class.

  1 B (The courses started on Wednesday.)
  2 C (They're making a kung fu film on the stairs.)
  3 B (There are fourteen dancers.)
  4 A (Robert's making an animation.)
  5 C (The show starts in thirty minutes, at 2.45 p.m.)

---

game on

Demonstrate the game by doing one of the actions and have students guess using the example structure, e.g. *Are you drinking water?* (*Yes, I am*).

Write up a few more actions on the board to include in the game: have a shower, read a book, shout, talk to a friend. To extend the game, students could play in groups and select some of their own actions, e.g. *playing volleyball, making an animation, taking the bus.* etc.

---

alternative ⇅

In groups students write up possible actions on post-it notes. Collects them and play charades with the class. Divide the class in half and have one student from each team come up to pick a post it and mime the action. The first team to guess what their team member is doing gets a point.

To finish

If the classroom overlooks the street, get students to look out of the window and say what people are doing. Alternatively, show a video (e.g. Mr Bean) and get students to call out or write down what he's doing. Another alternative is to re-use the set of pictures on page 127. Ask students to work in pairs and say what the boy is doing in each picture, e.g. *He is looking at a dinosaur at the museum. He is watching TV. He is listening to music. He is asking a question. He is talking on the phonew*

Presentation tool:	Unit 10, Listening
Workbook / Online Practice:	p92
Audioscript:	SB p150

SPEAKING SB p111

To start

See if students can remember any adverbs of frequency (e.g. sometimes, never, always, often). Replay track 3.5 and ask students to write down the adverbs they hear. Play again, pausing after each sentence and have students call out the adverb they heard.

Power up

1 Go through the rubric and example with the class. Ask students to write their own sentence then share it with a partner.

Possible answer

I often watch films at the cinema. I sometimes watch films at home too, but I usually watch TV.

2 Direct students to the questions in Ex 4 and 5 on that page, then work in pairs to answer the questions in the grammar quiz. Make it clear that they are doing the grammar quiz not answering the questions in Ex 4 and 5.

  1 A **2** A

Speak up

3 See how many of the words students can match, then go through the answers as a class. Point out that some films fit more than one category, e.g. *dance film, animated film, scary film.*

  A action film **B** science fiction film **C** sport film
  D superhero film **E** family film **F** animal film

4 Tell students what your favourite kind of film is (from the list in Ex 2), then give an example that they can relate to, e.g. *I like action adventure films like Star Wars.* Point out how *like* in this case is a word to introduce an example. If students want to, they could use other words they know to describe a film type, e.g. *dance film, scary film.*

Possible answer

I like funny films like *Paddington*.

5 🔊 10.4 Go through the instructions. Play the recording once for students to tick the questions, then a second time for students to tick the pictures talked about. Check as a class.

We hear question 2 *Do you like superhero films?* and question 3 *Why do you like sport films?*
They talk about photos D and C.

6 🅴 Put students in pairs to ask and answer the questions in Ex 5.

Possible answers

  1 Yes, they are usually interesting.
  2 Yes, I do.
  3 I like sports films because I like sports.
  4 I have watched ten films this year.

7 Ask students to work in pairs and write at least three questions using the words in the box. Circulate checking question forms. Students swap partners to ask and answer their questions.

Possible answers

A: Do you think animal films are great?
B: Yes, I do. I love animal films!

B: Do you think action adventure films are boring?
A: No, I think they're interesting.

A: Do you think cartoons are good?
B: Sometimes.

---

extra: mixed-ability classes

Brainstorm some questions as a class and write these on the board for use during the activity. Students can choose to ask the questions from the board as they are, or ask their own similar questions as they go, using the questions as a model.

Speaking extra

8 In pairs, tell students to work through the list of types of film from Ex 2, giving their opinions about each one. Conduct whole class feedback.

Possible answer

I love action adventure films because they are interesting. My favourite film is *A Wrinkle in Time*.

I usually like animal films because I love animals. I like *Happy Feet*. It's about a special penguin.

I don't often like cartoon films like *Cars*. I think they are boring, but my brother loves them!

I like family films because I can watch them with my family. They're fun! We like the *Harry Potter* films.

I love funny films like *Mr Bean* because I like laughing.

I don't usually like sport films. I think they're boring.

---

game on

Put students into groups of three or four. Encourage students to choose a famous moment from a film that most students have seen. As an alternative, they could act out a ten-second piece of the film. Give students a few minutes to prepare then take turns to present to the class for the other students to guess.

To finish

List the adjectives from Ex 5 in one column on the board: *boring, fun, good, great, interesting.* In a second column list some nouns: *job, animal, activity, subject, food.*

Ask students to work in pairs. Students take turns to choose one adjective and one noun for their partner, e.g. *fun activity.* Their partner needs to think of something that is a fun activity.

Presentation tool:	Unit 10, Speakng
Workbook / Online Practice:	p93
Audioscript:	SB p150

WRITING SB pp112–113

To start

Write the following riddle on the board, preferably in a spot where you can leave it displayed for the lesson. Alternatively, write it up line by line during the activity.

You went for a walk in a forest.
You didn't see it but you got it.
You didn't like it but you wanted to find it.
You went home with it because you didn't find it.
What was it?

Get students to work in pairs to look at the riddle line by line, checking they understand the meaning.it is a riddle and that the it throughout the riddle refers to something that they need to guess. Elicit guesses (students can guess in L1). If students don't guess it at this point, leave it on the board for fast finishers to come back to, and reveal the answer at the end of the class (answer: a splinter).

Whether students have guessed the answer or not, ask students to work in pairs to identify and write down any instances of the past simple tense they can see (went, didn't see it, got, didn't like, wanted, went, didn't find, was.) Get a student to come and underline the past simple forms on the board. Elicit the base verb form of *went* (go), *got* (get), *was* (be).

Power up

1 Elicit how the first question could be completed and write this on the board. Students complete the remaining questions then elicit some possible answers.

Possible answer
What did you **see**?
Who did you **go with**?
Where did you **go**?
Was it **good**?

2 Tell students that they should imagine that they went to the cinema at the weekend. They should think about how they would answer their questions with imagined answers. Then have students ask and answer in pairs.

Possible answer
(What did you see?) I saw *Coco.* It's an animated film.
(Who did you go with?) I went with my cousin.
(Where did you go?) We went to the Gold Cinema in the shopping centre.
(Was it good?) Yes, it was great! We loved it!

WRITING (Continued)

3 Direct students to the two reviews. Ask students to read the reviews and decide which they would rather see. Ask for a show of hands of who prefers each one. Elicit some reasons.

Possible answers

I want to watch *The Last Jedi* because it is exciting.
I want to watch *Coco* because it has a good story.

---

exam task: **Open Cloze**

In all the Cambridge English exams, this task type is a continuous text. In the Cambridge English A2 Key for Schools Reading and Writing Part 6 exam task (2020 onwards), there are six items, as here. In the current A2 Key for Schools Listening Part 7 exam task, there are ten items and one example. In the A2 Flyers Reading and Writing Part 6 exam task, there is one example and five items.

4 **e** Go through the example with the class, then students complete the cloze. Check as a class. Get stronger students to explain why each of these is the correct answer by highlighting relevant parts of the text.

1 the **2** it/this **3** but **4** his **5** we **6** was

---

5 Ask students to complete the grammar quiz then conduct whole class feedback. To revise the past simple in more detail, refer students to the Grammar reference on page 126.

Possible answer

1 past simple
2 things that happened in the past
3 yesterday
4 did
Four more examples of this tense on this page: loved, watched, enjoyed, laughed

Plan on

6 Students plan individually then compare their plans in pairs.

Possible answer

(What film did you see?) Jumanji: Welcome to the jungle.
(Add more details: Where?) home
(When?) Saturday
(Who with?) my family
(What is the film about?) action adventure film. Four young people are in a video game. It's a jungle.
(What happened?) They must win the game and escape.
(Opinion: was it a good film?) Yes. It was exciting and scary.

---

extra: mixed-ability classes

Don't limit stronger students to 30 words. They can write more if they want to!

Write on

7 **e** Students write their review. Circulate to provide assistance as required.

Possible answers

On Saturday I watched *Jumanji: Welcome to the Jungle* with my family. It's about four people in a video game. They must win the game and escape. It was exciting, but also scary!

Improve it

8 Elicit some things that students should check for, e.g. capital letters, full stops, check verb tense, have they included all the relevant information? Write these items on the board for students to use as they check their work.

9 Students could take turns to read their reviews. Keep a tally on the board of which films were chosen.

---

extra: digital

If you have an online class space, after editing their reviews, students could upload their answers in a forum post (with photos) to be able to read each other's reviews.

To finish

Ask students to work in pairs to think of any questions they have about English or the exam they are preparing for. Give students sticky notes or small pieces of paper, or do this in a collaborative online space. Collect in the questions. Ask each question to the class first and give them the opportunity to answer before you do.

---

extra: whole class

Consider planning a small celebration to mark the completion the course. For example, choose an appropriate English film to watch (with subtitles) in class, or repeat some of the games from the course for revision.

Presentation tool:	Unit 10, Writing
Workbook / Online Practice:	pp94–95

SWITCH ON VIDEOSCRIPTS

Unit 1

Narrator: Annabel is 18. She is a popular youtuber who vlogs about her tiny house. It's small, but it's hers and she loves it.

Annabel: Hey guys! So … welcome to my tiny house. My name is Annabel.

Narrator: Downstairs, there's a living room, … a bathroom and a kitchen. The kitchen is small but she can cook there, and make tea.

Annabel: I have knives here, I have cups up there.

Narrator: This is her living and dining room space. Her sofa is big for such a small house! Right next to the door, there are some shelves. She doesn't have a lot of space …, which means she only has things she really needs, like food, blankets and clothes.

Annabel: I have my clothes and all the clothes that you see is all the clothes that I have.

Narrator: These unusual stairs are a present from a Youtube friend.

Annabel: Thank you, thank you, thank you.

Narrator: There is one room upstairs: she calls it the loft.

Annabel: That's mainly it. I have this window here, I have that window there. This one opens, that one doesn't.

Narrator: Annabel reads, watches TV, and spends time taking photos, and making vlogs.

Annabel: Part of why I want to build a tiny house was to really only keep what I really wanted, what I really needed, what brought me happiness, what made me feel good I guess.

Narrator: In a small house you have very little space. So you choose the things that make you feel at home, the things that make you happy.

Unit 2

Narrator: In China, a lot of children want to be Kung Fu actors. They go to special schools. At the Shaolin Tagou School, there are thousands of boys and girls. They come from all over China. They have school lessons and kung fu training. They run, jump, kick and fight.

Narrator: One of the students is Qiao Tian Tian. She's sixteen years old. The school day is long. The students work from five in the morning to nine thirty at night – six days a week.

Tian Tian: We get one day off each week on a Sunday. But we can't go outside. We can only stay in the campus. We usually chat together, play cards or watch TV.

Narrator: In the morning, TianTian has normal lessons: maths, science and geography. And in the afternoon and evening she has kung fu training. She knows her lessons are important. She often goes to the school library because she loves reading.

Tian Tian: I like to read articles about true people and real-life stories. I like to read the *Reader's Digest* in my spare time. My dream is to become a kung fu actress in the future.

Narrator: TianTian often looks at the kung fu medals in the school. Her favourite Kung Fu actor is Jackie Chan. Who's the girl with the sword? It's TianTian!

Narrator: Kung Fu, of course, is a martial art. Some Kung Fu training is like dancing. It's very beautiful.

Unit 3

Narrator: These pandas are in a panda sanctuary. At the sanctuary, people take care of baby pandas. When the pandas get big … they move from the sanctuary and live in the mountains. At the sanctuary the young pandas drink milk. Panda mums clean the babies. And people weigh all the pandas …

Presenter: One point three. Very good. One point three kilos. That's very good.

Narrator: … To make sure they are all growing well.

Narrator: The babies usually go to bed at the same time. Sometimes it takes time to feel sleepy. Finally, they feel tired … and fall asleep.

Narrator: These pandas are a little older. They are good friends. Today they are having carrots for lunch.

Presenter: Oh you are absolutely gorgeous. So much bigger than the little ones. Do you want some carrot? No more. No more carrots. No, you can't have any more. You can't! Yes I know …

Narrator: Pandas need to move about … so chasing for carrots is good exercise.

Presenter: Come on poppet. You've got to move around a bit. I've taken a panda for a walk. This is crazy!

Narrator: They play with the helpers at the sanctuary. And they play with each other. When they play, they learn how to fight. And they often fall. It is important to learn to climb trees, too. The pandas here learn lots … and they grow fast. One day, they will be ready to leave the sanctuary … and go to live in the mountain forests of China.

Unit 4

Narrator: The journey to school. We all know it. Most of us don't really think about it. It's easy, it's comfortable, it's fast. But not for everyone … Some children travel for hours … in all kinds of weather, … to get to their schools.

Narrator: Monday. Half past five in the morning. A Rarámuri home in the Mexican Sierra. School starts at 9 o'clock. Teresa, Ángela and Filomena are almost ready. They go to school in the nearest village. It is two hours away on foot. Their journey to school is so difficult, they stay there all week and only come home on Friday.

Narrator: Vidal also takes two hours to get to school. And he does it every day. He gets there on a boat he made himself. Vidal lives with his family on a floating island on Lake Titicaca, in Peru.

Narrator: On the other side of the world, Sayana is just about to leave the house. She lives in Oymyakon, a small town in Siberia. It's the coldest village in the world. For Sayana, the cold is what makes her journey to school so difficult. It is minus fifty degrees outside. Sayana and her brother and sister walk one kilometre to the bus stop. There, they wait. But in this extreme cold, the road is dangerous for the school bus. Today, it's stuck in the snow.

Narrator: On lake Titicaca, Vidal is far from home now. He has to be careful. It's very windy. And it's easy to get lost. But Vidal knows the lake well: he does this twice a day. Once on his way to school, and once more on his way home.

Narrator: Teresa, Ángela and Filomena stop for a drink of water. They are near the school now, but first they must climb 300 metres on a very difficult path.

Narrator: Back in Siberia, Sayana is nervous. The bus is 15 minutes late. Finally, the bus arrives … and Sayana can get warm.

Narrator: After long and difficult journeys, all the children get to school. They are happy to see their friends, … and happy to start their classes.

Unit 5

Narrator: Welcome to the Ice Cream Museum: a very special kind of museum. At the Ice Cream Museum you don't *learn* about ice cream … you will leave having learned nothing about ice cream … but there is a lot to see and do.

Narrator: You can taste some ice cream. You can play on a swing. Or use the whipped cream cans to play a game. You can eat sweets and take photos of giant gummy bears.

Reporter: You can get lost in bananas and you can go swimming in a sprinkle-filled swimming pool. So it's the kind of thing you put on Instagram and your friends say 'What's that?' and they want to go check it out.

Visitor (Emily): You have to go for a swim in the sprinkle pool – a swimming pool full of sugar sprinkles, everyone loves it! They just have so many fun ideas. Who would have thought of a sprinkle pool but it's like the most popular attraction here and it's really fun.

Staff member: Welcome, would you like some mochi?

Narrator: Have another snack, and take another photo!

Visitor (Emily): I'm going to post the photos on Instagram and I really like this museum because of the colour theme. It's all like pink and pastel colours and the ice cream is actually really good.

Narrator: Before you leave, have a little more ice cream. This time, try peach!

Narrator: This museum is definitely fun and delicious. But is it really a museum, or something else?

Unit 6

Narrator: In the American TV series *Frontier House*, three families travelled back to 1883 . The Clune family moved from their home in California to a log cabin. Life was very different!

Narrator: The two girls, Aine, and her cousin Tracy, worked in the field … while Aine's brother, Justin, was busy with their father.

Narrator: Erinn Patton was on her family's farm too. She worked with the cows … and she was happy. Her brother Logan looked after animals and carried water. His life back home was very different!

Logan: My only friend here is work!

Narrator: In the 1880s, life in the countryside wasn't easy. Farm animals and sharp tools were dangerous. And wild animals were dangerous, too …! Like bears.

Tracy: I see it. I see it. I see it!

Narrator: In the 1880s, some teachers were very young – only 15 or 16. They often lived in the school. There were some books but there wasn't a library. All the students were in one classroom. They were at school for five months of the year. But a lot of children didn't go to school – they stayed on the farms. They worked and helped their parents.

Unit 7

Narrator: This is Zion. Zion is an eight year-old skateboarder.

Zion: My full name is Zion Gabriel Effs and I love skateboarding because it's the best thing in the world.

Narrator: Zion practises skateboarding all the time.

Zion: I skate all day every day wherever I go.

Narrator: Zion may only be eight years old, but he has already been skateboarding for five years! When Zion was three years old, his dad, Richie took him to a skate-park. At the skatepark they met a professional skate-boarder called Danny Fuenzalida.

Danny: They showed up at Grand Central, it was a public skatepark. And Richie came up and he was looking for someone to help teach his son to skate. I was like 'Man, this kid's awesome.' Like, I told him, I was like, 'if you ever want I'll do a class with you no problem.' I taught him for, like, two and a half years. And now we're just skate-buddies.

Narrator: Danny was Zion's teacher for a while. But now Zion is so good, he doesn't need lessons anymore. So Danny and Zion are just 'skate-buddies'. They skate together for fun – and try out new tricks.

Zion: My favourite thing about skateboarding is I get to learn new tricks all the time. I get to do them, perfect them and be happy when I land them.

Narrator: Zion wins **a lot of** skateboard competitions.

Zion: This year I've won like four competitions in a row. Sometimes I'll just like skate competitions for fun but I usually want to win.

Narrator: Zion has five brothers and sisters – and his youngest brother, Jax, also loves skateboarding. Jax is only *two* years old! The boys skateboard everywhere – even in the house!

Narrator: Richie thinks his sons' skateboarding is a good thing, because it means they are doing an outdoor activity.

Richie: Nowadays, most kids are not doing anything outdoors. Most kids are sitting inside on a computer on their phone.

Narrator: And Danny thinks that, if Zion continues to practise, one day his hobby might also be his full-time job!

Danny: I have no doubt in my mind that Zion will be a professional if he continues skating.

Narrator: But Zion is only eight years old, so he doesn't think much about the future. He just loves to skate!

Unit 8

Narrator: This is the Van Nes family. They are *famous* for one *big* thing. They are the *tallest* family in Britain! Miriam is 5 feet 11 inches tall. Her husband Frank is even taller: 6 feet 10 inches! Being tall runs in the family.

Frank: My grandparents were tall. My parents weren't that tall. But it was pretty obvious that Miriam and I were gonna have tall kids.

Narrator: The Van Nes children … Naomi, Franklin, Lucas, and Vincent … are all much taller than their friends. Sometimes people watch as they walk by: you don't see a family as tall as this every day! But with a family this big, how do you find a house the right size? … You build one.

Narrator: Everything here is bigger! And every room in the house is higher, from the bedrooms to the kitchen.

Frank: Normal kitchens are about 4 inch lower.

Narrator: The kitchen *has* to be big. From cereal, to milk … and bananas, … the family eat a *lot*.

Vincent: I usually have to eat every hour, at least.

Narrator: They have to buy food twice a week! The family's clothes are bigger too.

Miriam: Here's some jeans. They're quite long, as you can see.

Narrator: Finding good clothes can be hard when you're tall.

Naomi: It is hard to find clothes which are for my age and my height, 'cause, like, there's not very many people who are the same height as me, and 11.

Narrator: Everyone has something that makes them different: taller, smaller, good at a sport, or mad about gaming. Whatever it is, finding other people who are like you is great – and it's even better if you're in the same family!

Unit 9

Narrator: It's an exciting new day at *survival school* … A 12-day challenge: ten children between the ages of 12 and 15 have to survive in nature. For 12 days, they are going to have no mobile phones, no home-cooked food and no warm beds to sleep in. But they do have all the ingredients for a fun adventure.

Narrator: It's day seven at survival school and time for a new challenge. But after a rainy night, they wake up to a wet morning and some bad news. Two of the team members are ill. Callum has a stomachache and was sick during the night. Abigail has a cold. Also, Jasmine has twisted her ankle. The three of them will have to stay at camp if they want to get better. The rest of the team are not happy about the news.

Rubie: We are all tired and sad.

Narrator: But breakfast is over and it's time to go.

Leader: OK guys, ready to move?

Children: Yes

Leader: We move fast today 'cause it's wet and cold, come on, let's go.

Narrator: Facing the new challenge without their friends will be hard. But the team is ready and on their way. Today they are going to build a raft, … get across a lake … and climb up to safe ground. They are going to do it in two teams, boys against girls. Let the competition begin!

Children: Go! Come on! Run!

Narrator: With two girls ill, there are only three in the girls team.

The four boys grab most of the plastic barrels, which they need for the raft to float.

Girl: Those boys are selfish. Lauren!

Lauren: Yes.

Girl: Come now, we need to start building it, the boys are ahead of us! This is, like, for the middle, and these four are for, like, the four corners.

Narrator: Time is up and the race begins. But the boys didn't tie the knots very well, and their raft quickly falls apart. They have to swim to the other side … in the cold water.

Leader: Hold on team!

Narrator: The girls are first, winning the first part of the competition.

Girl: We did it guys, we're all done! High five!

Narrator: The boys are tired and wet, but they get to the other side too. Now, one boy and one girl must face the second part of the challenge. Jamie … and Lauren … are going to climb up the 15-metre ladder. The winner gets a point for their team. This time, Jamie is first.

Lauren: Oh, my arms! Oh!

Narrator: The day did not start well. But after some team fun, the boys and girls are happy … and ready for whatever comes next.

WORKBOOK ANSWER KEY

STARTER

p4

1 1 C (The verb 'to be' is used in the question, the short answer must contain 'be' and be in first person, e.g. Yes, I am.)

2 A (The question asks 'What's your name?' so the answer must be in the first person.)

3 B (The answer must contain a number and the verb 'be' to reflect the question 'How old are you?')

4 A (The answer needs to be an opinion. 'Not really' is a fixed expression to someone asking about your likes/dislikes.)

5 B (The answer needs to be a sport.)

6 C (The answer 'He's twelve' means that the question must about age. Tom is a boy, so 'he', not 'she'.)

2 **A** one   **B** six   **C** two   **D** seven   **E** three   **F** eight   **G** four   **H** nine   **I** five   **J** ten

3 Across: 1 basketball   **2** music   **3** cat
Down: 4 Mexican   **5** maths   **6** yellow

4 1 It is Daniel's ruler. ('It' requires a singular verb (is). The ruler belongs to Daniel – the apostrophe is added after his name.)

2 They are my family's dogs. ('They' requires a plural verb (are). The dogs belong to the family – the apostrophe is added after 'family'.)

3 She is my mum's sister. ('She' requires a singular verb (is). The woman is related to mum – the apostrophe is added after 'mum'.)

4 They are Josef's books. ('They' requires a plural verb (are). The books belong to Josef – the apostrophe is added after his name.)

5 It is my cousin's pen. ('It' requires a singular verb (is). The pen belongs to the person's cousin – the apostrophe is added after 'cousin'.)

6 He is my best friend's dad. ('He' requires a singular verb (is). The dad is related to the best friend– the apostrophe is added after 'best friend'.)

7 They are Molly's friends ('They' requires a plural verb (are). The friends belong to Molly– the apostrophe is added after 'Molly'.)

8 It is Sam's favourite colour. ('It' requires a singular verb (is). The favourite colour relates to Sam – the apostrophe is added after 'Sam'.)

p5

5

male	female	male or female
brother	mother	parent
grandad	sister	cousin
dad	grandma	grandparent
v	aunt	

6 Lily   grandma, 65
Tim   dad, 38
Ellen   mum, 34
Fluffy   cat, 13
Alex   brother, 14
Jenny   cousin, 11
Jill   aunt, 41
Charlie uncle, 49

7 1 Our (The whole family have the same surname so the possessive adjective must be plural and include the writer (first person).)

2 My (The possessive adjective refers to the writer (first person singular).)

3 Her (The possessive adjective refers to a woman (Lily), third person singular.)

4 Its (The possessive adjective refers to an animal and we don't know its gender.)

5 His (The possessive adjective refers to a boy (Alex), third person singular.)

6 Their (The possessive adjective refers to two people (Tim and Ellen), third person plural.)

7 His (The possessive adjective refers to a man, third person singular.)

8 1 The boy's cat is (very) old. (The verb 'isn't' needs to be changed to the positive.)

2 His parents aren't from Manchester./His parents are from London. (The verb 'are' needs to be changed to the negative.)

3 Mike's aunt is forty-one. (The verb 'is' needs to be changed to the negative.)

4 Jill isn't his uncle./ Jill is aunt. (The verb 'isn't' needs to be changed to the positive.)

5 Charlie and Jill are parents. (The verb 'aren't' needs to be changed to the positive.)

9 1 twenty-four (It is a list of consecutive numbers. 24 is next.)

2 forty (It is a list of consecutive numbers. 40 is next.)

3 sixty-nine (It is a list of odd numbers (counting in twos). 69 is next.)

4 fifteen (The numbers are in decreasing order. 15 is next.)

5 eighty-six (It is a list of even numbers (counting in twos). 86 is next.)

6 one hundred (The numbers go up in fives. 100 is next.)

10 1 are   2 is   3 are   4 is   5 are   6 are
Student's own answers.

p6

3 1 Edward   2 1st February (01/02)   3 Cheshire, England   4 Gemma   5 step-brother   6 White   7 Manchester

4 1 Is, it is ('pop music' is singular so the verb 'is' must be used. The prompt 'Yes' is given so the verb in the answer must be positive. The pronoun 'it' replaces 'pop music' (a thing, third person) (it is)

2 Are, I'm not (the question is directed to another person (you), so the verb must be second person of 'be' and the answer in the first person. The prompt 'No' is given so the verb in the answer must be negative (I'm not).)

3 Is, he is ('Harry' is singular, third person, so the verb 'is' must be used.
The prompt 'Yes' is given so the verb in the answers must be positive. The pronoun 'he' replaces 'Harry' (a man, third person masculine) (he is).)

4 Is, she is ('Gemma' is singular, third person, so the verb 'is' must be used.
The prompt 'Yes' is given so the verb in the answer must be positive. The pronoun 'she' replaces 'Gemma' (a woman, third person feminine) (she is).)

5 Are, they aren't (the question is about two people (Harry's parents), so the verb must be second person of 'be' and the answer in the third person. The prompt 'No' is given so the verb in the answer must be negative (they aren't).)

6 Is, it is ('birthday' is singular so the verb 'is' must be used. The prompt 'Yes' is given so the verb in the answer must be positive. The pronoun 'it' replaces 'Harry's birthday' (an event/thing, third person) (it is).)

7 Is, it isn't ('Liverpool/team' is singular so the verb 'is' must be used. The prompt 'No' is given so the verb in the answer must be negative. The pronoun 'it' replaces 'Liverpool' (a team/thing, third person) (it isn't).)

5 (The first number in each answer refers to the day and must be changed to an ordinal number. The second number refers to the month.

1 24th December '24th' is the abbreviation for 'twenty-fourth'. December is month 12.

2 3rd September '3rd' is the abbreviation for 'third'. September is month 9.

3 27th October '27th' is the abbreviation for 'twenty-seventh'. October is month 10.

4 10th August. '10th' is the abbreviation for 'tenth'. August is month 8.

5 5th November. '5th' is the abbreviation of 'fifth'. November is month 11.)

6 8 14th July.
  5 15th May.
  6 10th June.
  1 2nd January.
  4 3rd April.
  7 4th July.
  2 26th January.
  3 20th March.

p7

7 1 the USA **2** Turkey **3** Poland **4** Britain **5** Australia

8

-an	-sh	-ese
Russian	Spanish	Chinese
Brazilian	British	
Australian	Polish	

9 1 She is/'s Chinese ('China' is changed to nationality adjective 'Chinese'.)

2 They are/'re Spanish ('Spain' is changed to nationality adjective 'Spanish'.)

3 It is/'s British ('Britain' is changed to nationality adjective 'British'.)

4 They are/'re from Mexico (The nationality adjective is changed to the country name (Mexico). The word 'from' is added.)

5 He is/'s from Brazil (The nationality adjective is changed to the country name (Brazil). The word 'from' is added.)

6 It is/'s from the USA (The nationality adjective is changed to the country name (the USA). The word 'from' is added.)

10 1 E **2** D **3** F **4** A **5** B **6** C

11 1 Yes, she is. (Ala is a girl, so the pronoun 'she' is used. The answer is positive, so 'Yes' is added at the beginning. In a short answer, the verb is repeated from the question ('is').)

2 No, he isn't. (Victor is a boy, so the pronoun 'he' is used. The answer is negative, so 'No' is added at the beginning. In a short answer, the verb is repeated from the question, but here it is negative (isn't).)

3 Yes, he is. (Victor is a boy, so the pronoun 'he' is used. The answer is positive, so 'Yes' is added at the beginning. In a short answer, the verb is repeated from the question ('is').)

4 No, he isn't. (Luke is a boy, so the pronoun 'he' is used. The answer is negative, so 'No' is added at the beginning. In a short answer, the verb is repeated from the question, but here it is negative (isn't).)

5 Yes, they are. (The question is about two people, so the pronoun 'they' is used. The answer is positive, so 'Yes' is added at the beginning. In a short answer, the verb is repeated from the question ('are').)

6 No, they aren't. (The question is about two people, so the pronoun 'they' is used. The answer is negative, so 'No' is added at the beginning. In a short answer, the verb is repeated from the question, but here it is negative (aren't).)

UNIT 1

Vocabulary 1

1 1 desk **2** curtains **3** shelf **4** clock **5** chair **6** wardrobe **7** laptop

2 1 guitar **2** poster **3** bin **4** bat **5** book

3

electrical	on the wall	material
lamp	clock	bed covers
laptop	mirror	cushion
TV	noticeboard	mat
	pictures	
	shelf	

4 1 in **2** behind **3** under **4** on **5** in front of **5** above

Reading

1 1 He's Isobel's brother. (Part A says 'Isobel and her brother, Max …')

2 Next to the bed. (Part A says 'Next to the bed, there's a big box.')

3 Three. (Part C says 'There are three doors.')

2 1 box (Isobel says '… there's a big box. Can I look inside it?')

2 are above (Ana says 'There are five pictures … above the table.')

3 Britain (Ana says 'They [the pictures] are all from Britain.')

4 bin (Ana asks '… is there a bin in the room?' and answers 'No, there isn't.')

5 three doors in (Ana says 'There are three doors.')

6 secret door (Ana says 'There's a secret door behind this curtain.')

3 Student's own answers.

4 Student's own answers.

Grammar

1 1 D ('any' in phrase 1 means that the matching phrase must have a plural noun. The phrase starts with 'Are' so it must be a question.)

2 B (the phrase in 2 already has a verb and noun, so the matching phrase is likely to give some extra information, such as location ('on the shelf').)

3 E (the phrase in 3 is negative and after the word 'any' there doesn't have to be an article in the matching part. The noun has to be plural because the first phrase has 'aren't' ('curtains').)

4 C (the verb in phrase 4 is singular, so a noun with a singular article matches ('a cupboard').)

5 A (the article in phrase 5 is 'an' so the next word must begin with a vowel ('Italian book').)

6 F (the article 'a' is already there in phrase 6, so the next word must be a singular noun, which doesn't begin with a vowel ('desk').)

2 1 No, there aren't. (The question is about more than one item so the answer has a plural verb. They aren't in the picture, so the verb is in the negative form.)

  2 No, there isn't. (The question is about one item so the answer has a singular verb 'is'. The item isn't in the picture, so the verb is in the negative form.)

  3 Yes, there are. (The question is about more than one item so the answer has a plural verb. They are in the picture, so the verb is in the positive form.)

  4 Yes, there is. (The question is about one item so the answer has a singular verb 'is'. The item is in the picture, so the verb is in the positive form.)

  5 Yes, there are. (The question is about more than one item so the answer has a plural verb. They are in the picture, so the verb is in the positive form.)

3 1 Is there a pencil case in your bag? ('pencil case' is singular so the verb in the question is in the singular. 'a' is used because the question is about only one item. A pencil case can be found 'in' a bag so the phrase 'in your bag' is used.)

  2 Are there any books on your shelves? ('shelves' is plural so the verb in the question is plural. 'any' is used because this is a question about more than one item. Books are 'on' shelves so the phrase 'on your shelves' is used.)

  3 Is there a clock in your bedroom? ('clock' is singular so the verb in the question is in the singular. 'a' is used because the question is about only one item. Items are 'in' rooms so the phrase 'in your bedroom' is used.)

  4 Is there a mobile phone in your bag? ('mobile phone' is singular so the verb in the question is in the singular. 'a' is used because the question is about only one item. Items are 'in' bags so the phrase 'in your bag' is used.)

  5 Are there any computer games on your desk? ('computer games' is plural so the verb in the question is plural. 'any' is used because this is a question about more than one item. Items are 'on' desks, so the phrase 'on your desk' is used.)

4 1 Yes, there are. / No, there aren't. (Students must use the plural form 'are', whether the answer is positive or negative, to match the verb in the question.)

  2 Yes, there is. / No, there isn't. (Students must use the singular form 'is', whether the answer is positive or negative, to match the verb in the question.)

  3 Yes, there are. / No, there aren't. ((Students must use the plural form 'are', whether the answer is positive or negative, to match the verb in the question.))

  4 Yes, there is. / No, there isn't. (Students must use the singular form 'is', whether the answer is positive or negative, to match the verb in the question.))

  5 Yes, there are. / No, there aren't. (Students must use the plural form 'are', whether the answer is positive or negative, to match the verb in the question.)

5 1 's ('is' or 'are' must follow 'There'. 'school bag' is singular, so the answer must be singular 'is'. The abbreviated form is in the word choice box.)

  2 a (an article must follow 'There's'. 'banana' is singular to the answer must be 'a'.)

  3 isn't ('is' or 'are' must follow 'There'. The article 'a' after the gap means that the verb is singular, 'isn't' is the only singular verb form in the word choice box which hasn't been used.)

  4 any (after 'aren't' the word 'any' is used)

  5 some ('are' is plural, so the article which follows must also be plural)

  6 are ('is' or 'are' must follow 'There'. 'notebooks' is plural, so the answer must be plural 'are'.)

  7 aren't ('is' or 'are' must follow 'There'. 'pictures' is plural, so the verb is 'are', but the word after the gap is 'any' so it must also be negative.)

Vocabulary 2

1 1 garage **2** bathroom **3** lift **4** living room **5** balcony **6** kitchen

2 A Dad (The only other man's name in the word choice box is 'Dad'. So the man in the bathroom must be Dad ('There's a man in the bathroom.')

  B Grandma (The woman in the kitchen must be Grandma (as it isn't Ben's mum or his sister, and there is only one woman's name left in the word choice box).

  C Ben (The man in the garden is called Ben ('Ben is in the garden').)

  D Mum (Ben's mum must be in the bedroom because the only other room we can see upstairs is the bathroom and there's a man in the bathroom.)

  E Ben's cat (Ben's cat is on the stairs ('There's a pet on the stairs.'))

  F Jenny (Jenny must be in the living room, because his mum is 'upstairs'.)

3 1 lift I **2** bedroom I **3** garden O **4** garage B **5** balcony O **6** stairs I **7** bathroom I

4 1 kitchen (we can see two children in the kitchen through the window)

  2 the garage (we can see the car in the garage in the picture)

  3 one (there is a dog at street level (the other dog is upstairs, on the balcony))

  4 in the garden

  5 and 6 Student's own answers.

  Possible answers:

  There is a woman outside the house. The woman has got a dog. There's a balcony. There's a dog on the balcony. There are two children in the kitchen. The children are in the kitchen. There is a tree in the garden. There's a man in the garden.

Listening

1 1 an apartment This apartment is the same as our apartment.

  2 No, it hasn't. *Our apartment hasn't got a garden.*

  3 a dog.… *the same as our apartment. It's got a garage.*

  4 two *Our apartment has got two bedrooms …*

  5 No, it isn't … *but it isn't near the school.*

  6 on Saturday … *we can see the house on Saturday.*

2 1 A (It's an apartment with a garage, but no garden.)

  2 B (Their pet dog always sits on the balcony.)

  3 A (He shares a room with his sister. She says 'It's got two beds.')

  4 C (It's near the shops)

  5 A (The boy spells out the name.)

3 1 has (The verb must be in the third person singular (Angela) and it is positive.)

  2 has (The verb must be in the third person singular (my house) and is positive)

  3 has (The verb must be in the third person singular (the cat) and it is positive.)

  4 have (The verb must be in the first person plural (We) and it is positive.)

  5 have (The verb must be in the first person singular (I) and it is positive.)

  6 have (The verb must be in the third person plural (My parents) and it is positive.)

4 1 Has your house got a garden? No, it hasn't. (The short answer must be in the third person singular to match the question ('Has your house … ?') and the answer is negative.)

  2 Have you got stairs in your house? Yes, I/we have. (The short answer must be in the first person and it can be singular or plural The question is 'Have you … ?' and the answer is positive.)

3 Have you got a pet? No, I/we haven't. (The short answer must be in the first person and it can be singular or plural (the question is 'Have you … ?') and the answer is negative)

4 Has your apartment got a lift? Yes, it has. (The short answer must be in the third person singular to match the question ('Has your apartment … ?') and the answer is positive.)

5 Have you got a garage under your apartment? No, I/we haven't. (The short answer must be in the first person and it can be singular or plural (the question is 'Have you … ?') and the answer is negative)

6 Has your sister for a big room? Yes, she has. (The short answer must be in the third person singular to match the question ('Has your sister … ?') and the answer is positive.)

5 1 has (The verb must be in the third person singular ('it' after the gap refers to the windmill). No contractions are used in questions.)

2 It's (The verb must be in the third person singular ('It' before the gap refers to the windmill) and the verb can be contracted.)

3 got (After the form of 'have', the next word must be 'got' in a positive sentence.)

4 has (The verb must be in the third person singular ('your house', after the gap, is the subject of the verb. No contractions are used in questions.)

5 it's (The subject must go in the gap because the next word is the verb. A subject pronoun is used in order not to repeat 'house' from the question.)

6 you (The subject must be the second person singular because the verb form is 'Have' and because Eve's answer is about her bedroom 'My bedroom is …'. In a question, the subject comes after the verb 'Have you … ?'.)

7 haven't (This is a short answer, so the verb from the question above needs to be repeated, and the answer is negative.)

Speaking

4 1 07781 432987
2 01184 960325
3 07700 900784
4 01514 960591
5 02090 180672
6 07700 900162

5 1 B (The person making a phone call usually says 'Hello' to the person who answers by name (to check who they are))

2 C ('Is … there, please?' is a fixed expression to ask if the person you want to talk to is available. You usually say it after introducing yourself/saying your name.)

3 B ('Just a minute' is a fixed expression to ask someone to wait.)

4 A ('Yes, thanks' is a polite, fixed response when someone asks how you are.)

5 B (The caller asks about the date (not the time). Ethan is likely to know when his own party is, so the answer 'I don't know' is not valid.)

6 C ('Bye!' is the correct way to end an informal phone call.)

6 Friends and family: Thanks. Bye. Hi. Are you OK? No problem. People you don't know well: Goodbye. Hello. How are you? Thank you. Of course.

Writing

1 1 This is me in London in September. (Capital letters to begin the sentence, for cities and months. Full stop to end the sentence.)

2 My friend Will is Australian. (Capital letters to begin the sentence, for people's names and for nationalities. Full stop to end the sentence.)

3 This is my Chinese friend, Mai. (Capital letters to begin the sentence, for nationalities and names. Full stop to end the sentence.)

4 The party is on Saturday 10 March. (Capital letters to begin the sentence, for days of the week and months. Full stop to end the sentence.)

5 We've got a holiday house in Malaga, Spain. (Capital letters to begin the sentence, for cities and countries. Full stop to end the sentence.)

2 1 of (the preposition 'of' follows 'a photo/picture/poster')

2 from (the preposition 'from' comes before the name of a person who sent something (e.g. a postcard, email or letter)

3 from (the preposition 'from' comes before the name of a place, such as a café)

4 about (the preposition 'about' follows 'a book/story/film/DVD')

5 for (the preposition 'for' follows 'ticket')

6 card ('birthday card' is a compound noun)

3 1 A **2** A **3** C

4 1 Elena's grandparents ('This is a photo of my grandparents')

2 Forest ('Their names are Mary and Edward Forest')

3 London ('… they're in London, on holiday')

4 a concert ('The ticket is for a concert in London')

5 13 October (1963) (The date is visible on the ticket)

6 the Beatles (The name of the group is visible on the ticket and Elena mentions the name again at the end of the paragraph.)

5 Student's own answer.
Model answer in Ex 4

Unit check

1 1 stairs **2** poster **3** clock **4** lift **5** noticeboard **6** chair

2 1 on **2** between **3** on **4** behind **5** in front of **6** above

3 1 is **2** are **3** aren't **4** isn't **5** some

4 1 B (The answer must be a room you usually cook in.)

2 C (The answer must be something outside a house, a place where you can keep a car.)

3 A (The answer must be singular, since the word 'a' comes before the gap. It must be something outside an apartment.)

4 B (The answer must be somewhere people usually have a swimming pool.)

5 B (The answer must be a room you can have two of in a house.)

6 A (The answer must be a room inside a house, where you usually have a table and chairs.)

7 C (The answer must be something you usually use to do homework.)

5 1 've (The verb must be in the second person singular as the word before the gap is 'You')

2 has (The verb must be in the third person singular as the word before the gap is 'It' and the rest of the sentence doesn't contain 'any' so the verb must be positive.)

3 hasn't (The verb must be in the third person singular ('your house'), shows that it must be a negative verb (he says 'No, it hasn't got …').)

4 any (This word directly follows 'haven't got' before a plural noun ('stairs').)

5 got (The subject and verb are both missing in this sentence.)

6 It's ('Has' and 'got' are inverted in the question form.)

7 haven't (The verb must be in the first person singular, as the question is 'Have you got … ?' The answer is negative ('No, I …').)

UNIT 2

Vocabulary 1

1 Friday 5

Monday 1

Saturday 6

Sunday 7

Thursday 4

Tuesday 2

Wednesday 3

2 1 C   **2** E   **3** A   **4** F   **5** D   **6** G   **7** B

3 I got to school. 4

I have breakfast. 3

I go home. 5

I get up at seven. 1

I do my homework.

I go to bed. 7

I get dressed. 2

I have dinner. 6

4 **1** get ('get' collocates with 'up' (phrasal verb)

2 meet ('my friends' collocates with 'meet')

3 have ('lunch' collocates with 'have' (also 'have breakfast', 'have dinner'))

4 go ('go' can be followed by the preposition 'to')

5 play ('computer games' collocates with 'play')

6 do ('homework' collocates with 'do')

5 Student's own answer.

Reading

1 **1** E *I teach young actors in a theatre in London*

2 D *I work with children aged between 9 and 14.*

3 B *Then they study with me for three hours in the afternoon.*

4 A *Five days multiplied by three hours a day.*

5 C *I don't teach the children in a classroom. We use the dining room at the theatre.*

2 **1** B is (The sentence begins with a third person pronoun ('She') and talks about a profession. It must be 'be' in the third person: 'is'.)

2 C and (The word 'too' at the end of the sentence shows that the missing word is 'and' (connecting the things the children are).)

3 A in (The preposition 'in' is used with 'in the morning/afternoon/evening')

4 C have ('Breakfast' collocates with 'have')

5 A at (The preposition 'at' is used before times ('at 3.30'))

3 7.00–7.30 get up and have breakfast

7.30–11.30 work in the theatre

11.30–12.30 have lunch

12.30–3.30 study with Angela Barns

3.30 go home

Grammar

1 **1** I get up at 8.00 on Sunday. / I don't get up at 8.00 on Sunday.

2 I have breakfast with my parents. / I don't have breakfast with my parents.

3 I go to bed at 9.00 in the evening. / I don't go to bed at 9.00 in the evening.

4 I play computer games in my bedroom. / I don't play computer games in my bedroom.

5 I watch TV in the morning. / I don't watch TV in the morning.

2 **1** study (The subject of the sentence is 'They' so the verb which follows needs to be in the third person plural.)

2 has (The subject of the sentence is 'The school' so the verb which follows needs to be in the third person singular.)

3 get (The subject of the sentence is 'The students' (They) so the verb which follows needs to be in the third person plural.)

4 start (The subject of the sentence is 'Music lessons' (They) so the verb which follows needs to be in the third person plural.)

5 finishes (The subject of the sentence is 'The school day' so the verb which follows needs to be in the third person singular)

6 doesn't (The subject of the sentence is 'The school' so the verb which follows needs to be in the third person singular.)

3 **1** gets up at 6.30 in the morning.

2 has lunch at 12.30.

3 starts music lessons at 7.30.

4 doesn't have music lessons on Saturday. / doesn't go to music lessons on Saturday.

4 **1** loves (The subject of the sentence is 'She' so the verb must be in the third person singular.)

2 don't meet (The subject of the sentence is 'We' so the verb must be in the first person plural and negative (as the prompt is 'not meet').)

3 go (The subject of the sentence is 'we' so the verb must be in the first person plural.)

4 have (The subject of the sentence is 'we' so the verb must be in the first person plural.)

5 doesn't cook (The subject of the sentence is 'My dad' so the verb must be in the third person singular and negative (as the prompt is 'not cook').)

6 go (The subject of the sentence is 'My cousins' so the verb must be in the third person plural.)

Vocabulary 2

1 **1** volleyball   **2** have swimming   **3** the guitar   **4** play card games

2

	Sunday	Monday	Tuesday
Ben	**0** go to the beach	**1** play volleyball	have piano lessons
Rob	**2** play computer games	**3** have swimming lessons	**4** play football
Mary	**5** go to the beach	play the guitar	**6** have singing lessons
Anne	**7** go to the cinema	**8** play the guitar	play football

3 **1** go ('go' comes before 'to' and a place)

2 have ('have' collocates with 'swimming lessons')

3 play ('play' collocates with 'volleyball')

4 play ('play' collocates with 'card games')

5 go ('go' comes before 'to the cinema')

6 play ('play' collocates with 'computer games')

4 **1** the evening (The preposition 'in' is used with 'in the morning/afternoon/evening'.)

2 Wednesday (The preposition 'on' is used before days of the week.)

3 nine o'clock (The preposition 'at' is used before times.)

4 August (The preposition 'in' is used before months.)

5 May (The preposition 'in' is used before months.)

6 May (The preposition 'on' is used before specific dates.)

5 **1** on (The preposition 'on' is used before days of the week.)

2 on (The preposition 'on' is used before days of the week.)

3 in (The preposition 'in' is used before months.)

4 at (The preposition 'at' is used before times.)

5 in (The preposition 'in' is used with 'in the morning/afternoon/evening'.)

6 at (The preposition 'at' is used before 'the weekend/night'.)

Listening

1 Student's own answers.

2 1 F (Dillon says 'It's my 'walk to school' badge.')
   2 T (Dillon says 'We meet in the park …')
   3 F (Dillon says '… we get the badge at the end of the month.')
   4 F (Dillon says 'we walk with my friend's mum. Her name's Mrs Greenhow …')
   5 T (Dillon says 'Dad doesn't. He goes to work on the train.')
   6 T (Rob says 'I'm going now – my school starts in ten minutes!')

3 1 October *Because it's 'walk to school month. Do you mean this October? Yes.*
   2 8/eight *We meet in the park at eight o'clock in the morning.'*
   3 Greenhow (Rob spells out the name and Dillon says, *Well, she's the leader of the 'walk to school' group …')*
   4 Monday … *mum walks with us on parent's day. That's on Monday morning.*
   5 star *What's on the badge? Can I see? It's a star. Look! The picture is different every month.*

4 1 Does (The verb must be in the third person singular (your big brother).)
   2 do (The verb must be in the second person singular (you).)
   3 Does (The verb must be in the third person singular (your sister).)
   4 does (The verb must be in the third person singular (your guitar lesson).)
   5 Do (The verb must be in the third person plural (your parents).)
   6 does (The verb must be in the third person singular (the school bus).)

5 1 F (The question is to 'you' so the answer must be in the first person singular. Phrase 'F' has 'I love sport' so it matches 'football' in the question.)
   2 E (The question is about other people ('your parents') so the answer must be in the third person plural ('they'). Phrase 'E' has 'They love films' so it matches 'cinema' in the question.)
   3 D (The question is to 'you' so the answer must be in the first person singular. Phrase 'D' has 'His name is Pedro' so it matches 'brother' in the question.)
   4 A (The question is to 'you' so the answer must be in the first person singular. Phrase 'A' has 'I play the guitar', so it matches 'Do you have piano lessons?' in the question.)
   5 C (The question is about one other person ('your dad') so the answer must be in the third person singular and have the masculine subject 'he'.)
   6 B (The question is about other people ('your friends') so the answer must be in the third person plural ('they'). Phrase 'B' repeats the verb 'play' from the question.)

6 1 Do, get up (The verb must be in the second person singular (Do) because the subject is 'you'. 'get up' collocates with 'early' and 'in the morning'.)
   2 Does, teach (The verb must be in the third person singular (Does) because the subject is 'your tutor'. A tutor teachers students.)
   3 Do, meet (The verb must be in the third person plural (Do) because the subject is 'your friends'. 'meet' collocates with 'friends'
   4 Do, have (The verb must be in the second person singular (Do) because the subject is 'you'. 'have' collocates with 'singing lessons'.)
   5 Does, like (The verb must be in the third person singular (Does) because the subject is 'your mum'. The 'ing' form follows the verb 'like' ('like meeting').)

Speaking

4 1 nine o'clock   **2** ten thirty / half past ten   **3** twelve fifteen/ quarter past twelve   **4** two forty-five/ quarter to three   **5** four o'clock   **6** nine thirty / half past nine

5 Student's own answers.

7 1 time ('time' directly follows 'What' in the question 'What time does … ?')
   2 starts (The question for this answer uses the verb 'start'. The pronoun before the gap is 'It' so the verb must be in the third person singular.)
   3 Do (There is a gap for an auxiliary verb is at the beginning of the sentence and there is a question mark, so this must be a question. The verb in the question is 'have' so the auxiliary used must be *do/does*.)
   4 don't (The pronoun is second person singular 'you' so the form must be 'Do'. This is the short answer to the question in the previous line. The pronoun is 'I' so the verb must be in the first person singular (*do*). It must be negative because the word at the beginning of the answer is 'No'.)
   5 in (The preposition 'in' is always used before 'the morning/ afternoon/evening')(6 have('have' collocates with 'a lesson' It must be in the first person singular because the pronoun before the gap is 'I'.)

8 1 9.00   **2** 10.30   **3** 12.30   **4** 2.45   **5** sport   **6** science

Writing

1 1 My name's Elisa. (The words 'name' and 'is' are put together. An apostrophe replaces the letter 'i' in 'is'.)
   2 I've got a little sister. (The words 'I' and 'have' are put together. An apostrophe replaces the letters 'ha' in 'have'.)
   3 We're both at the same school. (The words 'We' and 'are' are put together. An apostrophe replaces the letter 'a' in 'are'.)
   4 Elisa doesn't like school. (The words 'does' and 'not' are put together. An apostrophe replaces the letter 'o' in 'not'.)
   5 She's got a pet rabbit. (The words 'She' and 'has' are put together. An apostrophe replaces the letters 'ha' in 'has'.)
   6 It's called Fluffy.(The words 'It' and 'is' are put together. An apostrophe replaces the letter 'i' in 'is'.)

2 1 you got (any) brothers or sisters (The answer is about how many brothers and sisters the person has and it's in the first person singular, so the question must be in the second person singular.)
   2 time does your school day start (The answer begins 'My school day starts' and includes a time, so the question must begin 'What time' and the auxiliary verb must be in the third person singular (does) because the subject is 'school day'. The verb 'start' must be used in the question, too.)
   3 your favourite subject (The question must be about the person's favourite subjects. The answer is in the third person singular and uses the verb 'be' 'History is …' so the question must use 'be' in the third person singular 'What's … ?' The possessive changes from 'my' in the answer to 'your' in the question.)
   4 sport do you like (playing) (The answer is in the first person singular ('I') and uses the verb 'like', so the question must be in the second person singular 'you' and use the auxiliary 'do'. The topic of the answer needs to be in the question 'Which sport …')
   5 do you do at the weekend (The answer is in the first person singular ('I') and uses the verb 'do', so the question must be in the second person singular 'you' and use the auxiliary 'do'. The complement from the answer needs to be at the end of the question ('at the weekend').)

3 1 Ashwood High   **2** 500   **3** geography, English, maths, drama
4 Student's own answers.

Unit check

1 1 have **2** go **3** in **4** play **5** have **6** on

2 1 art **2** geography **3** science **4** subject **5** history

3 1 C (The answer must be in the third person singular and use the pronoun 'he' because the question is 'Does your father … ?')

  2 A (The question asks 'What time … ?' so the answer must be a time.)

  3 C (The answer must be in the first person plural ('we') because the question is about 'you and your friends'.)

  4 B (The answer must be in the first person singular ('I') because the question is in the second person singular 'Do you … ?')

  5 A (The answer must be in the third person singular because the question is 'Does … ?' and the pronoun must be 'she' because the question is about 'your sister'.)

  6 C (The answer must be a time because it asks about a routine action which happens at a particular time of day 'go to bed'.)

4 1 doesn't start (third person singular: 'School')

  2 don't have (first person singular: 'I')

  3 don't play (first person plural: 'We')

  4 doesn't like (third person singular: 'My teacher')

  5 doesn't go (third person singular: 'My cousin')

  6 don't travel (third person plural: 'Those girls')

5 1 half past seven, seven forty-five

  2 seven forty-five, eight o'clock

  3 eight fifteen

  4 five o'clock, half past five

  5 six o'clock

REVIEW: UNITS 1–2

1 1 C (The answer must be a name. 'Why?' would be a very impolite answer.)

  2 A (The answer must be an age. The question is in the second person 'are you' so the answer must be in the first person singular or plural.)

  3 B (The answer must be a surname.)

  4 B (The same verb must be used in a short answer, but in the first person singular, as the question is 'Are you'.)

  5 A ('have got' must appear in the answer. 'No, I have.' is grammatically incorrect.)

  6 C (There answer must include the word 'there')

2 1 My favourite colour is red.

  2 Our house is number forty-three.

  3 The bed covers in my bedroom are blue.

  4 Where are the door keys?

  5 Are there any pictures in your living room?

  6 Have you got Charlie's mobile phone number?

  7 There are three bedrooms in our house.

  8 My room has got yellow walls.

3 1 from (The preposition 'from' is used before a place in the expression 'to be from'.)

  2 old ('be … years old' is a fixed expression)

  3 birthday (The rest of the sentence gives a date. The missing word is very likely to be birthday (as it can only be one word).)

  4 of (The preposition 'of' is used before 'picture/photo/poster')

  5 twins (If they are both five, the missing word must be 'twins')

  6 his (Possessive pronoun (referring to the writer's dog))

  7 My (Possessive pronoun (referring to the writer))

4 1 F Georgina's cats are British (Possessive apostrophe after the name of the owner. There is more than one cat so the verb is plural. Country name changes to nationality adjective.)

  2 E Tom's dog is American. (Possessive apostrophe after the name of the owner. There is only one dog so the verb is singular. Country name changes to nationality adjective)

  3 A Carmen's mouse is Spanish. (Possessive apostrophe after the name of the owner. There is only one mouse so the verb is singular. Country name changes to nationality adjective)

  4 C Yuri's dogs are Russian. (Possessive apostrophe after the name of the owner. There is more than one dog so the verb is plural. Country name changes to nationality adjective)

  5 B Natalia's dog is Brazilian. (Possessive apostrophe after the name of the owner. There is only one dog so the verb is singular. Country name changes to nationality adjective.)

  6 D Metin's cat is Turkish. (Possessive apostrophe after the name of the owner. There is only one cat so the verb is singular. Country name changes to nationality adjective)

5 1 laptop, lamp **2** clock **3** cushions **4** curtains **5** football

6 1 I don't play the drums. (First person singular ('I') auxiliary 'do', negative form.)

  2 My dad doesn't play card games. (Third person singular (My dad) auxiliary 'does', negative form.)

  3 There isn't a clock in our living room. (Verb 'be' in the third person singular, negative form 'isn't. The word 'a' needs to be added because 'clock' is singular. The preposition 'in' must be added before 'our living room'.)

  4 There aren't any pictures in their kitchen. (Verb 'be' in the third person plural, negative form 'aren't. The word 'any' needs to be added after the negative plural 'There aren't', before the noun. The preposition 'in' must be added before 'their kitchen'.)

  5 We haven't got a dining room in our house. (Verb 'have' in the first person plural, negative form 'haven't. The word 'a' needs to be added because 'dining room' is singular. The preposition 'in' must be added before 'our house'.)

  6 Silvia hasn't got a desk in her bedroom. (Verb 'have' in the third person singular, negative form 'hasn't. The word 'a' needs to be added because 'desk' is singular. The preposition 'in' must be added before 'her bedroom'.)

7 1 is she from (The answer is a country name.)

  2 family name (The answer is a surname.)

  3 old is she (The answer uses 'She is' and is a number, so must be her age.)

  4 (subject) does she (The answer is a subject name and the verb is 'teach'. So the question must be 'What subject …'.)

  5 she play (The verb 'play' collocates with 'guitar', so it must be used in the question.)

  6 's/is her favourite (The answer is a food, and the question begins 'What' so it must be 'What's her favourite food?')

8 1 are (After 'there' students must use 'is' or 'are'. Since there is a plural number (500) after the gap, the verb must be plural.)

  2 got ('got' follows 'have')

  3 lesson ('Spanish' collocates with 'lesson', as does 'teach a')

  4 starts/begins (The subject is 'School' so the verb must be in the third person singular. The time given looks like the beginning of the day, so the verb must be 'start' or 'begin'.)

  5 my (The gap is before a noun, so it is likely to be an article or an adjective. The possessive adjective fits because she is writing about travelling to work from her own house (in the morning).)

  6 don't (The subject is 'I' so the verb must be in the first person singular. There is already a main verb 'travel', so the verb in the gap must be an auxiliary. She lives near the school, so the verb is to make 'travel' negative: 'don't'.)

  7 at (The preposition 'at' is used before a time.)

  8 of (The preposition 'of' is used after 'picture'.)

  9 on (The preposition 'on' is used before days of the week.)

UNIT 3

Vocabulary 1

1 **1** kangaroo **2** dolphin **3** bear **4** shark **5** whale **6** lion

2 **1** jump, 2 swim, jump **3** walk, climb, run **4** swim
  5 swim, jump **6** walk, run

3 **1** climb **2** swim **3** jump **4** fly **5** walk

4 Student's own answers.

Reading

1 **1** four animals: dog, sheep, goat, pig
  2 Ellen's favourite month: April
  3 the name of Ellen's hobby: agility competitions

2 **1** family (The word must be someone/a group of people because the verb is 'live'. The text goes on to talk about Ellen's dad, so it must be 'family'. The word must describe humans (who own dogs) because the sentence ends 'our dog'.)
  2 morning (in the' collocates with 'morning')
  3 school ('finish' collocates with 'school')
  4 sheep (The word must be a noun because there is an article 'The' before the gap. The word must describe an animal which has babies and live in a field.)
  5 runs (The word must be a verb because there is a noun before the gap. The word must describe what the dogs do at the agility competition.)
  6 listen (The word must be a verb because there is an adverb of frequency before the gap. The reason the dog doesn't win is because he doesn't listen.)

3 **2** Me and my dog (The best title is 'Me and my dog' because Ellen doesn't describe a whole year on the farm and most of the post is about her dog, not the sheep.)

Grammar

1 **1** A always (Must be a positive word (because kangaroos live in Australia) so it can't be 'never'. The noun is plural 'kangaroos' so the answer cannot be 'doesn't' (third person singular).) B live (Must be a verb because there is an adverb before the gap. 'live' collocates with 'in groups')
  3 B always (The missing word can't be 'never' because the verb is negative already (aren't). 'aren't sometimes' doesn't make sense.)
  4 A never (In the previous sentence it says that kangaroos only eat plants, so they never eat spiders or beetles.)
  5 B sometimes (The beginning of the sentence says that kangaroos aren't usually dangerous, but this mean they can 'sometimes' attack people (but not often).)
  6 C are (The adverb 'often' comes after the verb 'to be'. After 'There' the verb must be is/are. The noun in the sentence is 'signs' so the answer must be 'are'.)

2 **1** My cat never has milk for breakfast.
  2 He often goes out at night.
  3 He doesn't always eat his food.
  4 He usually sleeps on my sister's bed.
  5 He is usually very happy.
  6 He always sits in front of the TV in the afternoon.

3 **1** usually (It must be an adverb and it can't be 'always' because the writer is describing a usual situation with a caveat 'but I am a bit nervous'.)
  2 don't (The problem in the post is that the writer doesn't like spiders. The word in the gap must be an auxiliary verb or an adverb.)
  3 are (The word in the gap must be 'are' because the noun is plural 'spiders' and the writer is using the adjective 'dangerous'.)

4 you (The auxiliary verb in the question is in the second person singular 'do' so the pronoun must be 'you'.)
  5 spiders (The subject is missing from the question. 'spiders' is the only noun in the box.)
  6 see (The missing word must be a verb, because it comes after the pronoun 'I' and is followed by a noun 'a spider'.)

4 **1** often see (The adverb of frequency 'often' goes before the verb 'see'.)
  2 aren't always (The adverb of frequency 'always' goes after the verb because the verb is 'be'.)
  3 don't often come (The adverb of frequency 'often' goes after the negative auxiliary verb 'don't' butbefore the main verb 'come')
  4 don't usually see (The adverb of frequency 'usually' goes after the negative auxiliary verb 'don't' but before the main verb 'see')
  5 don't usually like (The adverb of frequency 'usually' goes after the negative auxiliary verb 'don't' but before the main verb 'like')
  6 sometimes climb (The adverb of frequency 'sometimes' goes before the verb 'climb'.)

Vocabulary 2

1 **1** forest **2** jungle **3** lake **4** river **5** desert
  Students draw mountains.

2 **1** lakes **2** water **3** the mountains **4** desert **5** jungle
  6 lakes

3 **1** the **2** insects **3** fish **4** sea **5** drink **6** caves

4 Student's own answers.
  Possible answers:
  1 Parrots usually fly in the forest.
  2 Sharks always swim in the sea.
  3 Camels usually walk in the desert.
  4 Brown bears usually sleep in caves.
  5 People don't usually like crocodiles.

Listening

1 **1** in December *The tour starts in December …*
  2 parrots *I love parrots. They're my favourite birds.*
  3 snakes *Does it talk about snakes? I love snakes!*

2 **Day 1** A (monkeys) *Day 1… What do we see?… No, not snakes, Jake. Monkeys!*
  Day 2 F (caimen/crocodile) *On day two we … We usually see Caiman … Caiman are a type of crocodile.*
  Day 3 E (parrots) *listen to the description of day three. In the morning … we often see Macaws and parrots'*
  Day 4 D (frogs) *On Day 4 in the evening we … find interesting frogs.*
  Day 5 B (snakes) *Day 5 We go on a walk through the forest. This is often a good place to see snakes like the Green Tree Viper.*
  Day 6 C (hummingbirds) *And on day six of the tour … What animals and birds do we see?… we usually see butterflies and hummingbirds.*

3 **1** C (Where … ?' requires an answer which is a place ('In the mountains.'))
  2 D (What … ?' requires a noun as an answer ('Bamboo'))
  3 F (When … ?' requires an answer which is a time/time period ('At night.'))
  4 E (Why … ?' requires an answer which is a reason ('Because …'))
  5 B (How often … ?' requires an answer which describes frequency, e.g. an adverb ('Not very often.'))
  6 A (How … ?' requires an answer which describes an action/ method ('By walking around.'))

4 **1** Why do armadillos sleep a lot? (A reason, beginning with 'because' is underlined, so the question must start with 'Why'.)

2 Where do ducks live? (A place is underlined in the answer, so the question must start with 'Where'.)

3 How often do polar bears see penguins? (An adverb is underlined, so the question must start with 'How often'.)

4 When do bats sleep? (A time period is underlined, so the question must start with 'When'.)

5 What do ducks eat? (A list of nouns is underlined, so the question must start with 'What'.)

Speaking

1–4 **1** B (The question is 'Where … ?' so the answer must be a place.)

2 C (The question is 'What … ?' so the answer must be a noun (a type of food).)

3 A (The question contains 'Has it got … ?' so the answer must be 'Yes, it has.' or 'No, it hasn't.')

4 B (The question is 'Does it swim?' so the answer would usually be 'Yes, it does' or 'No, it doesn't.' Neither of these options is given, so 'Yes, sometimes' must be right ('Yes it sometimes does.' is the implied answer).)

5 A ('How long is it?' is the question, so the answer must contain a measurement of length.)

6 B (The question starts 'Is it … ?' so the answer must be 'Yes, it is.' or 'No, it isn't.')

5 **1** B **2** F **3** E **4** A **5** C **6** D

6 **1** one ('odd one out' is a fixed expression)

2 which (A question word is required and 'Which' is the word for choosing between different options (asking about one of a group))

3 sure ('I'm not sure' is one of the expressions students have practised in the Student's Book.)

4 because (The speaker is giving a reason for his opinion, so it begins with 'because')

5 think (This must be a verb because the pronoun 'I' comes before the gap, what follows is an opinion, so the verb must be 'think')

6 doesn't (This must be the auxiliary verb for making a regular verb negative in the present tense, third person ('it').)

7 **1** I think it's the duck because it hasn't got four legs. / I think it's the lion because it doesn't live on a farm.

2 I think it's the rabbit because it doesn't climb. / I think it's the monkey because it isn't a pet.

3 I think it's the kangaroo because it doesn't fly.

4 I think it's the panda because it doesn't live in the desert. / I think it's the snake because it hasn't got legs. / I think it's the camel because it doesn't climb.

5 I think it's the polar bear because it doesn't live in Africa / it lives in a cold place.

Writing

1 **1** Frogs make eggs, but they don't have nests.

2 They can jump, but they can't walk.

3 They hide in the day and come out at night.

4 They don't like cold places and they always live near water.

5 Some frogs sleep under water, but they can breathe.

2 Scorpions

Scorpions are amazing animals. They live all over the world, but they ~~live~~ in Antarctica. You can find them in jungles, forests and caves, but lots of scorpions live in the desert, under the ground. They go out in the day to look for food.

Scorpions are usually about 60 cm long.

Scorpions often eat insects, like beetles and spiders, but they don't eat a lot of food. Some scorpions only eat one insect in a day. Scorpions are never dangerous to people.

Mother scorpions usually have four to eight babies. Their nests are usually under the ground or under rocks. The babies live on their father's back.

3 **1** They go out at night to look for food.

2 Scorpions are usually about 6 cm long.

3 Some scorpions only eat one insect in a year.

4 Scorpions are sometimes dangerous to people.

5 The babies live on their mother's back.

4 **1** legs and a small **2** but they don't **3** get/are tired after **4** but they sometimes eat **5** they are **6** and they stay

Unit check

1 A duck B tiger C hippo D armadillo E penguin F bee

2 **1** B **2** C **3** E **4** A **5** D **6** F

3 **1** never **2** always **3** always **4** usually / often **5** often / usually

4 **1** Whales are always big. (The adverb goes after the verb 'be'.)

2 I often walk to school. (The adverb goes before the verb.)

3 Bears sometimes swim. (The adverb goes before the verb.)

4 Cheetahs don't usually eat at night. (The adverb goes between the auxiliary and the main verb.)

5 We never go to the beach in December. (The adverb goes before the verb.)

6 My aunt is always in her car. (The adverb goes after the verb 'be')

5 **1** Where do they **2** What do they **3** When do they **4** How old **5** What do you / we

UNIT 4

Vocabulary 1

1 A café B hospital C supermarket D bus stop E swimming pool F park

2 **1** square **2** sports centre **3** museum **4** shopping centre / souvenir shop **5** shopping centre / souvenir shop

3 **1** opposite **2** near **3** next to **4** near **5** next to **6** opposite

4 Students' own answers.

Reading

1 **1** C (Giolitti's café) **2** D (Borghese museum) **3** A (Navona square) **4** B (River Tevere)

2 **1** B ('in the morning' is a fixed expression)

2 A (The word must be a verb in the third person singular, because there is a singular subject 'The building' before the gap. At the end of the sentence is 'years old', so the verb is 'be')

3 B (The word is an adverb because it comes directly before a verb. The context of the sentence means the adverb is 'often')

4 B (The word is a possessive pronoun and it is in the first person singular (the whole article is written in the first person).)

5 C ('next' is followed by 'to' if it is a preposition)

3 **1** breakfast/ice cream … *have breakfast at a café … Giolitti's. They also serve fantastic ice cream*

2 almost 2,000 years old *The building is almost 2,000 years old!*

3 gardens *When you finish looking at the paintings, walk around the amazing gardens.'*

4 thirty-one/31 *There are 31 bridges across the river '… go to a restaurant in the evening – there are lots next to the river.*

5 (lots of) restaurants *go to a restaurant … there are lots next to the river.*

Grammar

1 **1** river **2** playground **3** cinema **4** bus stop **5** park **6** swimming pool

2 **1** Please don't run in the hospital.
2 Please don't talk in class at school.
3 Please don't eat or drink in the shop.
4 Please don't take photos in the museum.
5 Please don't walk on the grass in the garden / park.
6 Please don't pick the flowers in the park.

3 **1** must **2** must **3** mustn't **4** must **5** mustn't **6** mustn't

4 **1** You mustn't play football here. **2** You must sit down.
3 You mustn't talk during the film. **4** You mustn't be late.
5 You must close the doors.
(Students change positive imperatives to 'You must …' and negative imperatives to 'You mustn't …' They repeat the main verb from the original instruction.)

5 Student's own answers.
Possible answers: 1 8.30 (students write the time their school starts)/registration/the bell **2** school uniform/trousers and a jumper/comfortable clothes **3** mobile phones/sweets/chewing gum **4** must eat in the canteen/be quiet while you eat / mustn't leave rubbish on the floor **5** you must do it/you mustn't lose it **6** must be nice/mustn't fight

Vocabulary 2

1 **1** bus **2** plane **3** train **4** helicopter **5** lorry **6** tram

2 **1** B (The verb after the gap is 'cycle' so the word must be 'bike'.)
2 A (The sentence is about travelling the air, so the word must be 'plane'.)
3 C (The sentence is about a vehicle which stops to pick people up, so the word must be 'bus'.)
4 B (The sentence is about going to the shopping centre, so 'train' is the most logical answer.)
5 A (The sentence is about transport which travels between cities, so the word must be train, the other two are for travelling within one city.)
6 B (The type of transport must be one you would use for short journeys, so the word must be 'car'.)

3 **1** Dad – small, black car,
2 Mum – big, family car,
3 Flavia – bus,
4 Erik's uncle – lorry
5 Erik's grandparents – walk

4 **1** to (The preposition 'to' is used before a destination, after 'get' or 'go'.)
2 by (The preposition 'by' is used before methods of transport.)
3 roads (This must be a noun, and plural, because the verb afterwards is 'are'. 'busy' collocates with 'roads'.)
4 cars (This must be a noun, and plural, because sentence starts 'There are'. 'noisy' collocates with 'cars'.)
5 walk (This must be a verb because the word before the gap is an auxiliary verb.)
6 bike (This must be a noun and words in the sentence collocate with 'bike' ('bright clothes', 'helmet'))

5 **Possible answers (if students don't tick the sentence):**
1 I sometimes/never/don't walk to school. I don't always walk to school. **2** My parents have got a car. **3** I like/love cycling. **4** I don't travel by car every day./I sometimes/never travel by car. **5** I don't usually travel by train. I sometimes/never/always travel by train.

Listening

1 **1** woman **2** tables **3** eating **4** five
2 Madrid

3 Students colour the curtains of the café red, the woman's bike blue, the dog yellow and the train green. They write 'Coffee time' on the sign at the café.

4 **1** Mireia can swim. She can't speak English. She can't play volleyball. She can run 2 km.
2 Kirsten can swim. She can speak English. She can't play volleyball. She can't run 2 km.

5 **1** D (can) **2** B (can't) **3** F (can't) **4** E (can't) **5** A (can) **6** C (can)

6 **1** him (The subject of the sentence is 'I', students must choose the object pronoun 'him' (it's after the verb).)
2 I (The pronoun comes before the verb, so it must be the subject pronoun.)
3 it (The pronoun refers back the restaurant to students must choose 'it', not 'him'.)
4 She (The pronoun comes before the verb, so it must be the subject pronoun.)
5 me (The subject of the imperative 'Wait' is 'you', the object pronoun comes after the verb ('me').)
6 them (The subject of the imperative 'Don't walk' is 'you', the object pronoun comes after the verb ('them').)

Speaking

1 **A** 5 **B** 3 **C** 1 **D** 2 **E** 6 **F** 4

2 **1** He wants to go to the sports centre
2 She'd like to go to the cinema
3 He wants to go to the museum
4 She wants to go to the shops
5 He'd like to go to the supermarket
6 She'd like to go to the park

6 **1** Where are the famous paintings, please?
2 Can you help me, please?
3 I'm sorry, I don't understand.
4 Can you repeat that, please?
5 Can you say that again, please?
6 Can we get a bus to Trafalgar Square?

7 **1** me (Excuse me' is a fixed expression. An object pronoun must come after an imperative.)
2 help ('Can you help me?' is a fixed expression for asking someone for directions or help.)
3 please (The most likely word is 'please' because the person is asking someone they don't know for help, it is a polite question.)
4 want (The word must be a verb because the word before the gap is a subject pronoun 'I'. The words after the gap 'to go' collocate with 'want'.)
5 understand (After this sentence, the person giving directions repeats the information in a different way, so the first speaker must have said 'I don't understand.')
6 very ('Thanks very much' is a fixed expression.)

Writing

1 **1** D (A verb must follow 'Where' and 'are' is the only verb in the matching phrases.)
2 C ('Can you' is the beginning of a question, so the matching phrase must end with a question mark. The preposition 'to' can follow 'come' so c is the correct answer.)
3 E (Students match 'I'm sorry' with a possible reason ('I'm late' is the only phrase which could be a reason).)
4 A (The phrase ends with a conjunction ('when') so it must match to a clause with a subject and verb. It must be 'a'.)
5 F ('See you' is followed by a time or day. 'in 15 minutes' is the only time)
6 B ('Can you' is the beginning of a question, so the matching phrase must end with a question mark. 'meet me' must be followed by a place, so it must be 'b' (the bus station).)

2 1 on ('on' is used before street or road names)
 2 on ('on' is used before days of the week)
 3 at ('at' is used before times)
 4 to ('to' is used before destinations)
 5 at ('at' is used before 'the bus stop')
 6 in ('in' is usually used before public spaces, such as 'the square', 'the park')

3 1 me (An object pronoun must come after a verb. The question is 'Can you ...' so the next pronoun can't be 'you'. The email is written in the first person.)
 2 on ('on' is used before a street or road name)
 3 my (The possessive 'my' must come before 'birthday', because the email is written in the first person.)
 4 Be (This must be the imperative form.)
 5 to ('to' is used with destinations)
 6 you ('See you soon' is a fixed expression.)

4 1 Hi Mark,
 2 Meet me at the swimming pool in Barrack Street.
 3 Can you be there at 2.00?
 4 See you later.
 5 Tania

5 Student's own answers.
 Model answer:
 Please meet Tom after his guitar lesson.
 Be at the music room at 4.00.
 See you after work.
 Thanks.
 Dad

Unit check

1 1 school **2** square **3** hospital **4** bridge **5** bank **6** park

2 It's got wheels: bike, lorry, van
 It's got wheels / It travels in the air: plane
 It hasn't got wheels: boat
 It hasn't got wheels / it travels in the air: helicopter

3 1 me (The sentence is in the first person singular, so it must be 'me'.)
 2 her (The pronoun refers back to 'woman', so it must be third person singular, feminine: 'her'.)
 3 them (The pronoun refers back to 'souvenirs' so it must be third person plural: 'them'.)
 4 him (The pronoun refers back to 'David', so it must be third person singular, masculine: 'him'.)
 5 us (The sentence is in the first person plural, so it must be 'us'.)

4 1 Can you swim? **2** Can you play the piano? **3** Can you paint?
 4 Can you speak Spanish? **5** Can you cycle / ride a bike?

REVIEW: UNITS 1–4

1 1 Wednesday (the next day of the week.)
 2 always (the opposite of 'never'.)
 3 April (the month after 'March')
 4 Sunday (the day after 'Saturday')
 5 breakfast ('breakfast' collocates with 'have' and it is the only action left you might do in the morning before going to school)
 6 afternoon (the time of day between 'morning' and 'evening')

2 1 There's a monkey behind a tree. (the preposition needs to change)
 2 There are two frogs in the river. (the verb needs to change to plural form)
 3 There is one armadillo in the picture.. (the verb 'be' needs to change from the plural 'are' to the singular 'is' because the number of armadillo is one, not three)
 4 There are some birds flying above the water. (the preposition needs to change)

5 There isn't a dolphin in the picture. / There aren't any dolphins in the picture. (the verb needs to change to a negative singular or plural form)

3 1 E (The answer must be the name of an animal.)
 2 D (The answer must be 'Yes, I have' or 'No, I haven't' because the question uses 'have got' is in the second person singular (you))
 3 F (The answer must be 'Yes, I do' or 'No, I don't' because the question uses 'Do you ... ?')
 4 A (The answer must describe frequency)
 5 C (The answer must be a place)
 6 B (The answer must be a time)

4 Student's own answers.

5 1 of (the preposition 'of' follows 'a picture/photo/poster')
 2 is (this is a short answer, so it must repeat the verb in the question above)
 3 got ('He's' comes before the gap and after the gap is a noun, so the 's' represents 'has' and the next word must be 'got')
 4 old ('How old' is a fixed phrase in a question (and the answer is an age 'He's one'))
 5 likes/loves ((The verb after the gap is in the 'ing' form so the missing verb must be like/love. It must be in the third person because the pronoun is 'He'.)
 6 watching ('watch' collocates with 'TV' but it must be in the 'ing' form because it follows 'loves'.)

6 1 monkey (the rest live in water) **1** mountains (the rest are bodies of water) **2** bridge (the rest are places people live) **3** street (the rest are prepositions) **4** today (the rest are adverbs of frequency) **5** bus stop (the rest are vehicles)

7 1 stairs **2** kitchen **3** breakfast **4** weekend **5** frog **6** road

8 1 A (The question is about country of origin so the answer must contain the name of a country, not a nationality. The question is in the second person singular so the answer must be in the first person 'I'm from ...')
 2 C (The answer must be a place someone lives.)
 3 B (The answer must be a time or day.)
 4 A (The answer must be something cats usually eat.)
 5 B (The answer must be a place you can find toilets.)
 6 C (The answer must be a time.)

9 1 Polar bears eat fish.
 2 Elephants aren't small.
 3 There aren't (any) penguins in the desert.
 4 Don't / You mustn't play volleyball at the children's playground.
 5 Cars can't travel on water.

10 1 are (After the subject 'there' the verb must be is or are. The number later in the sentence is 'more than 40' so the verb must be plural 'are'.)
 2 must (The missing word must be an auxiliary or modal verb, given the meaning of the whole sentence, it must be an imperative. The intended meaning is 'It's important to plan your visit'.)
 3 walls (paintings are always 'on' walls)
 4 next ('to' follows 'next' in the preposition of place)
 5 usually (The missing word must be an adverb of frequency. The rest of the sentence explains that today is an exception, so the first part of the sentence is describing what usually happens.)
 6 mustn't (The missing word must be an auxiliary or modal verb. Given the meaning of the whole sentence, it is 'mustn't' (because people are not generally allowed to each in museums))
 7 don't (The missing word must be an auxiliary or modal verb. Given the meaning of the whole sentence, it must make a negative imperative (because people are not generally allowed to use a flash on the camera in museums).)

UNIT 5

Vocabulary 1

1 **1** salad **2** beans **3** bread **4** milkshake **5** fruit **6** cheese

2 fruit: apples, oranges, pineapples
vegetables: potatoes, carrots, onions
drinks: water, lemonade, milk

3 Student's own answers

4 **1** salad **2** sauce **3** cheese **4** onion **5** chicken **6** banana

Reading

1 **1** B 'Why … ?' in the question matches to 'because …' at the beginning of the paragraph ('We make pancakes because …').

　2 C Paragraph C explains what pancake tossing is.

　3 A The present continuous form in the question matches the form in the first sentence of the paragraph 'I'm mixing …'

2 **1** waits (Students find 'for half an hour' in the text and use the same verb ('wait'). They must change it to the third person 'waits' to match the subject of the sentence ('Louise's mum').)

　2 Tuesday (The preposition 'on' is used before a day of the week and 'Tuesday' is the day mentioned in section B.)

　3 finish the food (Students find 'in the house' in the text and use the same phrase as in the text 'finish the food' to complete the sentence.)

　4 isn't eating ((In the article, Louise's mum says 'I'm not eating chocolate in Lent …' Students change this to the third person (isn't eating) because they already have the subject ('Louise's mum') before the gap.)

　5 difficult (Students find 'Cooking is …' in the second sentence and find the adjective used to describe it ('difficult'). The missing word is an adjective because there the verb 'is' comes before the gap.)

　6 eating her (In the article, Louise writes 'I'm eating my pancakes with lemon juice and sugar.' Students repeat the gerund of the verb ('eating') but change the possessive pronoun to 'her' because the sentence is in the third person.)

3 Student's own answer.

Grammar

1 **A** 5 **B** 3 **C** 1 **D** 4 **E** 6 **F** 2

2 Sentence A is in the picture.

3 **1** 'm/am cooking (The subject of the sentence is 'I', so students must use the first person singular of the verb 'be' (am) and change the verb to the gerund by adding 'ing'.)

　2 're/are having (The subject of the sentence is 'We', so students must use the first person plural of the verb 'be' (are) and change the verb to the gerund by removing the 'e' and adding 'ing'.)

　3 's/is helping (The subject of the sentence is 'My brother', so students must use the third person singular of the verb 'be' (is) and change the verb to the gerund by adding 'ing'.)

　4 'm/am waiting (The subject of the sentence is 'I', so students must use the first person singular of the verb 'be' (am) and change the verb to the gerund by adding 'ing'.)

　5 's/is making (The subject of the sentence is 'My dad', so students must use the third person singular of the verb 'be' (is) and change the verb to the gerund by removing the 'e' and adding 'ing'.)

　6 are sitting (The subject of the sentence is 'The girls', so students must use the third person plural of the verb 'be' (are) and change the verb to the gerund by adding an extra 't' and adding 'ing'.)

4 **1** They aren't shopping for food at the bookshop.

　2 We aren't having lunch.

　3 I'm not watching a film.

　4 My mum isn't listening to music.

　5 My granddad isn't wearing jeans.

　6 The students aren't doing an exercise.

5 **1** Is he taking the train, he isn't

　2 Are they making a cake, they aren't

　3 Are you learning the piano, I'm not

　4 Is she drawing a picture, she isn't

　5 Are they playing a game, they aren't

6 **1** 'm/am learning (The subject before the gap is 'I', so students use the first person singular of 'be' and add 'ing' to the verb 'learn'.)

　2 's/is visiting (The subject before the gap is 'a chef' so students use the third person singular of 'be' and add 'ing' to the verb 'visit'.)

　3 's/is teaching (The subject before the gap is 'He' so students use the third person singular of 'be' and add 'ing' to the verb 'teach'.)

　4 're/are having (The subject before the gap is 'We' so students use the first person plural of 'be', remove the 'e' from the infinitive 'have' and add 'ing'.)

　5 'm/am sending (The subject before the gap is 'I', so students use the first person singular of 'be' and add 'ing' to the verb 'send'.)

　6 're/are watching (The subject before the gap is 'We' so students use the first person plural of 'be' and add 'ing' to the verb 'watch'.)

7 Student's own answers.

　Possible answers:

　1 I'm learning about the present continuous.

　2 No, I'm not. I'm wearing a skirt.

　3 My friend (name) is sitting next to me.

　4 I'm thinking about the weekend.

　5 Yes, it is./No, it isn't.

Vocabulary 2

1 **1** snowing **2** foggy **3** sunny **4** windy **5** raining **6** cloudy

2 **1** cold, raining. **2** warm, cloudy **3** cold, snowing

3 **1** spring **2** summer **3** autumn **4** winter

4 **1** autumn **2** winter **3** summer **4** spring **5** winter

5 **1** It's raining and very cold. "What's the weather like in London?" "… it's very cold and it's raining"

　2 It's raining and very hot. "It's raining here too. … it always rains a lot in summer, even if it's very hot."

　3 April and May. "… in autumn it's cloudy but there isn't so much rain. That's April and May."

　4 June, July and August. "I think it's so strange that winter for you is June, July and August!"

　5 It's very sunny and warm. "… in spring. That's when it's very sunny and warm."

　6 Because she wants to go to the beach on Christmas day. "I'd love to go to the beach on Christmas day!"

Listening

1 **1** T *"It's cloudy again. …"*

　2 T *"Who's your favourite member of the band?" "Nick."*

　3 F *"She never sings."*

　4 F *"He doesn't play any instruments."*

　5 T *"the one next to Lucy. Is she her sister?" "No, she's her cousin. Her name's May."*

　6 F *"What about your friend Tom?"*

2 Lines from: Nick – the drummer in the band *"The one playing the drums?" "Yes. That's Nick."*

Alice – the girl carrying a guitar *"Alice? Where is she?"*
"She's carrying her guitar …"

Mark – the man reading *"Mark's the one reading."*

May – the girl eating a sandwich *"The one eating a sandwich? … Her name's May."*

Tom – the boy eating a banana *"What about your friend, Tom? …" "Yes, there he is. He's eating some sweets."*

3 countable: banana, carrot, sandwich, potato
uncountable: bread, meat, fruit, rice

4 1 B ('bread' is uncountable and the sentence is a positive statement, not a question or negative)

2 B (This is a question and the missing word comes before a countable noun.)

3 B ('tomatoes' is a plural countable noun and the sentence is a positive statement, not a question or negative)

4 C ('sandwich' is a singular countable noun, and this is a statement not a question)

5 A (This is a negative sentence and missing word comes before a plural countable noun.)

6 B ('egg' is singular and because it begins with a vowel, students must use the article 'an'. They don't use 'any' because the sentence is a positive statement.)

5 1 some (This is a positive sentence, so 'some' is used before an uncountable noun.)

2 a (This is a negative sentence, so 'a' is used before a countable noun.)

3 some (This is a positive sentence, so 'some' is used before an uncountable noun.)

4 any (This is a question, so 'any' is used before a plural countable noun.)

5 any (This is a negative sentence, so 'any' is used before an uncountable noun.)

6 an (The article 'an' is used before a singular countable noun which begins with a vowel, in positive sentences questions or negative sentences.)

Speaking

1 B ✓ How do you say this in English?
D ✓ Are there any flowers in picture B?
E ✓ What's the English for this weather?

2 1 In the picture on the right it's snowing./It's snowing in the picture on the right.   **2** In picture B the man is listening to music.   **3** In the first picture the dog is under a tree.   **4** In the picture on the left the rucksack is green.   **5** In the second picture the boy is wearing sunglasses.   **6** In picture A there are five sandwiches on the plate.

3 1 a mobile phone   **2** It's raining.   **3** four.   **4** He's writing.   **5** six.   **6** a cat

4 1 writing. He's looking in his bag.
2 got any sandwiches.
3 are big. In picture A they're small.
4 has got a cup on his table. He hasn't got any juice.
5 aren't wearing coats. They're wearing T-shirts.

Writing

1 1 B   **2** D   **3** F   **4** E   **5** B   **6** A
2 1 RABIER   **2** fourteen/14   **3** E12 6VB   **4** 0171 564 312
5 louislovescooking@rmt.com
3 1 F *Send us your ideas for an amazing sandwich party*
2 T *you can win free lunches for a month*
3 F *our brilliant café Sandy's Sandwiches*
4 F *(thirty words) describe your new sandwich in thirty words*
5 T *(twelve or older) You must be 12 years or older*

4 Correct options:
3 how many people you want ✓
4 the time the party starts ✓
5 where the party is ✓
6 the food you want ✓

5 Student's own answers.
Model answer:
I want mushroom and chilli sandwiches. The party will start at 4pm. I want to invite my class of 30 people. We can have the party at my house!

Unit check

1 Hot weather: lemonade, orange juice, water
Cold weather: hot chocolate, soup, tea

2 1 cheese sandwich   **2** chicken sandwich   **3** bean and meat soup   **4** meat with vegetables and potatoes   **5** chicken salad

3 1 autumn   **2** spring   **3** foggy   **4** Winter   **5** cold

4 1 are flying (The subject before the gap is 'we', so students use the first person plural of 'be' and add 'ing' to the verb 'fly' (because 'fly' collocates with 'kites').)

2 'm/am sitting (The subject before the gap is 'I', so students use the first person singular of 'be', add an extra 't' and 'ing' to the verb 'sit' (because 'sit on the beach' makes sense).)

3 is making (The subject before the gap is 'my mum', so students use the third person singular of 'be', remove the 'e' and add 'ing' to the verb 'make' (because 'make sugar skulls' works as a phrase).)

4 are having (The subject before the gap is 'My friends and I', so students use the first person plural of 'be', remove the 'e' and add 'ing' to the verb 'have' (because 'have' collocates with 'hot chocolate').)

5 'm/am shopping (The subject before the gap is 'I', so students use the first person singular of 'be', add an extra 'p' and 'ing' to the verb 'shop' (because you 'shop for' something).)

6 're/are wearing (The subject before the gap is 'We', so students use the first person plural of 'be' and add 'ing' to the verb 'wear' (because 'wear' collocates with 'fancy dress').)

5 1 B (The sentence is positive and the word after the gap is plural, so students must choose 'some'.)

2 A (This is a question and the word after the gap is an uncountable noun, so students must choose 'any'.)

3 B (This is a question and it is about an uncountable noun (cheese) so the verb must be singular (is).)

4 C (This sentence is negative and it is about an uncountable noun, so students must choose 'any'.)

5 C (This is a question and it is about an uncountable noun (fruit) so the verb must be singular (is).)

6 A (The sentence is positive and the objects are plural nouns, so the missing verb must be 'are'.)

6 Student's own answers.

UNIT 6

Vocabulary 1

1 1 It's old and beautiful.
2 It's new and clean.
3 She's young and dirty.
4 They're ugly and loud.

2 1 large   **2** interesting   **3** quiet   **4** slow   **5** boring   **6** difficult

3 1 mobile phone *there's my mobile phone on the table*
2 radio *The radio is my dad's/*
3 records *Those are my grandad's his records*
4 laptop *That large, heavy laptop is Kate's.*
5 tablet *My mum always brings her tablet to the kitchen.*

Reading

1 **1** last week

2 1837

2 In a village.

2 **1** building (The article before the gap is 'an' so the students must choose a singular noun.)

2 small (The missing word is an adjective, a desk can't be 'easy' or 'difficult' and because the desks are in a museum, they can't be 'new', so 'small' is the answer.)

3 pens (Students must choose something you can write with.)

4 difficult (The missing word is an adjective. It must be 'difficult' because, reading ahead, Jenny says that her answers were wrong.)

5 laptops (The missing word is a plural noun, and also something which didn't exist in the past ('There weren't any gadgets, like …'), so the answer must be 'laptops'.)

3 A very different school (Students choose the title which best describes the topic of the whole text – it is about differences between modern and old schools, so the title is 'A very different school.')

Grammar

1 **1** were (The sentence is about 1837, so the verb must be in the past. The subject of 'be' is plural ('musical instruments') so the missing word is 'were'.)

2 are (The sentence is about 'modern British classes', so the verb must be in the present. The subject of 'be' is plural ('children') so the missing word is 'are'.)

3 Were (The question is about the school museum in the past. The subject of 'be' is plural ('whiteboards') so the missing word is 'Were'.)

4 is (The sentence is about now, so the verb must be in the present. The subject of 'be' is singular ('work') so the missing word is 'is'.)

5 was(The question is about yesterday, so the verb must be in the past. The subject of 'be' is third person singular ('she') so the missing word is 'was'.)

2 **1** There weren't any TVs at the school.   **2** The lesson wasn't very interesting.   **3** Old computers weren't very quick.

4 The weather wasn't nice.   **5** My parents weren't happy with me.

3 **1** was (The subject before the gap is 'I', so the verb must be in the first person singular, and it is positive.)

2 were (The subject of the sentence is third person plural 'gadgets', and the sentence is positive, so the students write 'were'.)

3 weren't (The subject of the sentence is third person plural 'CDs', and the sentence is negative, so the students write 'weren't'.)

4 were (The subject of the sentence is third person plural 'machines', and the sentence is positive, so the students write 'were'.)

5 wasn't (The subject before the gap is 'the sound', so the verb must be in the third person singular, and the meaning of the sentence is negative (the sound wasn't like modern CDs).)

6 were (The subject of the sentence is third person plural 'gramophones', and the sentence is positive, so the students write 'were'.)

4 **1** was (The subject before the gap is 'the city' so the verb must be in the third person singular, and the meaning of the sentence is positive (the city was different from in the past), because the speaker says 'Wow!' at the beginning.)

2 were (The subject of the question is third person plural 'those things', and it is a positive question.)

3 were (The subject of the sentence is third person plural 'They' and the speaker is explaining what she thinks the word means, so it's positive.)

4 weren't (The subject of the sentence is third person plural 'cars', and the sentence is negative, because there aren't any cars in the photograph.)

5 weren't (The speaker is talking about the same subject (cars) so the verb is third person plural, and the sentence is negative, because she is agreeing with the previous statement ('you're right').)

6 were (The subject of the sentence is third person plural 'hats' and people are wearing hats in the photo, so it's positive.)

5 **1** Yes, they were. / No, they weren't.   **2** Yes, he was. / No, he wasn't.   **3** Yes, there was. / No, there wasn't.   **4** Yes, I was. / No, I wasn't.   **5** Yes, there were. / No, there weren't.   **6** Yes, it was. / No, it wasn't.

Vocabulary 2

1 **Across: 3** stay   **4** travel   **7** arrive

Down: 1 change   **2** text   **5** visit   **6** walk

2 **1** A ('travel' collocates with 'by car')

2 C ('arrive' is usually followed by 'at' or a time (so 'in the morning' matches))

3 D ('talk about' needs to be followed by a topic (football))

4 B ('tidy' collocates with 'garage' (and it doesn't require a preposition (so it isn't 'F'))

5 F ('help in the garden' works as a phrase)

6 E (a noun is required after 'wash', they are more likely to wash the dog than the garage, so it must be 'E')

3 **1** B (There is no preposition after the gap, so the answer must be 'visit' ('talk' is always followed by 'to' or 'with', 'arrive' is usually followed by 'at' or 'in'.)

2 C ('stay' collocates with a period of time ('for a week'), whereas you can't 'arrive' for a week and 'am' is grammatically incorrect)

3 C ('travel' collocates with 'by car', you can't 'walk by car' and 'goes' is grammatically incorrect)

4 A ('arrive' is usually followed by 'at' or 'in' – it collocates with 'in the evening')

5 B ('walk' collocates with 'on the beach', you can wash on the beach, but it is an unlikely thing to do on holiday, 'visit' is not followed by a preposition (it takes a direct object))

6 A ('talk' is the only activity in the options which you could do 'for hours')

4 **1** washes her hair   **2** She helps her   **3** arrive at eight   **4** stays at the   **5** usually visit her   **6** clean the street

Listening

1 **1** In York (England)   **2** Norway   **3** Because it has 'time travel' train rides. / Because it helps visitors experience life in Viking times.

2 **1** B *'It's in a shopping centre!'*

2 C *'… my grandma, my sister and I were inside.*

3 B *'In the Time Machine there was a real computer.*

4 B *They usually had fish and meat with bread*

5 A *And in the garden of the house was a real Viking toilet!*

3 + ed: talked, stayed

double consonant + ed: travelled, stopped

change y to ied: carried, tidied

+ d: changed, arrived

4 **1** John Lennon didn't play the drums.

2 Columbus didn't arrive in America in 1942.

3 Julius Caesar didn't travel by bus.

4 In 1750 people didn't clean their teeth every day.

5 Children didn't play computer games in 1960.

5 **1** arrived ('arrive' collocates with 'home', it must be positive because the rest of the text is about what Mason does after he gets home.)

2 didn't travel ('travel' collocates with 'by helicopter', it must be negative, because the previous sentence says 'doesn't like flying.')

3 changed ('change' collocates with 'his clothes', it is positive because he is likely to change his clothes after a concert)

4 washed ('wash' collocates with 'his hair')

5 didn't talk (you can talk 'a lot' or 'not much', so 'talk' is the correct verb, it is negative because the rest of the sentence says he was 'tired from singing')

6 helped (There is a direct object ('his parents') after the gap, 'help' is usually followed by a reference to the person you help, no preposition is used. It is positive because if he likes cooking (as stated at the beginning of the sentence) Mason would help his parents make dinner.)

Speaking

1 1 on ('on' is used before days of the week or dates)

2 last ('last weekend' is a fixed expression (also 'last month', 'last week'))

3 last ('last night' is a fixed expression (but we say 'yesterday morning/afternoon/evening'))

4 last ('last' is used before years or months)

5 x (no preposition is required before 'yesterday')

6 in ('in' is used before references to decades)

2 1 C **2** D **3** F **4** B **5** A **6** E

3 1 C **2** A **3** B **4** B **5** A **6** C

4 2 I think I do. ✓
3 I'm not sure. ✓
4 I think the answer is … ✓
5 Well done! ✓
6 Yes, that's right. ✓
8 That's a good idea. ✓

5 1 I think I do. (The phase must be positive because the word before the gap is 'Yes', and it must answer 'Do you …?' (the auxiliary from the question is repeated in the response))

2 That's a good idea. (Maria has just made a suggestion with 'Let's …' so the response needs to be a reaction to this.)

3 I think the answer is (The phrase is introducing an answer ('Italy').)

4 Yes, that's right. (Since Ana says 'I remember now' at the end of the line, this phrase must be about being sure of an answer.)

5 I'm not sure. (Since Ana asks 'what do you think?' at the end of the line, this phrase must be about being unsure of an answer.)

6 Well done! (Ana is saying that Maria has got two questions right, so she is praising/congratulating her at the end of the conversation.)

Writing

1 1 Where **2** Who **3** How **4** What time/When **5** What did **6** What is/was

2 A 6 very interesting place, the view was beautiful (The adjectives give the person's opinion of the trip, so 'What was your opinion …' is the matching question.)

B 3 travelled to the island on a boat (The answer contains a method of transport so 'How did you travel there?' matches.)

C 4 arrived at ten in the morning (The answer contains a time, so the question 'When did you arrive?' matches.)

D 5 listened to information about the history of the lighthouse, climbed to the top (119 stairs) (The answer is about what the person did (listened, climbed) so the question 'What did you see and do?' matches.)

E 1 Red Point Lighthouse on an island near Scotland (The answer is a place, so the question 'Where was it?' matches.)

F 2 with my parents (The answer is about the people and contains 'with' so the question 'Who were you with?' matches.)

3 1 parents ('with my' parents means the missing word is the people she went on holiday with)

2 boat ('travelled … by' before the gap means the missing word is method of transport)

3 history ('talked about the' before the gap means the missing word is the topic of the information she listened to)

4 stairs (students find the number in the notes and the noun which follows it)

5 beautiful ('It' in the sentence refers back to the 'view'. Students look at the notes to find the adjective the writer uses to describe the view ('beautiful').)

4 Student's own answers.
Model answer in Ex 3

Unit check

1 1 surprised (The adjective must describe an emotion someone feels (Dad).)

2 record ('record player' is a compound noun)

3 exciting (a trip can be described as 'exciting' but not 'modern')

4 fun (The first sentence recommends that someone goes to the museum, so the students must choose the positive adjective.)

5 different (The first sentence suggests that the speaker wants to go to a different place (because the park is 'boring').)

6 new (Students circle the adjective which is an antonym for 'old-fashioned'.)

2 1 dirty **2** small **3** loud **4** slow **5** terrible

3 1 stay (the preposition 'at' follows 'stay')

2 tidy / clean ('tidy' and 'clean' collocate with 'bedroom', a direct object follows both verbs)

3 tidy / clean ('tidy' and 'clean' collocate with 'bedroom', a direct object follows both verbs)

4 text / visit / help ('text', 'visit' and 'help' collocate with 'my friends', a direct object follows all three verbs)

5 text / visit / help ('text', 'visit' and 'help' collocate with 'my friends', a direct object follows all three verbs)

6 text / visit / help (text', 'visit' and 'help' collocate with 'my friends', a direct object follows all three verbs)

7 walk / travel (the preposition 'to' and a place follow 'walk' and 'travel')

8 walk / travel (the preposition 'to' and a place follow 'walk' and 'travel')

4 1 was (The subject before the gap is 'The bus', so students use the third person singular ('was'), which is positive because the words after the gap are adjectives describing the bus (if the verb was negative, the connector between the two adjectives would be 'or').)

2 were (The subject of the sentence is 'people', which is a countable plural noun, so the verb is in the third person plural 'were'.)

3 Was (The subject of the question is 'your brother', so the verb is in the third person singular.

4 wasn't (The subject is 'my teacher', so the verb is in the third person singular, it is negative ('wasn't') because the meaning of the sentence is that the teacher was unhappy that the writer talked in class.)

5 Were (The subject of the question is 'you' so the verb is in the second person. It doesn't make sense to ask 'Where weren't you …?' so it must be positive.)

6 weren't (The subject is 'CD players' so the verb is in the third person plural, the meaning of the sentence is that CD players didn't exist until 1982, so the verb must be negative.)

5 1 B **2** F **3** E **4** A **5** C **6** D

6 1 visited **2** didn't visit **3** played **4** didn't play **5** didn't tidy **6** tidied

REVIEW: UNITS 1–6

1 vehicles: car, van, lorry
animals: bee, whale, sheep
food and drink: milk, carrot, cake

2 1 understand ('I don't understand' explains why you would ask someone to repeat something.)
 2 play ('play' collocates with football)
 3 meet ('meet' collocates with 'my friends', especially since a meeting place is given in the second half of the sentence)
 4 have ('have a party' is a fixed expression)
 5 help ('Can you help me, please?' is a way to stop a stranger and ask for directions (the following sentence suggests that the person needs directions))
 6 say ('How do you say … in English?' is a common expression, which students practised in Unit 5.)

3 1 'm doing (The person is currently doing homework (at the moment of speaking) so the present continuous form must be used.)
 2 mustn't (People generally can't play loud instruments at night, so 'mustn't' is the correct answer.)
 3 any (This is a question about a countable, plural noun, so 'any' is the correct answer.)
 4 is (The subject of the verb is 'he' so 'is' is the correct answer (third person singular))
 5 'm enjoying (The person is currently reading the book (at the moment of speaking), because of the word 'this', so the present continuous form must be used.)
 6 speak (After 'can' the infinitive form is used, not the continuous.)

4 1 E **2** C **3** F **4** B **5** A **6** D

5 1 How are you? (This is a standard way to ask about someone's health and the usual answer is 'I'm fine, thanks.')
 2 What do pandas eat? (The answer is about pandas' diet. Students repeat the verb 'eat' in the question, with 'do' in the third person plural (because 'pandas' is plural).)
 3 Where's the supermarket, please? (The reply gives directions, so the question must be 'Where's …'. The place mentioned is the supermarket, so students put that in the question.)
 4 What's the weather like? (This is a standard way to ask about the weather.)
 5 What's your sister doing (at the moment)? (The answer is in the present continuous, so the question must be in the same form. The speaker is talking about his/her sister, so the question must be about 'your sister' (and the verb must be in the third person singular).)

6 1 Do (The verb in the question is 'come' so the question in the present simple is formed with the verb 'do'. The subject of the question is 'you', so 'do' must be in the second person singular.)
 2 This (Ala is introducing her cousin to someone else. 'This is my …' is a fixed expression for doing this.)
 3 do (In the short answer, the same auxiliary verb from the question must be repeated 'do'. The answer is positive, so it's 'do', not 'don't'.)
 4 eating (Kasia can't understand Marta, and the reason is that she is eating cake ('Christmas cake') comes after the gap, so the verb must be 'eating'.)
 5 Are (The question is in the present continuous, so the missing words must be the auxiliary verb 'be'. The subject of the question is 'you' so the form must be the second person singular 'Are'.)

7 1 bicycle (the rest have four wheels and motors)
 2 bus stop (the rest are things people visit)
 3 pasta (the rest are drinks)
 4 change (the rest are adjectives)
 5 forest (the rest are bodies of water)
 6 boring (the rest are positive adjectives)

8 A clock **B** bridge **C** bat **D** shower **E** desert **F** motorbike
9 1 C **2** D **3** E **4** A **5** F **6** B
10 1 C (Students choose the correct auxiliary verb to make 'arrive' negative (didn't).)
 2 B (Students choose the past tense form of 'text' – it is a regular verb so forms the past with –ed (texted).)
 3 A (Students choose the correct auxiliary verb to make 'help' negative (didn't).)
 4 A (Students choose the past tense form of 'watch' – it is a regular verb so forms the past with –ed (watched).)
 5 B (The auxiliary must be negative because it isn't a good idea to play computer games before bed, 'isn't play' is grammatically incorrect, so the answer is 'mustn't'.)
 6 C (Students choose the correct auxiliary verb to make 'go' negative in the present, also in the third person singular (the subject of the sentence is 'We'), so the answer is 'don't'.)

11 1 visited (The verb must be in the past simple (+ed) and it must take a direct object -'visited' (her) fits the gap.)
 2 pictures/photos (The preposition 'of' follows 'pictures' and 'photos'.)
 3 got ('have got' is used to say how many children/grandchildren someone has. The 's before the gap means 'has' so the next word must be 'got'.)
 4 are (After the gap there is an adjective, so the verb is 'be'. The subject of the sentence is 'We' and the adverb 'always' means it is in the present simple ('are').)
 5 helped ('help' takes a direct object ('my mum') and afterwards has 'to' + infinitive. The sentence begins 'On Saturday' so it is in the past (students add 'ed').)
 6 was (The sentence is describing a cake – the verb is 'be' in the past. The subject is 'It' so 'be' needs to be in the third person singular.)
 7 didn't (Students need to make the verb negative in the past, so they use the auxiliary 'didn't'.)

UNIT 7

Vocabulary 1

1 A doctor **B** scientist **C** photographer **D** basketball player
 E farmer **F** artist
2 1 C **2** E **3** A **4** F **5** D **6** B
3 Student's own answers.

Reading

1 1 Chris Haas
 2 hands-on basketball
 3 *Kids Inventing, Shooting for Your Dreams*
2 1 USA ('from' before the gap means the missing word is a place or country, the article 'the' means the answer must be 'USA', since countries made up of states/smaller political entities need the article (e.g. 'the UK', 'the UAE').)
 2 help (the direct object and infinitive 'to play' after the gap fit the pattern for 'help' (help someone to do something).)
 3 competition at (The event described in the text is a competition. Students need to add 'at' before the place.)
 4 big sports company bought (Students find the people/company that bought the idea in the text.)
 5 famous (Students look for the verb 'became' in the text to find the corresponding adjective.)
 6 wrote a book (The title of the book is given after the gap, so the phrase must be 'wrote a book'.)
3 Student's own answers.
4 Student's own answers.

Grammar

1 1 had **2** wrote **3** came **4** read **5** were

2 1 Suzanne Collins wrote *The Hunger Games* in 2008.
2 Barack Obama became president of the USA in 2009.
3 Ed Sheeran had his first hit song in England in 2011.
4 One Direction made their first album in 2011.
5 Germany won the football World Cup in 2014.

3 1 Did, see **2** Did, buy **3** Did, go **4** Did, have **5** Did, write **6** Did, make **7** Did, read

4 1 Did Justin Timberlake sing a song at his wedding? ('sing' collocates with 'a song'. Students use 'did' and the infinitive form to make the question.)
2 Did Borge Ousland walk across the Antarctic? ('across' can follow the verb 'walk'. Students use 'did' and the infinitive form to make the question.)
3 Did Emma Watson play hockey at college? ('play' collocates with sports like 'hockey'. Students use 'did' and the infinitive form to make the question.)
4 Did Rafal Nadal want to be a tennis player? ('to be' follows 'want'. Students use 'did' and the infinitive form to make the question.)
5 Did Enrique Iglesias live in Spain when he was young? ('live' collocates with 'in Spain'. Students use 'did' and the infinitive form to make the question.)

5 1 Yes, I did. / No, I didn't.
2 Yes, they did. / No, they didn't.
3 Yes, he/she did. / No, he/she didn't.
4 Yes, I did. / No, I didn't. + Student's own answers.
5 Yes, they did. / No, they didn't.
6 Yes, I did. / No, I didn't.

Vocabulary 2

1 1 give **2** go **3** learn **4** see **5** make **6** take

2 1 left **2** thought **3** said **4** could **5** found **6** had **7** built

3 1 C (The end of the sentence 'for my birthday' is a clue that it is about giving a present. There is also a direct object (me) after the gap.)
2 A (The adjective in the sentence suggests it is about an opinion, so 'thought' is the correct choice.)
3 B ('took' collocates with 'some pictures')
4 A ('train' collocates with 'left')
5 C (There is a score at the end of the sentence and 'football match' after the gap, so 'won' is the correct verb.)
6 B ('went' is followed by 'to' and a place)

4 1 was (Before 'born' students need to put the correct form of 'be'. The subject of the sentence is Alma Deutscher, so 'be' needs to be in the third person singular.)
2 could (There is already a main verb ('sing') so the verb in the gap must be an auxiliary ('can'). There is only one past form ('could').)
3 learnt (The words after the gap are 'to play', so 'learn' is the best fit.)
4 wrote (The words after the gap are 'a piano sonata' so 'write' is the best fit.)
5 saw (You can see an orchestra play (e.g. at a concert).)
6 made ('make' collocates with 'a TV programme')

Listening

1 Student's own answers.
Correct answer: 2 (to break a record)

2 1 Milan *'Why did you go to Milan?' … 'There was a special event there for people who love building.'*
2 35/thirty-five *'It was 35 metres tall in the end.'*
3 5/five *'And how long did people work on the tower?' 'Five days.'*

4 Cattelan *'… his name was Alessandro Cattelan. C-A-T-T-E-L-A-N.'*
5 seven *'They gave seven Euros for every centimetre of the tower!'*
6 work *My family and I learnt to work with other people and together.'*

3 1 *Who* (The answers are all people and 'go with' in the question suggests the question is asking about 'who'.)
2 Where (The answers are all country names.)
3 When (The answers are all dates.)
4 Did (Short answers are given, so the question needs to be formed with the auxiliary, in the past ('Did').)
5 What (The question is about Bruno's opinion ('What' is the correct question word).)

4 1 A
2 B
3 C
4 A
5 C

5 1 Why did she write that message?
2 What was your favourite picture?
3 When did the train leave?
4 Where did your sister go to school?
5 Who did you see at the café?
6 How long did you stay in Madrid?
7 When did you visit the museum?
8 What did you do in the evening?

Speaking

1 1 E ('Where' in the question matches the place in the answer (Paris), and the verb 'go' is followed by the preposition 'to'.)
2 A ('When' in the question matches a time in the answer (in August))
3 F ('How' in the question matches 'by' + a method of transport in the answer (by train))
4 C ('Who' in the question matches 'her parents' in the answer.)
5 D (The order of pictures show what she did on the first day (go on rides))
6 B (The last picture shows what she did on the next day (play tennis))

2 1 and (The second clause adds extra information / description to the first. There is no contrast or change in time.)
2 when (The beginning of the sentence is about the time of day, 'when' connects this to what happened.)
3 when ('when' is used to show that one event happened after soon after another (they arrived/they went to the theme park).)
4 but (The second clause has a negative verb, so 'but' connects this to the positive beginning of the sentence.)
5 then (The order of events in the day is shown by the connector 'then'.)
6 and (The second clause adds extra information about what Rita did. There is no contrast or change in time.)

3 Students tick: 3, 4, 5 and 6

4 1 Last ('Last' collocates with the name of a month (or day of the week/ 'month'/ 'week' /'year'))
2 When ('when' is used to show that one event happened after soon after another (they arrived/they had to wait).)
3 knew ('know' collocates with 'face' (you can 'know a face'))
4 said (The gap comes after some direct speech, so 'said' is the correct choice.)
5 but (The second clause has a negative verb, so 'but' connects this to the positive beginning of the sentence.)

Writing

1 **1** was (The whole article is in the past, so the correct choice is 'was'.)
  2 up ('grow up' is a phrasal verb)
  3 go (After 'didn't' the infinitive of the verb is used.)
  4 was (The subject of the sentence is 'He' so the verb must be in the third person singular.)
  5 When ('when' is used to show that one event happened after soon after another)
  6 sang ('singed' is grammatically incorrect, because 'sing' is an irregular verb)

2 **1** D ('When' in the question matches a date in the answer (In 1989))
  2 H ('Where' in the question mateches a place in the answer (London))
  3 E ('When' in the question matches a time period in the answer (When they were young.). The answer reflects the subject of the question (his parents – they))
  4 F (The question is formed with the auxiliary (Did) so a short answer must match. The question is about school, so the answer containing 'He went to a regular school.' fits.)
  5 A ('When' in the question matches a time period in the answer (When he was ten years old.') This is a logical answer to when he began acting.)
  6 G ('How old' in the question matches an age in the answer (he was eleven))
  7 C (The question is formed with the auxiliary (Did) so a short answer must match. The question is about Daniel's work in America, so the answer about theatre matches.)
  8 B (The question is formed with the auxiliary (Did) so a short answer must match. The subject of the short answer 'they' matches the subject of the question 'people'.)

3 **1** He's from Spain. **2** She was born in 1993. **3** She started to play tennis when she was three (years old). **4** She won the French Open (in 2016). **5** Because when you win everything is beautiful, but when you lose it's hard.

4 Student's own answers.
  Model answers in Ex 1 and 3

Unit check

1 **1** buy, bought **2** win, won **3** think, thought **4** sing, sang
  5 give, gave **6** write, wrote

2 **1** said **2** learnt **3** could **4** built **5** did **6** went

3 **1** wasn't (The subject before the gap is 'It', so students use the third person singular ('was'), but they make it negative because of the adverb 'always' before 'fun'.)
  2 saw (The object after the gap is 'the same ten people' which collocates with 'see'. The verb is positive because the writer is describing what she saw every day.)
  3 didn't have ('have' collocates with 'time'. The word 'much' after the gap means that the verb must be negative.)
  4 knew (The words after the gap 'that it was cold' follow after 'know'. The verb is positive because the writer is describing a thing she knew.)
  5 took ('with me' at the end of the sentence collocates with 'take'. The verb is positive because she is describing what she took.)
  6 made ('make' collocates with 'friends'. The verb must be positive, because she says the experience was 'amazing' (it wouldn't have been if she didn't make friends))
  7 didn't win (The second part of the sentence says 'I was second' so it's clear that she 'didn't win'.)

4 **1** is he from (The answer is a place.)
  2 was he born (The answer is a date (in the past).)
  3 did he study (The answer is the name of a university, so 'did he study' fits the question)

4 did he become ('become' collocates with a profession, such as 'film-maker'.)
  5 was his first film (The verb 'was' is used in the answer, so it needs to be in the question too. The question needs to have the same subject 'His first film'.)
  6 did he win/get / did they give him (An Oscar is a prize, so the verbs 'win', 'get' and 'give' all collocate.)

UNIT 8

Vocabulary 1

1 one: neck, mouth, head, back
  two: shoulders, legs, arms, hands, feet
  ten: toes

2 **1** face **2** hand **3** leg **4** foot

3 **1** She's got long curly hair. It's dark. (Third person singular 'She's got' as it is a woman in the photo.)
  2 He's got short wavy hair. It's brown/dark. (Third person singular 'He's got' as it is a man in the photo.)
  3 They've got short curly hair. It's fair/blonde. (Third person plural 'They've got' as there are two people in the photo.)
  4 She's got short straight hair. It's fair/blonde. (Third person singular 'She's got' as it is a woman in the photo.)
  5 They've got long straight hair. It's brown/dark. (Third person plural 'They've got' as there are two people in the photo.)
  6 He's got long straight hair. It's fair. (Third person singular 'He's got' as it is a man in the photo.)

Reading

1 **1** F 'Actor Scarlett Johansson is from New York …'
  2 T 'She acted for the first time in a theatre when she [was] eight years old …'
  3 T 'Hunter was in one film, with his sister, in 1996 …'
  4 F 'Patricia, her twin, is five minutes younger than her famous sister.'
  5 T '… they both went to modelling school when they were thirteen.'
  6 F 'She was much taller and thinner than the other children in her class at school. "It wasn't fun," she says.'

2 **1** A (on) (The preposition 'on' is used before 'TV'.)
  2 B (was) (The verb 'be' is used to talk about ages in English, not 'have' or 'have got'.)
  3 A (got) (The verb phrase 'have got' is used to describe eye colour.)
  4 B (has) (Before the gap there is a subject, so the verb is missing from the sentence. 'have' must be in the third person singular, because of the subject (she).)
  5 A (the) (The definite article is missing.)
  6 C (that) (The missing word is a conjunction – to link the two parts of the sentence.)

Grammar

1 **1** Kasia She's got long, fair hair
  2 Anastasia They look the same, but we always know who is who because Anastasia's hair is longer than Ala's
  3 Ala They look the same, but we always know who is who because Anastasia's hair is longer than Ala's.'
  4 Jan … my dad, Jan. Boris is my dad's younger brother, but he's taller than him.
  5 Dobry My cousin Dobry is 11. His hair is short like mine, but it's curlier and much blonder.
  6 Boris … my dad, Jan. Boris is my dad's younger brother, but he's taller than him
  7 Marek Marek is Dobry's younger brother.

2 **1** older **2** curlier **3** than **4** nearer **5** worse **6** than

3 **1** better **2** bigger **3** easier **4** darker **5** happier **6** louder

4 1 The book is sadder than the film. **2** Our kitchen is dirtier than our living room. **3** Your singing is worse than my singing. **4** Running is easier than skiing. **5** My school is bigger than your school.

5 Student's own answers.
Possible answers:
1 My English is better than my parents' English.
2 My bedroom is smaller than my parents' bedroom.
3 My bag is lighter than my friend's bag.
4 My dad is taller than my friend's dad.
5 My hair is longer than my friend's hair.

Vocabulary 2

1 1 sunglasses **2** jeans **3** boots **4** hoodie **5** shorts **6** hat
2 1 shirt **2** tshirt **3** boots **4** across: skirt **4** down: sandals **5** shoes **6** jeans **7** shorts
3 1 A ('walking in the mountains' at the end of the sentence means the right footwear is 'boots', not sandals and tights are not 'strong')
2 B ('swimsuit' is the only item people usually wear at the beach)
3 C (people usually play tennis in trainers, not boots or sandals)
4 B (a swimsuit is not appropriate)
5 B ('socks' is the only item which, if worn, would make boots smaller)
6 B (people usually stand on boots and shoes, so the answer must be 'sunglasses' because of the negative imperative)
7 A (a 'cap' would be the only thing that could be worn to hide a haircut)
8 B ('tights' are usually the only item worn with a skirt)
4 1 shorts ('shorts' collocates with 'T-shirts' and is it something you would wear in hot weather)
2 shirts ('shirts' is the only formal item of clothing in the word box)
3 sandals ('sandals' are a type of footwear, and are worn at the beach)
4 boots ('boots' are a type of footwear, and are for the winter)
5 trainers (The phrase 'because we aren't a sports shop' after the gap means the missing word must be something sold at a sports shop.)
6 jeans (The item must be something which is almost always blue.)
5 Student's own answers.

Listening

1 1 C … the world's first fashion designer. … she lived about 300 hundred years ago in France
2 D The wedding dress with the longest train in the world. … was made in China in 2017.
3 A They are the highest shoes in the world, … A man called James Syiemiong made them in India.
4 E the most people wearing sunglasses in the dark … people got together in Valladolid, Spain, to set this record.
5 B people say the British are the people who dress the worst in Europe'
2 1 queen Her name was Rose Bertin … One of her most famous clients was Marie Antoinette, the queen of France.
2 month This dress was made in China in 2017. It took 22 people one month to make it …
3 94/ninety-four They are the highest shoes in the world, at 94 centimetres
4 September On 6th September 2015, 6,774 people got together in Valladolid, Spain, to set this record.'
5 70/seventy British people spend the most on clothes … in 2015 it was 70 million euros!'

3 1 the slowest **2** the biggest **3** the funniest **4** bad **5** the saddest **6** the best
4 1 I think this is the worst DVD I've got. **2** I've got three cousins. Rafael is the tallest. **3** This is the happiest day of my life. **4** Our classroom is the coldest in the school. **5** They've got three dogs. Pablo is the loudest.
5 1 fastest (The speed given at the end of the sentence means the adjective must be to do with speed, 'fast' is the only one. Students use the superlative.)
2 smallest (The end of the sentence describes just two rooms, so the adjective must be 'small'. Students use the superlative.)
3 longest (The distance given at the end of the sentence means the adjective must be to do with length, 'long' is the only one. Students use the superlative.)
4 youngest (The age given at the end of the sentence means the adjective must be to do with age, 'young' is the only one. Students use the superlative.)
5 most (The remaining word in the box is 'more', superlative form 'most'.)

Speaking

1 A the USA B Antarctica C India D Bolivia E Austria F Chile
2 Student's own answers.
3 A the USA B Antarctica C India D Bolivia E Austria F Chile
4 1 D (the highest capital city on Earth)
2 A (the oldest tree in the world)
3 E (the best place to live in the world)
4 F (the driest place on Earth)
5 C (the wettest place on Earth)
6 B (the coldest place on Earth)
7 1 summer Even in summer the temperature in higher parts of Antarctica is around minus 20.
2 89/eighty-nine … the lowest temperature recorded there was -89 degrees Celsius
3 desert The Atacama Desert, in Chile has less than one millimetre of rain per year.
4 rain There are around 11,000 millimetres of rain there every year.
5 above This amazing city is 3,600 metres above sea level.
6 2015 In a survey in 2015, experts discovered that people who live there had the best quality of life.

Writing

1 1 at (The preposition 'at' follows 'look' before something you can see.)
2 like ('look like' is a phrasal verb)
3 – (After the gap there is an adjective, so 'look' shouldn't be followed by a preposition.)
4 for (The preposition 'for' follows 'look' when the meaning of 'look' is 'search'.)
5 – (After the gap there is an adjective, so 'look' shouldn't be followed by a preposition.)
6 at (The preposition 'at' follows 'look' before something you can see.)
7 like (phrasal verb 'look like' means 'similar to')
8 for (The preposition 'for' follows 'look' when the meaning of 'look' is 'search'.)
2 1 'I need to see Grandma,' says Mum.
2 'Can I come too?' asks Daniel.
3 Mum says, 'Yes that's a good idea.'
4 'I'm going to look for my shoes,' says Daniel.
5 'I think they're in the kitchen,' says Mum.
6 'Yes, here they are,' says Daniel.

3 Student's own answers.

Model answer:

Oliver and Robert are twins. They are in their bedroom doing their homework. Oliver takes his brother's homework. Robert isn't looking.

The next day they go to school. Oliver gives some homework to the teacher but Robert can't find his homework. 'I don't understand!' he says.

Later the teacher is asking questions about the homework. 'I don't know the answer,' says Oliver. 'I think Olivertook my homework, Miss!' says Robert. He's very angry.

Unit check

1 1 C   2 D   3 B   4 E   5 A

2 1 head   2 neck   3 shoulder   4 arm   5 hand   6 finger   7 leg

3 Student's own answers.

4 1 world ('world record' is a fixed expression and it collocates with 'break', 'break a pop record' is unlikely (the article is about traditional Irish dancing))

   2 most (Students choose the superlative form – 'more' would be used before an adjective to make a comparison, but there is no adjective after the gap and no 'than' in the second half of the sentence.)

   3 than ('than' comes after a comparison)

   4 straight ('straight' collocates with 'arms', but 'wavy' is for describing hair ('wavy hair'))

   5 feet ('feet' are used in dancing, 'teeth' aren't)

   6 louder (Students choose the comparative form because the sentence compares two things and the word 'than' is after the gap.)

   7 like ('look like' is a phrasal verb)

5 1 Anna 'Anna's got the curliest hair.'

   2 Eva 'Marta's hair is shorter than Jana's and Eva's hair. Eva's mouth is bigger than Jana's mouth.'

   3 Heidi 'Heidi's hair is the longest.'

   4 Isobel 'Isobel has got dark, wavy hair. It isn't the shortest hair.'

   5 Jana 'Marta's hair is shorter than Jana's and Eva's hair. Eva's mouth is bigger than Jana's mouth.'

   6 Marta 'Marta's hair is shorter than Jana's and Eva's hair.'

REVIEW: UNITS 1–8

1

things in a room	verbs	jobs
bin	help	dentist
mirror	sing	teacher
mat	teach	singer

2 1 C   2 H   3 B   4 A   5 G   6 D   7 F   8 E

3 1 above (A shelf can be 'above' a bed.)

   2 from ('from' is used after 'be' and before a city/country of origin)

   3 on ('on' is used before days of the week)

   4 by ('by' is used before methods of transport)

   5 at ('at the weekend' is a fixed expression)

   6 in ('in front of' is a preposition made up of three words)

   7 for ('go for a walk' is a collocation)

   8 to (go 'to' a place)

4 1 I don't meet my friends in the evening. (Students use the auxiliary 'do' in the first person, negative form. 'meet is in the infinitive form)

   2 You mustn't take photos. (Students add 'n't' to 'must'.)

   3 There isn't any rice in the cupboard. (Students add 'n't' to 'is' and change 'some' to 'any'.)

   4 We didn't go to a basketball match yesterday. (Students use the auxiliary 'do' in the past tense, negative form. They change 'went' to the infinitive 'go'.)

   5 She didn't lose her suitcase at the airport. (Students use the auxiliary 'do' in the past tense, negative form. They change 'lost' to the infinitive 'lose'.)

   6 I'm not having breakfast (Students use 'not' in front of the gerund of the verb)

   7 My sister doesn't always walk to school (the negative auxiliary verb 'doesn't' goes before the adverb of frequency 'always' and the main verb 'walk')

5 1 because (The interviewer asked 'Why' so the reply must include 'because')

   2 have ('have' collocates with 'singing lessons' (first person singular because the subject of the sentence is 'I'))

   3 my (The word after the gap is noun, so a possessive pronoun fits.)

   4 When (The question is about a date, so 'When' is the best question word.)

   5 was ('be' is used to refer to age. The subject of the sentence is 'I' so students change it to the first person singular (in the past).)

   6 at ('at' collocates with 'school' ('at' is used with public places e.g. 'at the library', 'at the hospital').)

   7 didn't (This is a short answer, so the auxiliary 'did' needs to be used. It must be negative because the answer starts with 'No'.)

6 1 play   2 climb   3 travel   4 tidy   5 wash   6 write

7 1 played ('Play' collocates with 'card games'. Students form the past simple by adding -ed.) 2 climbed ('Climb' collocates with 'hill'. Students form the past simple by adding -ed.)

   3 travelled (The preposition 'to' often follows 'travel' (and there is a named destination). Students form the past simple by adding the letter 'l' (doubling the consonant) and adding -ed.)

   4 washed (Rain can wash snow away. Students form the past simple by adding -ed.)

   5 wrote ('Write' collocates with 'on the board'. 'write' is an irregular verb, students use the simple past form 'wrote'.)

   6 tidied ('Tidy' collocates with the name of a room ('the kitchen'). Students form the past simple by removing the 'y' and adding -ied.)

8 1 Tuesday   2 bread   3 wheels   4 May   5 clock   6 bridge

9 1 Do you live in a village? (Yes, I do. / No, I don't.)

   2 Is there a noticeboard in your classroom? (Yes, there is./ No, there isn't.)

   3 Has your best friend got fair hair? (Yes, he/she has. / No, he/she hasn't.)

   4 Do you play a musical instrument? (Yes, I do. / No, I don't.)

   5 Did your parents go to work yesterday? (Yes, they did./ No, they didn't.)

10 1 coldest (The word 'the' before the gap and the description in the rest of the sentence means the missing word is a superlative adjective. Since the temperature mentioned is very low, the answer must be 'coldest'.)

   2 must (The missing word is an auxiliary verb, because the main verb 'wear' is after the gap, with the subject before. Given the meaning of the previous sentence, the verb has to be 'must'.)

   3 can (The missing word is an auxiliary verb, because the main verb 'be' is after the gap, with the subject before. The sentence is positive, and describes a possibility, so the verb has to be 'can'.)

   4 difficult (A question can be 'easy' or 'difficult'. The rest of the sentence means students should choose 'difficult' (it goes on to say that it's hard to choose a season to visit Moscow).)

   5 worst (The word 'the' before the gap, with a noun afterwards suggests the missing word is a superlative adjective. 'best' and 'worst' both collocate with 'time', but the rest of the sentence leads students to choose 'worst' as it describes bad weather.)

UNIT 9

Vocabulary 1

1 1 rock climbing   2 dancing   3 tennis   4 skiing   5 swimming
6 yoga

2 Student's own answers.

3 1 do   2 go   3 play   4 go   5 do   6 play

4 Student's own answers.

5 1 B (sailing) ('go sailing' collocates with 'on a boat')
2 B (surfing) (The word must be something you can do 'on the sea', so it can't be 'cycling' and if it were 'skiing' the word 'water' would be needed before the gap.)
3 C (volleyball) ('volleyball' is the only option which collocates with 'play')
4 A (mountain biking) (In the first part of the sentence the writer mentions her bike, with the two phrases connected with 'and' the next part must also be about cycling.)
5 A (skateboarding) ('skateboarding' and 'skiing' both collocate with 'go' (before the gap) but the sport must be something to do 'at the park' so the answer must be 'skateboarding')
6 C (basketball) ('basketball' and 'baseball' both collocate with 'go' (before the gap) but the sport must be something you can play either inside or outside. The writer also says 'It helps that I'm tall', so it must be 'basketball'.)

Reading

1 1 C   2 A   3 B   4 A   5 B   6 A   7 C

2 Joe: London Eye, Buckingham Palace, British Museum
Patricia: Switzerland
Max: train station

3 Student's own answers.

Grammar

1 1 They're going to go rollerblading.   2 They're going to play football.   3 They're going to play tennis.   4 They're going to ski/go skiing.   5 He's going to play basketball.   6 She's going to surf/go surfing.

2 1 We aren't going to win.   2 He isn't going to sing in the show.
3 They aren't going to have a party.   4 I'm not going to go camping.   5 You aren't going to clean your bedroom.
6 She isn't going to go cycling.

3 1 are, going to (Students use 'are' because the subject of the question is 'you' (second person singular))
2 's/is going to (The sentence must be positive because the speaker is talking about when a birthday is going to be. The subject is 'he' so the verb 'be' needs to be in the third person singular ('is').)
3 'm going to (The sentence must be positive because the speaker is talking about buying something. The subject is 'I' so the verb 'be' needs to be in the first person singular ('am', abbreviated to 'm').)
4 is going to (The sentence must be positive and the subject is 'it' so the verb 'be' must be third person singular (is))
5 are going to (This is a positive sentence. The subject is 'parents' so the verb 'be' is in the third person plural ('are').)
6 're/are going to (This is a positive sentence. The subject is 'We' so the verb 'be' is in the third person singular ('are').)

4 1 Are you going to go to France in the summer?   2 Are you going to travel by plane?   3 Is the weather going to be hot?
4 Is your sister going to go with you?   5 Are you all going to stay in a hotel?   6 Is your dad going to try to speak French?

5 1 Yes, I am. / No, I'm not.   2 Yes, they are. / No, they aren't.
3 Yes, I am./No, I'm not.   4 Yes, they are./No, they aren't.
5 Yes, they are. / No, they aren't.   6 Yes, she is. / No, she isn't.

Vocabulary 2

1 1 She's got a cold.   2 She's got stomachache.   3 She's got a sore throat.   4 She's got a headache.   5 He's got toothache.
6 He's got earache.

2 1 B   2 A   3 C   4 C   5 B   6 C

3 Across: 2 matter   4 sunburn   5 cough   6 well
Down: 1 cut   3 temperature

4 1 Have you got (Students must use 'have got' before 'a temperature'. They use the subject 'you' and invert the subject and verb because it is a question.)
2 a sore ('sore' collocates with 'throat' and students must use the article beforehand.)
3 doctor ('see a doctor' is what you should do if you are ill.)
4 a (The article 'a' must be used before 'cold'.)
5 to drink (The word after the gap is 'water' and so the main verb must be 'drink' (good advice if you have a sore throat). Students must use the infinitive with 'to' after 'need'.)

5 Student's own answers.

Listening

1 A 4 *'How was your guitar lesson?'*
B 2 *'I want to swap to the after-school tennis club.'*
C 5 *'we can leave early tomorrow and have all weekend away'*
D 3 *'But I don't like speaking in front people.'*
E 1 *'Your mother and I are thinking about the holiday in August.'*

2 1 C *'I like staying in the flat with Grandma and Grandpa.'*
2 B *'It's just that I don't like playing basketball any more. I want to swap to the after-school tennis club.'*
3 A *'I know there are going to be lots of parents listening …'*
4 B *'Don't you want to be a pop star?' 'Not a pop star, Mum, a classical guitarist.'*
5 C *'I really want to pack my phone!'*

3 1 to be (The word after the gap is 'a dancer', so the verb must be 'be'. Students use the infinitive 'to be' after 'want'.)
2 tidying (The word after the gap is the name of a room, so the verb must be 'tidy'. Students use the gerund 'tidying' after 'like'.)
3 to watch ('a film' is after the gap, so the verb must be 'watch'. Students use the infinitive 'to watch' after 'want'.)
4 listening ('listen' collocates with 'to music'. Students use the gerund 'listening' after 'love'.)
5 swimming ('swim' collocates with 'in the sea'. Students use the gerund 'swimming' (adding an extra 'm') after 'like'.)
6 to stay ('stay' collocates with 'at home'. Students use the infinitive 'to stay' after 'want'.)

4 1 travelling   2 watching   3 having   4 to be   5 to write

Speaking

1 2 Cinema

2 1 an exhibition about the history of sports
2 Cam's sister My sister said it's not that interesting.
3 It's raining. But it's raining.
4 some boots I need some boots.
5 There are always lots of people (on Saturday). … there are always lots of people at the shopping centre.
6 They go online (and see what's on). We can go online and see what's on.

3 1 D (How about' is the beginning of a question, option 'c' already has the word 'about', so the answer must be 'D')
2 F ('sure' is used after the verb 'be')
3 B ('Let's' needs to be followed by the infinitive (without 'to'))
4 A (The matching phrase must have both a subject and a verb (missing from the first part of the sentence.)
5 C ('What' matches with 'about' to make a fixed phrase used to make suggestions)
6 E ('Good idea' is a fixed expression.)

4 1 How about **having a party?**

2 Let's **go swimming**.

3 What about **playing baseball?**

4 How about **going cycling?**

5 I want to **play tennis**.

6 What about **doing yoga?**

5 1 How/What ('How' or 'What' comes before 'about' to make a fixed phrase used to make suggestions.)

2 sure ('sure' is used after the verb 'be', in response to a suggestion (usually to preface a rejection of the suggestion))

3 doesn't (Since the subject and verb are both already given, the missing word must be an auxiliary verb. 'doesn't' can be used before 'like' in the present to make the verb negative. Students use the third person singular because of the subject ('Ben').)

4 right ('right' is used after the verb 'be', in response to a suggestion when the speaker is agreeing/accepting it.)

5 idea ('good idea' is a fixed expression.)

6 Let's (The sentence is a suggestion, with the main verb already given. The answer can't be 'How about' because the verb is in the infinitive (without 'to'), so it must be 'Let's'.)

Writing

1 1 Y (The sentence is in the past simple.)

2 N (The sentence is in the present continuous.)

3 T (The sentence includes 'going to', so it refers to a future plan.)

4 T (The sentence includes 'going to', so it refers to a future plan.)

5 Y (The sentence is in the past simple.)

2 1 (Hi Louis,)

7 (Love Maggie)

4 (Tomorrow I'm …)

2 (I'm having a …)

5 (I can't wait!)

6 (See you soon,)

3 (It was a lot of fun.)

3 1 play ('play' is used before sports, such as tennis)

2 visit ('visit' collocates with 'a museum')

3 go ('go' is used before outdoor pursuits, such as swimming)

4 meet (You usually meet a person/some people. Since there is a name after the gap, 'meet' is the best fit.)

5 have ('have' is used before meals (breakfast/lunch/dinner))

6 walk ('walk' collocates with 'on the beach'.)

4 1 played (The sentence begins 'Yesterday' so students use the past tense.)

2 visited (The description continues in the past.)

3 'm going to go (The sentence begins 'Later this morning' so students use 'be going to' (because it's a plan). The subject is 'I' so they use the first person singular (I'm).)

4 'm going to meet (This sentence is also about future plans. Again the subject is 'I'.)

5 to have (The verb before the gap is 'want' so students use the infinitive with 'to'.)

6 are going to walk (The sentence describes future plans so students use 'be going to'. The subject is 'we' (Carla and I) so students use the first person plural 'are'.)

5 Student's own answers.
Model answer in Ex 4

Unit check

1 1 skiing **2** volleyball **3** shopping **4** rollerblading **5** sailing

2 1 F **2** E **3** A **4** B **5** C **6** D

3 1 to do (The infinitive with 'to' is used after 'want'.)

2 doing (The gerund 'ing' is used after 'love'.)

3 to go (The infinitive with 'to' is used after 'want'.)

4 playing (The gerund 'ing' is used after 'like'.)

5 to play (The infinitive with 'to' is used after 'want'.)

6 going (The gerund 'ing' is used after 'like'.)

7 to have (The infinitive with 'to' is used after 'want'.)

4 1 's/is going to be (There is an adjective after the gap, so the verb must be 'be'. The subject is 'My mum' so students use the third person singular of 'be'.)

2 'm/am going to have ('have' collocates with 'a shower'. The subject is 'I' so students use the first person singular of 'be'.)

3 aren't going to travel ('travel' can be followed with 'by' and a method of transport. The subject is 'We' so students use the first person plural of 'be'.)

4 Are, going to walk ('walk' collocates with 'home'. The subject of the question is 'you' so students use the second person singular 'Are' (which is at the beginning, since subject and verb are inverted in a question))

5 'are going to watch ('watch' collocates with 'TV'. The subject is 'Carla and her brother' so students use the third person plural.)

6 's/is going to see ('see' collocates with 'a concert'. The subject is 'he' so students use the third person singular.)

5 1 meeting/seeing (The object after the gap is 'my friends' so the missing verb must be 'meet' or 'see'. Students use the gerund because the verb before the gap is 'like')

2 playing ('play' collocates with 'computer games'. Students use the gerund because the verb before the gap is 'like')

3 to (After 'want' the infinitive with 'to' must be used. 'to' is missing before 'be'.)

4 'm/am (The verb 'be' is used before 'going to' to talk about a future plan (the sentence ends 'next week'). Students use the first person singular because the subject is 'I'.)

5 are (The verb 'be' is used before 'going to' to talk about a future plan. Students use the third person plural because the subject is 'My friends')

REVIEW: UNITS 1–9

1 1 singer (the rest are medical professionals that deal with health problems) **2** tall (the rest can describe hair) **3** jeans (the rest are worn on the feet) **4** toes (we only have two of the other parts of the body, but ten toes) **5** helped (the rest are irregular past forms) **6** new (the rest can be used to describe hair)

2 A mirror **B** postcard **C** scientist **D** socks **E** sweatshirt **F** cold

3 1 A **2** E **3** F **4** C **5** D **6** B

4 1 food / milk

2 colourful bird

3 drive / road

4 insect/animal / eight legs

5 someone who works un a hospital

6 it to cross over water

5 1 city (Liverpool is a city, 'city' is the only available noun that is a place where people can live)

2 upstairs (The answer needs to be an adjective that describes the position of the bedroom)

3 bathroom (The answer must be a room that isn't in Betty's house. It cannot be 'garden' because of the sentence that follows, describing the position of the toilet.)

4 garden (The answer must be a place outside, which is where the toilet is)

5 plane (The answer must be a mode of transport because the sentence says 'travel … by' before the gap)

6 difficult (The answer must be an adjective. It has to be a negative adjective because the previous adjective in the text is 'long' and the connector is 'and')

7 beautiful (The answer must be an adjective because the gap is before a noun 'house'. A house cannot be 'difficult' (the only other adjective available) and from the context is must be a positive adjective 'beautiful')

6 1 She didn't grow up in London.
  2 There aren't any photos of the inside of the house.
  3 The house didn't have three bedrooms.
  4 There wasn't a toilet inside the house.
  5 Betty's family didn't go to Australia by plane.
  6 Emma isn't going to visit Sheffield one day.

7 1 lighter (A sword can be 'light'. The word after the gap is 'than' so the sentence is a comparison. Students form the comparative by adding 'er'.)
  2 best (Because the next sentence says 'They're great!' the adjective is 'good'. The word before the gap is 'the' so the missing word must be a superlative form. Students use the superlative of 'good', which is irregular.)
  3 dangerous (Because the next sentence says 'I haven't got any cuts.' the writer is clearly saying that fencing isn't dangerous.)
  4 good (The word after the gap is 'at' followed by a sport/skill, so the missing word is either 'good' or 'bad'.)
  5 quick ('quick' could be used to describe feet, when they have to move fast in a sport. The writer uses 'faster' in the next sentence.)
  6 interesting (The phrase 'it's a very good way to learn' is another way of saying that something is interesting.)

8 1 We sometimes go skiing in January.
  2 Football players aren't always tall.
  3 I don't really like playing tennis in winter.
  4 Don't go rollerblading in the children's playground.
  5 My sister usually plays basketball at the sports centre.
  6 You mustn't go swimming when you've got a temperature.

9 1 are you (The reply is 'I'm fine, thanks', so the question must be 'How are you?')
  2 did you start (The answer is 'I started playing when I was 11' so the question must also be in the past simple and use the verb 'start' with the auxiliary verb 'did'.)
  3 were you (The answer is 'no, I wasn't', so the question must also be in the past simple and be an inversion of the subject and verb, with the verb 'be' in the second person singular.)
  4 did you (The question already has the question word 'how' and phrasal verb 'get better', so the auxiliary verb 'did' and subject 'you' are needed.)
  5 Do you like (The answer is 'Yes, I do. I love it.' so the question must be 'Do you like …'. 'Love' is only used in response to the question and never in the question.)
  6 are you doing/are you training for (The reply is in the present continuous, so the question needs to be in the present continuous with the subject 'you' as the reply is 'I'. The question could use the same verb and collocation 'training for' as the reply or could be more general 'what are you doing'.)

10 1 A (The answer must be a date.)
  2 C (The question begins 'When' so the answer must be a date, day or time.)
  3 B (The subject of the question is 'it' (family name) so the answer which begins 'It's …' is correct.)
  4 B (The question is in the second person singular, but the reply must be in the first person, so A and C are both impossible. 'Yes, of course' is a common response to a request for help.)
  5 B (The question is not an offer, so 'No, thank you' (C) is an incorrect reply. The answer must include 'yes' or 'no'. The subject of the question is 'there' so the short answer would be 'Yes, there is' (A is incorrect).)
  6 A (The question 'What's the weather like?' must be answered with a description of the weather, not how you feel (so C is incorrect). 'like' mustn't be repeated in the answer so B is incorrect.)

7 C (The person is asking what the problem is, so the usual reply would be a specific answer)
8 B (The question is a suggestion 'How about …' so 'Great idea' is the suitable answer, as the other two options are answers to closed questions (starting with 'Do you' or 'Are you').)

UNIT 10

Reading

1 1 join **2** work **3** wear **4** have **5** learn
2 1 Young people aged eighteen to twenty-five *Are you aged between 18 and 25?*
  2 £100 *We pay £100 a day …*
  3 seven thirty *'… extras need to arrive at seven thirty*
  4 three *We can't tell [you] the name or subject of the film, but we can say that three famous actors are making it with us.*
3 1 C ('look for' is a phrasal verb. The verb must be in the gerund because the auxiliary 'are' is before the gap, so it's the present continuous.)
  2 C (The preposition 'at' must be used before 'night'.)
  3 A (The subject is missing (because the word after the gap is a verb), so 'they' is the correct choice ('their' is a possessive adjective and 'them' is an object pronoun).)
  4 B ('get up' is a phrasal verb)
  5 C ('we don't/never work long hours' doesn't make sense, when the rest of the sentence is about wanting to complete a scene. 'we sometimes work long hours' is both grammatically correct and makes sense.)
  6 A (An object pronoun is needed after 'tell'. Because the rest of the advert is directed at the reader, the pronoun which fits is 'you'.)
4 Students' own information – name must be in capitals.
5 1 B (Emma asks 'Is your throat better?', so Clare may be sick.)
  2 A (Take three people with you because the sign says: 'Free drinks for every table of four people or more.')
  3 A ('My brother's got three tickets for a concert tonight. Are you free?' The answer can't be 'B' because Ed says 'we only need to pay him £20'. Ed doesn't talk about 'meeting' Sam, he says 'tell me before 5 p.m.'.)
  4 B ('Only children older than 12 can watch this film.')
  5 C (It can't be 'A' because Leslie says they are 'beautiful', it can't be B because she says they have 'nice personalities' so it must be C, as she says 'We have three adults, so these little ones need a new home.')
  6 B ('There is a special volleyball match at 11.30. It's free to watch …')

Listening

1 1 'Do you like the food here?' **3** 'What time did you start work?' **5** 'What's the film about?' and **7** 'What's the weather like?'
2 1 B *It's half past seven in the morning and I'm eating breakfast!'*
  2 B *'… I got up at six thirty this morning!*
  3 C *In the film I'm going to be talking with some friends.*
  4 A *I'm listening to some music while I wait on the beach …*
  5 C *It's cloudy and it's raining. No more filming today.*
3 1 A month ago. *'This is my friend, Karen. We started work together last month.'*
  2 Before the extras. *'I did the stars' make-up first. They start work before the extras, you know.'*
  3 Because it's never boring. *'… I love it because it's never boring.'*
  4 Some dolphins. *'Yesterday I saw some dolphins!'*
  5 It's cloudy and it's raining. *'It's cloudy and it's raining.'*
  6 Sunday *'We're not going to work tomorrow because it's Sunday.'*

4
1 She's having breakfast.
2 She's practising her scene.
3 She's waiting on the beach.
4 She's having lunch.
5 She's going home.

Speaking

1 **Students tick: 1** I love … **3** What about you? **4** I'm not sure.
6 Well, I think they're OK. **8** Really?

2 1 B (The question starts with 'Where' so the answer must give a location.)
2 C (The question is about types of film, so the answer must be a genre/film type.)
3 B (The question requires a yes/no answer or an opinion. 'They're OK.' is the best response.)
4 A ('What do you think …' is asking for an opinion. 'I'm not sure.' is the only answer which says what the person thinks/feels.)
5 A ('I love …' is a statement. The speaker could be agreeing or disagreeing. 'You're boring' is not an appropriate response (very impolite), 'I love, too' is grammatically incorrect because the object 'them' is missing. 'Really?' is an appropriate response – showing that the speaker is surprised.)
6 C (The question requires a yes/no answer, with the same verb ('be'). The short answer 'Yes, they are' is correct because it also repeats the same subject (films = 'they').)

4 Student's own answers.
Possible answers:
1 I like animal films because they're interesting.
2 I like action films because they're exciting.
3 I don't like cartoons because I prefer human characters.
4 I love kung fu films because they're different.
5 I think sport films are interesting and inspiring. I don't like 3D films because I don't like wearing the glasses.

Writing

1 1 D (The matching phrase must be an adjective followed by a noun (because the article 'a' is at the end of the first phrase).)
2 C ('have' collocates with 'a good time')
3 E ('enjoy' collocates with 'a lot'. The matching phrase must also contain an object (film).)
4 F ('about' follows 'be sure')
5 B ('watch' collocates with 'film'. It can't be 'e' because there is no article, so it must be 'b' ('this film'))
6 A ('like' is followed by a direct object ('the characters').)

2 1 I don't want to read the next book in the series. (Students make the sentence negative using the auxiliary 'don't' and the verb in the infinitive (without 'to').)
2 I didn't have a very good time at the concert. (Students make the sentence negative using the auxiliary 'didn't' and the verb in the infinitive (without 'to'))
3 My sister and I laughed. (The main verb is 'laugh'. Students add 'ed' to make the positive past form. An auxiliary verb isn't necessary.)
4 I didn't think it was an interesting programme. / I thought it was a boring programme. (Students make the sentence negative using the auxiliary 'didn't' and the verb in the infinitive (without 'to'). Alternatively, they change the positive adjective 'interesting' to 'boring'.)
5 My family enjoyed watching the film. (The main verb is 'enjoy'. Students add 'ed' to make the positive past form. An auxiliary verb isn't necessary.)
6 The characters were very funny. (Students make the sentence positive by changing the 'be' verb from negative to positive in the third person plural.)

3 1 What was (The answer is the topic of a book, so the question word is 'What'. Students use the same verb and tense as in the answer ('be' in the past simple, third person singular to match the subject (the book).)
2 Who were/are (The answer is about people, so the question word is 'Who'. There is no tense in the answer, so the question could be in the present or the past ('be' in the past or present simple, third person plural to match the subject (the characters).)
3 happened (The answer is a description of the plot, so the verb must be 'happen'. Students use the same tense as in the answer (past simple), by adding 'ed' to the infinitive.)
4 Who, you (The answer is about who the book came from, so the question word is 'Who'. The answer is in the first person, so the question needs to be in the second person singular (you).)
5 Who (The answer is a person's name so the question word must be 'Who'.)
6 When (the answer is a time (2017), so the question word must be 'When'.)
7 What, think (The answer is an opinion, so the question must be 'What did you think … ?')

4 1 Four stars *The group was called 'Four stars'*
2 The life of a dancer. *It was about the life of a famous Russian dancer*
3 Pablo *The main character, Pablo …*
4 Russia *'… a famous Russian dancer'*
5 An hour *We stayed for an hour and then we went home*
6 In a pet shop. *He worked in a pet shop and that's when he had the idea and he wrote the book.*

5 1 an 2 at 3 are 4 the 5 swam 6 to

6 1 'Explore Australia' It was called 'Explore Australia'
2 Because he studied Australia at school last year. We learnt a little about Australia at school last year …
3 Camels and red kangaroos. The presenter took a trip into the desert and she saw camels and red kangaroos there.
4 Sharks. Then she swam with sharks in the ocean
5 Visit Australia. I want to visit Australia now!

7 Student's own answers.
Model answer in Ex 5

A1 MOVERS: WORDLIST

Grammatical Key

adj adjective
adv adverb
conj conjunction
det determiner
dis discourse marker
excl exclamation
int interrogative
n noun
poss possessive
prep preposition
pron pronoun
v verb

A

above *prep*
address *n*
afraid *adj*
after *prep*
age *n*
all *adj + adv + det + pron*
all right *adj + adv*
along *prep*
always *adv*
another *det + pron*
any *det + pron*
app *n*
around *prep*
asleep *adj*
at *prep of time*
aunt *n*
awake *adj*

B

back *adj + adv + n*
bad *adj*
badly *adv*
balcony *n*
band (music) *n*
basement *n*
bat *n*
be *called v*
beard *n*
because *conj*
before *prep*
below *prep*
best *adj + adv*
better *adj + adv*
blanket *n*
blond(e) *adj*
boring *adj*
both *det + pron*
bottle *n*
bottom *adj + n*

bowl *n*
brave *adj*
break *n*
brilliant *adj*
Brilliant! *excl*
bring *v*
build *v*
building *n*
bus station *n*
bus stop *n*
busy *adj*
buy *v*
by *prep*

C

café *n*
cage *n*
call *v*
car park *n*
careful *adj*
carefully *adv*
carry *v*
catch (e.g. a bus) *v*
CD *n*
centre (US center) *n*
change *v*
cheese *n*
cinema *n*
circle *n*
circus *n*
city *n*
city/town centre
(US center) *n*
clever *adj*
climb *v*
cloud *n*
cloudy *adj*
clown *n*
coat *n*
coffee *n*
cold *adj + n*
come on! *excl*
comic *n*
comic book *n*
cook *v*
cook *n*
cough *n*
could (as in past of can
for ability) *v*
country *n*
countryside *n*
cry *v*
cup *n*
curly *adj*

D

dance *n + v*
dangerous *adj*
daughter *n*
dentist *n*
difference *n*
different *adj*
difficult *adj*
doctor *n*
dolphin *n*
down *adv + prep*
downstairs *adv + n*
dream *n + v*
dress up *v*
drive *n*
driver *n*
drop *v*
dry *adj + v*
DVD *n*

E

earache *n*
easy *adj*
e-book *n*
elevator (UK lift) *n*
email *n + v*
every *det*
everyone *pron*
everything *pron*
exciting *adj*
excuse me *dis*

F

fair *adj*
fall *v*
famous *adj*
farm *n*
farmer *n*
fat *adj*
feed *v*
field *n*
film (US movie) *n + v*
film (US movie) *star n*
fine *adj + excl*
first *adj + adv*
fish *v*
fix *v*
floor (e.g. ground, 1st, etc.) *n*
fly *n*
forest *n*
Friday *n*
frightened *adj*
funfair *n*

G

get dressed *v*
get off *v*
get on *v*
get undressed *v*
get up *v*
glass *n*
go shopping *v*
goal *n*
granddaughter *n*
grandparent *n*
grandson *n*
grass *n*
ground *n*
grow *v*
grown-up *n*

H

have (got) to *v*
headache *n*
helmet *n*
help *v*
hide *v*
holiday *n*
homework *n*
hop *v*
hospital *n*
hot *adj*
how *adv*
how much *adv + int*
how often *adv + int*
huge *adj*
hundred *n*
hungry *adj*
hurt *v*

I

ice *n*
ice skates *n*
ice skating *n*
idea *n*
ill *adj*
inside *adv + n + prep*
internet *n*
into *prep*
invite *v*
island *n*

J

jungle *n*

K

kangaroo *n*
kick *n*
kind *n*
kitten *n*

L

lake *n*
laptop *n*
last *adj + adv*
laugh *n + v*
leaf/leaves *n*
library *n*
lift (US elevator) *n*
lion *n*
little *adj*
look *for v*
lose *v*
loud *adj*
loudly *adv*

M

machine *n*
map *n*
market *n*
matter *n*
mean *v*
message *n*
milkshake *n*
mistake *n*
model *n*
Monday *n*
moon *n*
more *adv + det + pron*
most *adv + det + pron*
mountain *n*
moustache *n*
move *v*
movie (UK film) *n*
must *v*

N

naughty *adj*
near *adv + prep*
neck *n*
need *v*
net *n*
never *adv*
noise *n*
noodles *n*
nothing *pron*
nurse *n*

O

o'clock *adv*
off *adv + prep*
often *adv*
on *adv + prep of time*
only *adv*
opposite *prep*
out *adv*
out *of prep*
outside *adv + n + prep*

P

pair *n*
pancake *n*
panda *n*
parent *n*
parrot *n*
party *n*
pasta *n*
penguin *n*
picnic *n*
pirate *n*
place *n*
plant *n + v*
plate *n*
player *n*
pool *n*
pop *star n*
practice *n*
practise *v*
present *n*
pretty *adj*
puppy *n*
put *on v*

Q

quick *adj*
quickly *adv*
quiet *adj*
quietly *adv*

R

rabbit *n*
rain *n + v*
rainbow *n*
ride *n*
river *n*
road *n*
rock *n*
roller skates *n*
roller skating *n*
roof *n*
round *adj + adv + prep*

S

safe *adj*
sail *n + v*
salad *n*
sandwich *n*
Saturday *n*
sauce *n*
scarf *n*
score *v*
seat *n*
second *adj + adv*
send *v*
shall *v*
shape *n*
shark *n*
shop *v*

A1 MOVERS: WORDLIST

shopping *n*
shopping centre (US center) *n*
shoulder *n*
shout *v*
shower *n*
sick *adj*
skate *n + v*
skip *v*
sky *n*
slow *adj*
slowly *adv*
snail *n*
snow *n + v*
someone *pron*
something *pron*
sometimes *adv*
son *n*
soup *n*
sports centre (US center) *n*
square *adj + n*
stair(s) *n*
star *n*
station *n*
stomach *n*
stomach-ache *n*
straight *adj*
strong *adj*
Sunday *n*
sunny *adj*
supermarket *n*
surprised *adj*
sweater *n*
sweet *adj*
swim *n*
swimming pool *n*
swimsuit *n*

T
take *v*
take off (i.e. get undressed) *v*
tall *adj*
tea *n*
teach *v*
temperature *n*
terrible *adj*
text *n + v*
than *conj + prep*
then *adv*
thin *adj*
think *v*
third *adj + adv*
thirsty *adj*
Thursday *n*
ticket *n*
tired *adj*
tooth / teeth *n*
toothache *n*
toothbrush *n*
toothpaste *n*
top *adv + n*
towel *n*
town *n*
town/city centre (US center) *n*
tractor *n*
travel *v*
treasure *n*
trip *n*
Tuesday *n*

U
uncle *n*
up *adv + prep*
upstairs *adv + n*

V
vegetable *n*
video *n*
village *n*

W
wait *v*
wake (up) *v*
walk *n*
wash *n + v*
water *v*
waterfall *n*
wave *n*
weak *adj*
weather *n*
website *n*
Wednesday *n*
week *n*
weekend *n*
well *adj + adv*
wet *adj*
whale *n*
when *adv + conj + int*
where *pron*
which *pron*
who *pron*
why *int*
wind *n*
windy *adj*
work *n + v*
world *n*
worse *adj + adv*
worst *adj + adv*
would *v*
wrong *adj*

X
(No words at this level)

Y
yesterday *adv + n*

Z
(No words at this level)

Letters & Numbers
Candidates will be expected to understand and write numbers 21–100 and ordinals 1st to 20th.

Names
Candidates will be expected to recognise and write the following names:

Charlie	Jack	Lily	Sally
Clare	Jane	Mary	Vicky
Daisy	Jim	Paul	Zoe
Fred	Julia	Peter	

Appliances

camera
CD (player)
cell phone
clock
computer
cooker
digital camera
DVD (player)
electric
electricity
fridge
gas
heating
lamp
laptop
lights
mobile (phone)
MP3 player
PC
phone
radio
telephone
television / TV
video
washing machine

Clothes and Accessories

bag
bathing suit
belt
blouse
boot
bracelet
cap
chain
clothes
coat
costume (swimming)
dress
earring
fashion
glasses
glove
handbag
hat
jacket
jeans
jewellery / jewelry

jumper
kit
necklace
pocket
purse
raincoat
ring
scarf
shirt
shoes
shorts
skirt
suit
sunglasses
sweater
swimming costume
swimsuit
T-shirt
tie
tights
trainers
trousers
try on v
umbrella
uniform
wallet
watch
wear v

Colours

black
blue
brown
dark
golden
green
grey
light
orange
pale
pink
purple
red
white
yellow

Communication and Technology

address
at / @
by post

call v
camera
CD (player)
cell phone
chat
click v
computer
conversation
digital
digital camera
dot
download n & v
DVD (player)
email n & v
envelope
file
information
internet
keyboard
laptop (computer)
mobile (phone)
mouse
MP3 player
net
online
PC
phone
photograph
photography
printer
screen
software
talk
telephone
text n & v
video
web
web page
website

Documents and Texts

ad / advertisement
article
bill
book
card
comic
diary
diploma
email

form
letter
licence
magazine
menu
message
newspaper
note
notebook
passport
postcard
project
text n & v
textbook
ticket

Education

advanced
beginner
biology
blackboard
board
book
bookshelf
chemistry
class
classmate
classroom
clever
coach
college
course
desk
dictionary
diploma
eraser
exam(ination)
geography
history
homework
information
instructions
know
language
learn
lesson
level
library
mark
maths/mathematics

note
physics
practice n
practise v
project
pupil
read
remember
rubber
ruler
school
science
student
studies
study v
subject
teach
teacher
term
test n
university

Entertainment and Media

act
actor
adventure
advertisement
art
article
board game
book
card
cartoon
CD (player)
chess
cinema
classical (music)
competition
concert
dance n & v
dancer
disco
draw
drawing
drum
DVD (player)
exhibition
festival
film n & v

fun
go out
group
guitar
hip hop
instrument
keyboard
laugh
listen to
look at
magazine
MP3 player
museum
music
musician
news
newspaper
opera
paint *v*
painter
photograph
photographer
photography
piano
picture
play *n*
pop (music)
practice *n*
practise *v*
programme
project
radio
read *v*
rock (concert)
screen *n*
show *n*
sing
singer
song
television / TV
theatre
ticket
video (game)
watch *v*

Family and Friends
aunt
boy
brother
child
cousin
dad(dy)
daughter

family
father
friend
friendly
girl
grand(d)ad
grandchild
granddaughter
grandfather
grandma
grandmother
grandpa
grandparent
grandson
granny
group
guest
guy
husband
love *n & v*
married
Miss
mother
Mr
Mrs
Ms
mum(my)
neighbour
parent
pen-friend
sister
son
surname
teenager
uncle
wife

Food and Drink
apple
bake
banana
barbecue
biscuit
boil
boiled
bottle
bowl
box
bread
break *n*
breakfast
burger
butter

cafe/café
cafeteria
cake
can *n*
candy
carrot
cereal
cheese
chef
chicken
chilli
chips
chocolate
coffee
cola
cook *n & v*
cooker
cream
cup
curry
cut *n*
dessert
dinner
dish *n*
drink
eat
egg
fish
food
fork
fridge
fried
fruit
garlic
glass
grape
grilled
honey
hungry
ice
ice cream
jam
juice
kitchen
knife
lemon
lemonade
lunch
main course
meal
meat
melon

menu
milk
mineral water
mushroom
oil
omelette
onion
orange
pasta
pear
pepper
picnic
piece of cake
pizza
plate
potato
rice
roast *v & adj*
salad
salt
sandwich
sauce
sausage
slice *n*
snack *n*
soup
steak
sugar
sweet *n & adj*
tea
thirsty
toast
tomato
vegetable
waiter
waitress
wash up
yog(h)urt

Health, Medicine and Exercise
accident
ambulance
appointment
arm
baby
back
blood
body
brain
break *v*
check *v*
chemist

clean *adj & v*
cold *n*
comb *n*
cut *v*
danger
dangerous
dead
dentist
die
doctor
Dr
ear
exercise
eye
face
fall *v*
feel *v*
finger
fit
foot
hair
hand
head
health
hear *v*
heart
hospital
hurt *v*
ill
leg
lie down
medicine
neck
nose
nurse
pain
problem
rest *n*
run
sick
soap
stomach
stomach ache
swim
temperature
tired
tooth
toothache
toothbrush
walk
well *adj*

Hobbies and Leisure

barbecue
beach
bicycle
bike
book
camera
camp
camping
campsite
CD (player)
club
collect *v*
computer
dance *n & v*
draw
DVD (player)
festival
go out
guitar
hobby
holidays
join
magazine
member
MP3 player
museum
music
musician
paint *n & v*
park
party
photograph *n & v*
picnic
quiz
tent
video game

House and Home

address
apartment
armchair
bath(tub)
bathroom
bed
bedroom
blanket
bookcase
bookshelf
bowl
box
carpet
chair
clock
computer
cooker
cupboard
curtain
desk
dining room
door
downstairs
drawer
DVD (player)
entrance
flat *n*
floor
fridge
furniture
garage
garden
gas
gate
hall
heating
home
house
key
kitchen
lamp
light
live *v*
living room
pillow
refrigerator
roof
room
safe *adj*
shelf
shower
sink
sitting room
sofa
stay *v*
toilet
towel

Measurements

centimetre / centimeter
day
degree
gram(me)
half
hour
kilo(gram[me])/kg
kilometre/km/kilometer
litre / liter
metre / meter
minute
moment
quarter
second
temperature
week
year

Personal Feelings, Opinions and Experiences (adjectives)

able
afraid
alone
amazing
angry
bad
beautiful
better
big
bored
boring
brave
brilliant
busy
careful
clear
clever
cool
different
difficult
excellent
famous
fast
favourite
fine
free
friendly
funny
good
great
happy
hard
heavy
high
hungry
important
interested
interesting
kind
lovely
lucky
married
modern
nice
noisy
old
pleasant
poor
pretty
quick
quiet
ready
real
rich
right
slow
small
soft
sorry
special
strange
strong
sure
sweet
tall
terrible
tired
unhappy
useful
well
worried
wrong
young

Places: Buildings

apartment (building)
bank
block
bookshop
bookstore
building
cafe/café
cafeteria
castle
cinema
college
department store
disco
elevator
entrance
exit
factory
flat
garage
grocery store
guest-house
hospital
hotel
house
library
lift
museum
office
pharmacy
police station
post office
railway station
school
shop
sports centre
stadium
supermarket
swimming pool
theatre
university

Places: Countryside

area
beach
campsite
farm
field
forest
hill
island
lake
mountain
path
railway
rainforest
river
sea
sky
village
wood

Places: Town and City

airport
bridge
bus station
bus stop
car park
city centre
corner
market
motorway

park
petrol station
playground
road
roundabout
square
station
street
town
underground
zoo

Services

bank
cafe / café
cafeteria
cinema
dentist
doctor
garage
hotel
library
museum
petrol station
post office
restaurant
sports centre
swimming pool
theatre
tourist information centre

Shopping

ad / advertisement
assistant
badminton
ball
baseball
basketball
bat
bathing suit
beach
bicycle
bike
bill
boat
bookshop
buy *v*
cash *n & v*
catch *v*
cent
change *n & v*
cheap
cheque

climb *v*
close *v*
closed
club
coach *n*
competition
cost *n & v*
credit card
cricket
customer
cycling
department store
dollar
enter (a competition)
euro
expensive
fishing
football
football player
for sale
game
goal
golf
hockey
kit
luck
member
open *v & adj*
pay (for)
penny
play *v*
player
pool *n*
pound
practice *n*
practise *v*
price
prize
race *n & v*
racket
receipt
rent
rest *n & v*
ride *n & v*
riding
rugby
run *v*
sailing
sea
shop
shop assistant
shopper

shopping
skate *v*
skateboard *n*
ski *v*
skiing
snowboard *n*
snowboarding
soccer
spend
Sport
sport(s)
sports centre
stadium
store
supermarket
surf
surfboard
surfboarding
swim
swimming
swimming costume
swimming pool
swimsuit
table tennis
team
tennis
tennis player
throw *v*
ticket
tired
trainers
try on
v / versus
volleyball
walk *v*
watch *v*
win *v*
windsurfing
winner

The Natural World

air
autumn
beach
bee
country
countryside
desert
east
explorer
field
fire
flower

forest
grass
grow
hill
hot
ice
island
lake
moon
mountain
north
plant
rabbit
river
sea
sky
south
space
spring
star
summer
tree
water
west
winter
wood
wool
world

Time

a.m./p.m.
afternoon
appointment
autumn
birthday
calendar
century
clock
daily
date
day
diary
evening
half (past)
holidays
hour
January – December
meeting
midnight
minute
moment
Monday – Sunday
month

monthly
morning
night
noon
o'clock
past
quarter (past/to)
second
spring
summer
time
today
tomorrow
tonight
week
weekday
weekend
weekly
winter
working hours
year
yesterday

Travel and Transport

(aero)/(air)plane
airport
ambulance
backpack
boat
bridge
bus
bus station
bus stop
car
case
coach
country
delay *n & v*
delayed
drive
driver
driving/driver's licence
engine
engineer
explorer
far
flight
fly
garage
helicopter
journey
leave
left

light
luggage
machine
map
mechanic
mirror
miss *v*
motorbike
motorway
move
oil
park *v*
passenger
passport
petrol
petrol station
pilot
platform
railway
repair *v*
return *n & v*
ride
right
road
roundabout
sailing
seat
ship
station
stop
straight on
street
suitcase
taxi
ticket
tour *n*
tour guide
tourist
tourist information centre
traffic
traffic light
tram
travel
trip
tyre
underground *n*
visit
visitor
way *n*
wheel
window

Weather
cloud
cloudy
cold
fog
foggy
hot
ice
rain
snow
storm
sun
sunny
thunderstorm
warm
weather
wet
wind
windy

Work and Jobs
actor
artist
boss
break *n*
business
businessman
businesswoman
chemist
cleaner
coach *n*
company
computer
cook *n & v*
customer
dentist
desk
diary
diploma
doctor
Dr
driver
earn
email *n & v*
engineer
explorer
factory
farm
farmer
footballer
football player
guest
guide

instructions
job
journalist
king
letter
manager
mechanic
meeting
message
musician
nurse
occupation
office
painter
photographer
pilot
police officer
queen
receptionist
secretary
shop assistant
shopper
singer
staff
student
teacher
tennis player
tour guide
uniform
waiter/ waitress
work
worker
writer

A1 MOVERS EXAM OVERVIEW

Listening Test

Parts (25 minutes)	What is the skills focus?	What you have to do
1 (5 questions)	Listening for names and descriptions	Draw lines to match names to people in a picture
2 (5 questions)	Listening for names, spellings and other information	Write words or numbers in gaps
3 (5 questions)	Listening for specific information	Match pictures with illustrated items by writing a letter in a box
4 (5 questions)	Listening for specific information	Tick a box under the correct picture
5 (5 questions)	Listening for words, colours and specific information	Colour and write something on the picture

Reading & Writing Test

Parts (30 minutes)	What is the skills focus?	What you have to do
1 (5 questions)	Matching short definitions to words and pictures Writing words	Copy the correct word next to the definition
2 (6 questions)	Reading a dialogue and choosing the correct response	Choose the correct response by circling a letter
3 (6 questions)	Reading for specific information and gist Copying words	Choose and copy missing words correctly Tick a box to choose the correct title for the story
4 (5 questions)	Reading and understanding a factual text Copying words	Complete a text by selecting the correct words and copying them in the gaps
5 (7 questions)	Reading a story Completing sentences	Complete sentences about a story by writing one, two or three words
6 (6 questions)	Writing about a picture	Complete sentences about a picture, answer questions and write two sentences

Speaking Test

Parts (5–7 minutes)	What is the skills focus?	What you have to do
1	Describing two pictures using short responses	Identify four differences between two pictures
2	Understanding the beginning of a story Continuing the story using the picture prompts provided	Describe each picture in turn
3	Suggesting which picture of four is different and saying why	Identify the odd one out and give a reason
4	Understanding and responding to personal questions	Answer personal questions

A2 KEY FOR SCHOOLS EXAM OVERVIEW

Cambridge English Qualification A2 Key for Schools Exam, otherwise known as *Cambridge Key for Schools*, is an examination set at A2 level of the Common European Framework of Reference for Languages (CEFR). It is made up of **three papers**, each testing a different area of ability in English: Reading and Writing, Listening, and Speaking.

Reading and Writing	1 hour	50% of the marks
Listening	35 minutes (approximately)	25% of the marks
Speaking	8–10 minutes for each pair of students (approximately)	25% of the marks

All the examination questions are task-based. Rubrics (instructions) are important and candidates should read them carefully. They set the context and give important information about the tasks. There are separate answer sheets for recording answers for the Reading and Writing paper and the Listening paper.

Paper	Format	Task focus
Reading and Writing Seven Parts 32 questions	**Part 1:** three-option multiple choice. Reading six short texts and choosing the correct answer	**Part 1:** reading short texts for the main idea, detail, and writer's purpose.
	Part 2: matching. Reading three short texts or paragraphs on the same topic and matching the correct text or paragraph to the question.	**Part 2:** reading for detailed understanding.
	Part 3: three-option multiple choice. Five multiple-choice questions.	**Part 3:** reading for main idea(s), detail, opinion, attitude and writer's purpose.
	Part 4: three-option multiple-choice cloze. Reading a text with six gaps and selecting the correct word to complete each gap.	**Part 4:** reading and identifying appropriate word.
	Part 5: open cloze. Short text with six gaps. Completing the text with one word in each gap.	**Part 5:** reading and writing appropriate word to fill in the gap.
	Part 6: guided writing; writing a short message. Reading an email or reading about a situation and writing an email.	**Part 6:** Writing an email to a friend including three pieces of information. 25 words or more.
	Part 7: guided writing; writing a short narrative. Three pictures which show a story.	**Part 7:** Writing the short story shown in the three pictures. 35 words or more.
Listening Five Parts 25 questions	**Part 1:** three-option multiple choice. Listening to five short dialogues and choosing the correct picture for each answer.	**Part 1:** listening to identify key information.
	Part 2: gap fill. Listening to a longer monologue and writing the missing word, number, date or time in five gaps.	**Part 2:** listening and writing down information.
	Part 3: three-option multiple choice. Listening to a longer dialogue and choosing the correct answer to five questions.	**Part 3:** listening to identify key information, feelings and opinions.
	Part 4: three-option multiple choice. Listening to five short dialogues or monologues and choosing the correct answer for each text-based question.	**Part 4:** listening for gist, main idea or topic.
	Part 5: matching. Listening to a longer dialogue and matching five questions with seven options. An example is given.	**Part 5:** listening to identify specific information.
Speaking Two Parts	**Part 1:** interview: examiner-led conversation. 3–4 minutes	**Part 1:** giving personal information.
	Part 2: collaborative task: two-way conversation with visual prompt. Examiner asks two more questions to broaden the topic. 5–6 minutes	**Part 2:** asking and answering simple questions, expressing likes and dislikes and giving reasons.